THIRD EDITION

Exploring Medical Anthropology

Donald Joralemon
Smith College

Prentice Hall
Boston Columbus Indianapolis New York San Francisco Upper Saddle River Amsterdam Cape Town Dubai London Madrid Milan Munich Paris Montreal Toronto Delhi Mexico City Sao Paulo Sydney Hong Kong Seoul Singapore Taipei Tokyo

I dedicate this book to my wife, Phoebe Ann Porter,
for her patience and support.

Editorial Director: Leah Jewell
Editor in Chief: Dickson Musslewhite
Acquisitions Editor: Nancy Roberts
Editorial Project Manager: Vanessa Gennarelli
Director of Marketing: Brandy Dawson
Marketing Manager: Nicole Kunzmann
Marketing Assistant: Jen Lang
Production Manager: Kathleen Sleys
Cover Designer: Axell Designs
Manager, Cover Visual Research & Permissions: Karen Sanatar
Cover Art: © Rune Hellestad/Corbis
Full-Service Project Management/Composition: Shiji Sashi/Integra Software Services, Ltd.
Printer/Binder/Cover Printer: Courier Companies, Inc.
Text Font: 10/12 Janson Text

Credits and acknowledgments borrowed from other sources and reproduced, with permission, in this textbook appear on appropriate page within text.

Library of Congress Cataloging-in-Publication Data

Joralemon, Donald.
Exploring medical anthropology/Donald Joralemon.—3rd ed.
p. cm.
Includes bibliographical references.
ISBN-13: 978-0-205-69351-1
ISBN-10: 0-205-69351-2
1. Medical anthropology. I. Title.
GN296.J65 2010
306.4'61—dc22

2009021875

10 9 8 7 6 5 4 3 2 1

Prentice Hall
is an imprint of

www.pearsonhighered.com

ISBN 13: 978-0-205-69351-1
ISBN 10: 0-205-69351-2

CONTENTS

PREFACE

Medical anthropology studies the human experience of disease in cross-cultural, historical, and evolutionary perspective. It provides a point of connection for biological, cultural, and applied research. No other anthropological specialization holds as much promise for the integration of biological and cultural views of humankind.

Among the social sciences that study health and disease (e.g., medical sociology and medical economics), medical anthropology is the new kid on the block. However, despite its comparative youth, the field has already made significant theoretical and empirical contributions to our understanding of the cultural embeddedness of medical knowledge and practice, the dynamics of the healer's role, the impact of general political and economic forces on the health of individuals and communities, and the interplay between social structures (e.g., political and economic arrangements), ecological settings, and disease-causing agents.

Because of these contributions, medical anthropologists now teach in major medical schools and serve as consultants in hospitals, in clinics, and on national and international health projects. Most anthropology departments have at least one medical anthropologist, and undergraduate and graduate classes in the field typically have large enrollments.

This book is a concise and personal introduction to medical anthropology. I have not set out to write an exhaustive survey of the field nor to summarize medical anthropology research from around the world. Rather, I keep the focus on regions and topics with which I am familiar and limit myself to a few of the most important insights of anthropological research on health and disease. Specifically, I use ethnographic material from Andean South America and from the United States to illustrate the following points:

1. *Biology and culture matter equally in the human experience of disease.* Every aspect of the illness experience, from the individual's recognition of symptoms to assessments of treatment outcome, is shaped by the cultural frameworks of the sufferer and of those to whom he/she turns for help. A **biocultural** perspective is essential to avoid reductionist views of disease.

2. *The political economy is a primary epidemiological factor.* A society's economic system, and the political structures that support it, has a critical role to play in the kinds of health risks people face and the treatment resources they have available.

3. *Ethnography is an essential tool to understand human suffering due to disease.* Both as the foundation of a cross-cultural database and as a research method, ethnography is the sine qua non for a holistic understanding of sickness and healing.

4. *Medical anthropology can help to alleviate human suffering.* Anthropological research can assist in the planning, execution, and evaluation of health interventions by providing cultural information on the community and individuals involved, as well as on the medical practitioners and health care institutions that undertake such interventions.

After introducing the special perspectives of medical anthropology (Chapter 1), I turn to my research on Peruvian shamanism and organ transplantation in the United States to illustrate the questions and methods of medical anthropology (Chapter 2). Then, I take an extended look at a cholera outbreak in Peru to review the theoretical models and current debates in medical anthropology (Chapters 3 and 4). Chapter 5 considers the impact of re/emerging diseases and bioterrorism. Chapters 6 and 7 contain a discussion of how medical anthropology understands the position of healers—folk and biomedical—in the contemporary world and the relationship medical anthropologists believe they should have with biomedical professionals. What anthropology has to offer to the study and practice of medical ethics is considered in Chapter 8. Innovative research on biotechnologies is introduced in Chapter 9. The text concludes with a look at the relevance of medical anthropology to contemporary health issues and career paths in the field in Chapter 10.

Acknowledgments

I thank those who have helped to keep my language clear, my discussions sharp, and my errors to a minimum: Gail Joralemon, Brian Hansen, Lynn Morgan, James Trostle, and Lynnette Leidy. I am also grateful to my development editor, Sylvia Shepherd, who understood my vision and helped to make it real. To Phoebe Porter, my love and appreciation.

I would like to acknowledge the following reviewers: Joci Caldwell-Ryan, Southern Methodist University; Helen Cho, Davidson College; Erica Gibson, University of South Carolina; Bonnie Glass-Coffin, Utah State University; Clarence C. Gravlee, University of Florida; Sallie Han, State University of New York College at Oneonta; Linda Jerofke, Eastern Oregon University; John Olmstead, Fullerton College.

CHAPTER

1 What's So Cultural about Disease?

North coast of Peru, 1980: It's three in the morning; the ocean breeze is wet and cold. It is not clear if my present nausea is attributable to the mescaline-bearing San Pedro (*Trichocereus pachanoi*) brew with which I began the evening, or to the vile black-leaf tobacco sludge I have been asked to snort repeatedly. For the moment the **shaman's** rattling and chanting have stopped. In the partial light of the moon, I can see my fellow participants huddled under blankets up against the reed windbreak: some doze, while others talk in hushed voices. I hear one, in the dune behind me, retching and coughing.

The shaman's head is down, his gaze fixed on the objects arrayed in front of him (see Photo 1.1). Two assistants sit on stools by his side. Nineteen adults and one ten-year-old boy have entrusted him with their care; they expect him to learn the source of their suffering and to put things right. There are poor and middle-class men and women, some from close by and others from far away. A few have come alone, but most have spouses, friends or close family members at their side.

The shaman will tell most of them that their pains and incapacities, their bad fortune and sorrows, result from the injurious actions of envious neighbors, jealous competitors, or the illicit lovers of their mates. The label he will apply to their suffering is *daño* ("harm"), a sickness category linked to the malicious work of sorcerers. The shaman's task is to cleanse each person of the sorcerer's poisons and, in some cases, to reverse the harmful effects so as to punish the responsible party.

What are we to make of this event and of the diagnosis of daño? The ritual is certainly unlike the practices of medical practitioners with which we are more familiar. The idea of sorcery-induced illness brings with it negative associations built on Hollywood visions of voodoo ceremonies. It would only be in the spirit of cultural sensitivity that we would apply the term "medical" to the body of knowledge on which the Peruvian shaman depends in treating his clients; in unguarded moments we might even be tempted to use less flattering adjectives, like superstitious or primitive.

The assumption guiding our response to the Peruvian healing ceremony is that there are two kinds of knowledge about sickness, scientific and nonscientific. To diagnose a set of symptoms and organic manifestations as a viral infection, for example, is

Photo 1.1 José Paz Chapoñan and his assistants, Lambayeque, Peru, 1980. (Courtesy of Donald Joralemon)

to employ an objective, biologically based scientific concept. Naming a group of symptoms as daño, on the other hand, is to apply a cultural category that has no scientific standing. What distinguishes contemporary biomedicine from healing traditions like that described above is precisely that it is founded on scientific notions of disease that are supposedly free of any cultural content.

Culture in Medicine

Peter Sedgwick, a political scientist from the University of Leeds, challenges the assumption that there is a culture-free way of thinking about disease: "Outside the significance that man voluntarily attaches to certain conditions, there are no illnesses or diseases in nature" (Sedgwick 1981:120–121). Anticipating our response, he continues:

> What, are there no diseases in nature? Are there no infectious and contagious bacilli? Are there not definite and objective lesions in the cellular structures of the human body? Are there not fractures of bones, the fatal ruptures of tissues, the malignant multiplications of tumorous growths? Are not these, surely, events of nature? Yet these, as natural events, do not—prior to the human social meanings we attach to them—constitute illnesses, sicknesses, or diseases. The fracture

> of a septuagenarian's femur has, within the world of nature, no more significance than the snapping of an autumn leaf from its twig: and the invasion of a human organism by cholera-germs has no more the stamp of "illness" than does the souring of milk by other forms of bacteria (p. 121).

Disease in Other Cultures and Times

Sedgwick's view of disease, that it is an imposition of human meanings on naturally occurring processes, is somehow less controversial when we study other societies' beliefs about illness. It seems obvious that the Peruvian shaman's idea of daño is a culturally laden concept. We can even feel at ease with Sedgwick's position when examples are drawn from closer to home, provided they are historically remote from our contemporary medical practices. A case in point is the eighteenth-century European and American discussion of "onanism," a disease that was considered responsible for epilepsy, blindness, vertigo, loss of hearing, headache, impotency, memory loss, rickets, and irregular action of the heart (Engelhardt 1981). We know this dread disease by its modern name, masturbation. The influence of sociocultural values on this disease concept is irrefutable; the fact that the example is two hundred years old makes it easy for us to deny any implications for current biomedicine.

A century closer to the present, it is still possible to point with confidence to the cultural content of American medicine. Publishing in the prestigious *New Orleans Medical and Surgical Journal* (May 1851), the eminent Dr. Samuel A. Cartwright coined the term "drapetomania" to describe the disease of the mind that "induces the negro to run away from service." The physician reassured his readers that "with the advantage of proper medical advice, strictly followed, this troublesome practice that many negroes have of running away, can be almost entirely prevented, [even if] the slaves be located on the borders of a free State, within a stone's throw of the abolitionists" (Cartwright 1981:319).[1] No objective science here, but, we reassure ourselves, this is still prior to the real development of scientific medicine.

Feminist scholars contribute additional historical illustrations of the link between medicine and culture in the United States. Barbara Ehrenreich and Deirdre English, in their book *For Her Own Good: 150 Years of the Experts' Advice to Women* (1978), describe the nineteenth-century medical view that a woman's personality and physiology are completely controlled by her ovaries. They cite one authority, Dr. W. W. Bliss, who, in 1870, referred to the:

> gigantic power and influence of the ovaries over the whole animal economy of woman—that they are the most powerful agents in all the commotions of her system; that on them rest her intellectual standing in society, her physical perfection, and all that lends beauty to those fine and delicate contours which are constant objects of admiration, all that is great, noble and beautiful, all that is voluptuous, tender, and endearing. . . . (in Ehrenreich and English 1978:120–121).

The logic of this view led to the diagnosis of an ovarian basis for a wide variety of "diseases," from tuberculosis and consumption to "simple cussedness" and erotic tendencies. The cure? Ovariotomy, the surgical removal of the ovaries. This operation, by one estimate, had been performed on 150,000 American women by 1906 (Ehrenreich and English 1981:290). It is hard to deny the link between this medical practice and the sociocultural assumptions about gender that helped to define social relations at the turn of the century.

Drs. Cartwright and Bliss were, no doubt, certain that their work rested on firm scientific foundations; they would likely have denied the links that appear so obvious from an early twenty-first-century vantage point between their medical speculations and culturally rationalized forms of social inequality. Could the same be said of physician/researcher and drug promoter Robert Wilson, author of the 1966 best-selling *Feminine Forever*? Convinced of the value of "estrogen replacement therapy" (ERT) for the treatment of menopausal symptoms, Wilson warned that without ERT "no woman can be sure of escaping the horror of this living decay" (p. 43). His psychiatric colleague David Reuben agreed that menopause was a terrible threat to women. In *Everything You Always Wanted to Know About Sex* (1966), Reuben wrote that when menstruation ends, "a woman becomes not really a man but no longer a functional woman; these individuals live in the world of inter-sex" (p. 365; see also, MacPherson 1981).

Wilson and Reuben, like their nineteenth-century medical predecessors, seem to have allowed some culturally derived prejudices into their science. They transform a normal process of aging into a disease and link a woman's social worth and identity to the functioning of her reproductive organs. Whatever may prove to be the advantages and disadvantages of hormonal replacement therapies,[2] the significance that Wilson and Reuben attach to menopause is just as value-laden as the examples of ovariotomies, onanism, and drapetomania (see Martin 1987, Lock 1993). A parallel development for male aging is presented in Box 1.1.

But wait: These examples do not come from some historically distant period; they are just decades old. What happened to our scientific, culture-free medicine that seemed so clearly to contrast with the Peruvian shaman's practice?

The Impact of Culture on Contemporary Biomedicine

The fact is that these are just a few illustrations from a growing body of social science and historical research supporting Sedgwick's view of the social and cultural embeddedness of *all* notions of disease and the medical practices they inspire. And it is not just the observations of individual practitioners that have been the focus of this work; medical knowledge, both past and present, has also been analyzed for its sociocultural logic. For example, why do we find North American biomedical texts and popular media of all varieties drawing so heavily on mechanical and combat metaphors to describe organic parts and processes? Why do we speak of the heart as a pump and viruses as invading forces attacking the body's defense system? Psychologist Samuel Osherson and anthropologist Lorna AmaraSingham (1981) trace the rise of a mechanical metaphor for the functioning of the human anatomy, the body-as-machine, to the shift from a rural, farm economy to an industrial economic base (p. 229). They argue that thinking about the body in mechanical terms has contributed to a dehumanization of clinical practice. They cite the medical management of childbirth: The machine metaphor contributes to the

BOX 1.1
From ERT to TRT

Do a Goggle™ search for "male menopause"—also called "andropause," "androgen deficiency in aging males" (ADAM), "partial androgen deficiency in aging males" (PADAM), "viropause," and "male climacteric"—and you may find the site for reNEWMAN (http://renewman.com), an organization dedicated to "combating the aging process in men." You will learn that when men reach their mid-forties "hormone levels have dropped to the extent that the erection which once greeted them in the morning ceases, while their muscle definition fades and they notice they are getting a bit flabby around the middle." But there is an anti-aging cure: testosterone replacement therapy or TRT. Energy returns, depression lifts, sexual interest is recharged, muscles regain definition, and thinking sharpens. At least that's the promise.

The Federal Drug Administration has approved testosterone treatment for men—irrespective of age—who suffer from medical conditions (e.g., cancer or injury) that trigger testicular or hypothalamic–pituitary dysfunctions that result in low concentrations of testosterone. The accompanying symptoms are bone loss, muscle weakness, lack of energy, diminished sex drive, impaired cognition, and depressed mood. Approval for this limited use does not stop physicians from prescribing TRT more widely.

Entrepreneurial pharmaceutical companies and some physicians argue that the benefits of replacing lost testosterone ought to apply as well to aging men, who experience a reduction in the quantity of this important hormone at a rate of about 1 percent per year after the age forty. This promotion of the drug comes despite a shortage of studies evaluating the safety of TRT, especially over the long term, and in the face of concern that artificially elevating levels of testosterone in older men could contribute to prostate cancer, breast cancer, liver disease, and blockages of blood vessels resulting in heart attacks. Prescriptions for TRT in the United States—available as an injection, in tablets, and as skin patches and gel—increased from 648,000 in 1999 to nearly two million in 2002 (Brody 2004).

At a 1995 gathering of the American Academy of Anti-Aging Medicine (A4M) in Las Vegas, Nevada, Dr. Julian Whitaker of the Whitaker Wellness Institute asked, "Are we going to give hormones only to women, while men are supposed to just wither away? Rather than making jokes about grumpy old men, we should keep searching for ways to restore optimal neurochemistry for both sexes" (quoted in *Life Extension Magazine*, August 2002; http://www.lef.org). For testosterone, "optimal" is defined as the levels of the hormone found in healthy twenty-year-old men (Gould and Petty 2000; Matsumoto 2003); any level below the range in young men is defined as "testosterone deficiency."

TRT has found a niche in the arsenal of potions aimed at an aging baby-boom generation, including the massively promoted remedies for "erectile dysfunction" and antiaging skin creams. The disturbing déjà vu of an inadequately studied hormonal replacement therapy marketed as a "cure" for the normal effects of life's later stages seems not yet to have overcome the wish for a fountain of youth.

---

transformation of delivery rooms into factories where "birth [is] the processing of a machine by machines [under the control of] skilled technicians" (Wertz and Wertz, in Osherson and AmaraSingham 1981:236).

Anthropologist Emily Martin (1990, 1994) finds the metaphor of disease-as-combat to be pervasive in popular journals and in immunology texts. She suggests that this way of thinking about disease resonated well with the priorities and concerns of the American nation-state during the Cold War. A 1986 *National Geographic* article, titled "Our Immune System: The Wars Within" (Jaret 1986), makes Martin's point. The entire text is organized around the combat metaphor, with references to "combatants," "defenders," and "penetrations of our defenses." The arch villain, the AIDS virus, is described as a "virulent scourge that relentlessly disarms the immune system." Not surprisingly, in an accompanying illustration the invading virus is represented as a red star and the immune system's parts are miniature "biological arms factories." Former president Ronald Reagan (1980–1988), known for his anticommunist views, could not have put it any better.[3]

Just as the machine metaphor has implications for the actual practice of medicine in America, so too does this linked metaphor of disease-as-combat. Expensive high-tech approaches to curing disease find the same compelling justifications as Pentagon budgets: When it comes to conquering the enemy, no cost is too high. Surrender is unacceptable, either on the battlefield or in the hospital. Metaphorical frameworks like these may make complex biological processes easier to understand, but they can also influence the organization and allocation of medical care and even limit our ability to conceive of alternative ways of caring for the sick.

These examples and many others like them confirm Sedgwick's observation that "The medical enterprise is from its inception value-loaded; it is not simply an applied biology, but a biology applied in accordance with the dictates of social interest" (1981:122). This is the opening for a social science of medicine: an analysis of the connections between cultural frameworks, social organizational realities, and those human conditions that are captured under the rubric "disease."[4] A basic premise of social science approaches is that these connections shape the knowledge and practice of surgeon and shaman alike—that cultural assumptions and social structures have an impact on the way that both healers and patients think about and respond to disease.

Development of Medical Anthropology

Anthropology is well positioned among the social sciences to take full advantage of the insight that culture matters when it comes to the human experience of and response to disease. After all, the concept of **culture**[5] is central to the discipline: anthropology may be defined as the study of humankind's biological and cultural capacities. Furthermore, anthropology is committed to understanding culture in relationship to the evolution of human biological capacities (i.e., in "biological" or "physical" anthropology). This focus on the interface between culture and biology serves the discipline well in the study of disease.

Physical anthropologists have always been interested in the topic of human health and disease, as is evident in their studies of skeletal material (e.g., to identify cause of death or to assess the health of ancient societies) as well as in their research with living populations (e.g., to evaluate growth patterns and nutrition) (Bogin 1988; Goodman et al. 1988). Cultural anthropologists were slower to come to the study of health and disease. At first, they raised the issue only in the context of describing "primitive" healing rituals in chapters on "magic" or "religion," but not as a subject worthy of attention in its own right. Just during the past forty years has there been a concerted effort to treat knowledge about and treatments for disease as subjects of independent inquiry in cultural anthropology.

It is worth reviewing how and why cultural anthropologists came to pay greater attention to the topic of health and disease, because in this intellectual and professional history are the seeds of present divisions in medical anthropology. A good place to start is with the scholars who understood the importance of beliefs and practices related to disease before there was a recognized specialty called medical anthropology. I have selected two of the most noteworthy (see Wellin 1977).

Medicine as a Social Process: William H. R. Rivers

In the early part of the twentieth century, anthropologists became obsessed by reconstructions of the historical **diffusion** of cultural traits from a point of origin outward to ever more distant societies. The first step in diffusion studies[6] was to derive a classification system: For a given cultural domain (e.g., religion), what subtypes can be distinguished in the ethnographic record (e.g., animism, polytheism, and monotheism)? The resulting classifications were then used on a sample of world societies to code ethnographic descriptions of the cultural domain under study. Colored pins or flags representing each subtype would be stuck in a world map as this coding proceeded (e.g., colored pins representing animistic beliefs would be inserted into the map at spots corresponding to societies that were reported to have such beliefs). A concentration of particular colored pins/flags would be taken as evidence that the related subtype of the cultural domain under investigation had originated in that geographic location and then diffused outward.

The physician and experimental psychologist William Halse Rivers Rivers (born 1864, died 1922) applied this strategy to medical beliefs around the world, concentrating on ideas about the cause(s) of illness. Rivers began his anthropological work as a reluctant recruit on a scientific expedition organized by A. C. Haddon to the Torres Straits (north of Australia). He is best known for his landmark work on the cultural variability of color perception, but Rivers was also interested in non-Western medicines. His Fitzpatrick Lectures, "Medicine, Magic and Religion" (Royal College of Physicians, 1915–1916; Rivers 1924), offered a classification of disease causation beliefs and a diffusionist analysis of the geographic centers for each type. Diseases are believed to be caused by human agency (e.g., magical means), spiritual or supernatural agency (e.g., taboo), and/or natural agency. One of the conclusions of Rivers's world survey was that Australian indigenous societies must have been the wellspring for the idea that human agency is behind disease episodes.

More important for the development of medical anthropology than his diffusionist reconstructions was Rivers's declaration that "the practice of medicine is a social process, subject to the same laws, and to be studied by the same methods as other social processes" (p. 55). He must have astonished his physician audience when he took this observation a step further, insisting that the healing practices of "primitive people" are logical and systematic, "in some respects more rational than our own" (p. 52). Whatever we make of Rivers's classification efforts and diffusionist speculations, his call for a social analysis of medical beliefs and practices and his recognition that his own culture's healing science had no monopoly on rationality were truly prescient.

Functional Views of Medicine: Erwin Ackerknecht

The expedition in which Rivers took part was an early example of a new anthropological preference for doing firsthand fieldwork in individual societies rather than relying on secondary sources such as accounts written by explorers, missionaries, or colonial administrators. With the contribution of pioneers like A. R. Radcliffe-Brown and Bronislaw Malinowski, anthropology came to champion long-term participant observation as its distinctive method. Associated with this development was a growing recognition of how interconnected aspects of social life are. From kinship systems to religious practices, anthropologists demonstrated how the many parts of the social fabric function together as a coherent whole. This **functional** theory compared the relationships among social institutions to the workings of the various parts of the body, or to the integrated components of a smoothly operating machine. Each part can be seen to contribute to the maintenance of the whole.

Another physician-turned-anthropologist, Erwin Ackerknecht (born 1905, died 1988), showed how functional theory might be applied to the ethnographic study of medical beliefs and practices. Ackerknecht's German medical training was supplemented with studies of ethnology under the famous French sociologist Marcel Mauss. But it was not until he came to the United States and made the acquaintance of Columbia University anthropologist Ruth Benedict that he abandoned speculations about the origin and evolution of cultural customs in favor of functional analyses of cultures.[7] In his own words, he was finally "liberated from the evolutionary obsession" (Ackerknecht 1971:9). Although he did not carry out his own fieldwork, Ackerknecht embraced the ethnographer's commitment to **holistic** accounts of sociocultural systems.

In a series of essays written during the 1940s and 1950s, subsequently published in *Medicine and Ethnology: Selected Essays* (1971), Ackerknecht explored how ideas about the causes of disease can reflect lines of social tension in a society (e.g., attributing disease to witchcraft performed by political enemies). He also argued that the very threat of a disease (or of being accused of causing one) can serve as a powerful social sanction supporting the status quo against those who are inclined to deviate from social norms. Ackerknecht may also have been the first to argue for a cultural construction of disease concepts: "What is disease is, in the last instance, not a biological fact but a decision of society" (p. 167).

If Rivers and Ackerknecht provided the legitimation for an anthropology of medical practices and theoretical frameworks by which to link health-related practices to broader social realities, there were more pragmatic impulses behind the final coalescence of a field called medical anthropology. The consulting work on international health care projects done by anthropologists in the 1950s was the final catalyst for anthropological research focused specifically on health and disease.

The Applied Roots of Medical Anthropology

In the aftermath of World War II, the United States sought to extend its influence in the world via foreign assistance programs modeled on the successful Marshall Plan that helped to rebuild devastated Europe. Among the development projects supported by the International Cooperation Administration, precursor to the Agency for International Development (AID), and later by the United Nations' World Health Organization (WHO), were many which sought to eradicate **epidemic** diseases and improve basic sanitation in poor countries. Often, these public health campaigns foundered because of what the development specialists called "cultural obstacles": resistance or opposition that seemed to relate to cultural misunderstandings between the developers and the "recipient peoples." When this occurred, anthropologists were hired to identify and remove cultural impediments blocking the success of the projects.

An early example of anthropological work on international health projects was Richard N. Adams's (1955) analysis of village resistance in Guatemala to a child nutrition program supported by WHO and the Pan American Sanitary Bureau and directed by the Institute of Nutrition of Central America and Panama (INCAP). Local ethnographic work revealed that community members interpreted INCAP as a communist organization, a very serious assessment given the country's right-wing ruling class and its violent anticommunism campaigns. They also considered the project's requirement that children have blood samples taken as detrimental to their health. Guatemalan Indians believe that blood is a nonregenerative vital fluid, so the samples were seen as a permanent loss of strength. In addition, the idea that outsiders would wish to fatten up the children of the village was linked to popular mythology, dating back to the time of the conquest, that whites capture Indian children to eat them. There were many good reasons, from the viewpoint of the villagers, to keep children out of the program.[8]

The involvement of anthropologists as cultural experts on international health campaigns directed new attention to disease and healing as subjects for anthropological analysis. The notion of an "applied anthropology in medicine" (Caudill 1953) predates the widespread use of the term "medical anthropology," which indicates how central this work was to the development of a discrete anthropological subfield focused on medicine. One of the earliest collections of essays properly considered "medical anthropology" (Paul 1955) was a series of case studies of applied work in international and domestic public health projects. The first general literature review of medical anthropology (Scotch 1963) shows the preponderance of research directly related to international health projects. The application of anthropological theory and methods in both preventive and curative medicine still remains a core component of medical anthropology.

Medical Anthropology Today

In 1971, a "Society for Medical Anthropology" was formed under the administrative structure of the American Anthropological Association (AAA). By 2004, the Society had 2,293 members, or about 12 percent of the total membership of the AAA; it is among the largest of the specialized societies in the organization. Over the past twenty-five years, major new journals and new sections of existing journals have appeared which are either completely or partly dedicated to the publication of research in medical anthropology: *Medical Anthropology Quarterly*, *Medical Anthropology*, *Culture, Medicine and Psychiatry*, *Social Science and Medicine*, and *Ethnomedizin*. Many major academic publishers now have specialized series in medical anthropology. In short, after a slow beginning, medical anthropology has caught on and now is among the most vibrant and productive subfields of the discipline.

As the earlier discussion suggests, part of what medical anthropologists do is to explore how sicknesses are "culturally constructed." How are a society's understandings of and responses to disease shaped by cultural assumptions about such things as the beginning and end of life, the workings of the human organism, and the causes of ill health and misfortune? The **cultural-constructivist** or **interpretive** approach to medical anthropology addresses this question.

A second concentration in medical anthropology, the **ecological** or **ecological/evolutionary** approach, analyzes the interaction between sociocultural patterns and the biological and environmental parameters within which humans operate. The approach draws upon evolutionary theory and the concept of **adaptation** to explore the short- and long-term implications for human health of different environments and social and cultural arrangements.[9] For example, what new patterns of disease accompanied the shift from hunting and gathering to sedentary agriculture in tropical regions? What were the short-term physiological and long-term (i.e., evolutionary) genetic consequences of this change in subsistence practices (Cohen 1989)?

Medical anthropologists have recently been challenged to pay more attention to the fundamental role that socioeconomic arrangements have on human health. Inspired by the literature in the political economy of health and Marxist theory,[10] **critical medical anthropologists** ask how the distribution of wealth and power and the division of labor affect disease patterns and health care access. Although sometimes presented as a challenge to the interpretive and ecological approaches, I argue in the following chapters that many of the priorities of the critical perspective can and should be incorporated into the research of all medical anthropologists.

A final approach to medical anthropology relates to its application in the context of health care. As I noted earlier, anthropologists have long been involved as social science consultants on health-related projects both nationally and internationally. Their role is most often that of a culture broker, an intermediary between biomedical practitioners and groups whose cultural assumptions might be at odds with those underlying scientific medicine. From programs sponsored by the WHO to American hospitals serving ethnically diverse communities, **applied medical anthropology**[11] pursues more effective health interventions.

The four currents in medical anthropology—interpretive, ecological/evolutionary, critical, and clinically applied—have had largely independent trajectories in the profession. The tendency for medical anthropologists to specialize in one approach has limited the opportunity for a cross-fertilization of ideas. Paradoxically, it was the assault launched by critical medical anthropologists on all four perspectives (e.g., Singer 1989a) that initiated conversations about the possibility of an integrative approach to medical anthropology. A central objective of this text is to move closer to this integration—to develop an approach to the study of health and disease which (1) pays attention to ecological, biological, *and* cultural factors; (2) considers the political and economic forces that influence disease patterns and affect access to health care resources; and (3) offers an opportunity for health-promoting interventions.

Summary: Placing Medical Anthropology among the Social Sciences of Medicine

Medical anthropology starts with two insights: (1) cultural premises, which are oftentimes implicit and difficult for the insider to recognize, shape the health-related knowledge and healing practices of every society; and (2) disease patterns, social norms, and socioeconomic arrangements are intricately interrelated. The latter insight brings medical anthropology close to the perspective of **epidemiology**, the public health field which analyzes the "distribution and determinants of disease" (Trostle and Sommerfeld 1996:253).

Among the social sciences of medicine, medical anthropology is distinct in at least three ways. First, its temporal and geographic scope is wider than any other medical social science. From **paleontological** and **archaeological** investigations of human/disease interactions in early human societies to contemporary **ethnographies** of medical systems around the world, anthropology embraces the full sweep of humankind's experience with suffering.

Second, medical anthropology, more than its sister disciplines, seeks to consider both the cultural and biological parameters of disease. Health and disease is the ideal meeting ground for anthropology's biological and cultural divisions. Although we will see in the following chapters just how difficult it has proven to be to realize a **biocultural** perspective in medical anthropology, it will also be clear just how important it is to move in that direction.

Finally, the commitment of medical anthropology to a research strategy that builds on long-term participant observation also distinguishes it from other social sciences of medicine. Medical sociologists have certainly engaged in research that resembles anthropological fieldwork, but no other social science has so thoroughly grounded its contribution to the study of health and disease on a combination of **qualitative** (e.g., participant observation and open-ended interviews) and **quantitative** (e.g., surveys and questionnaires) **methods** of investigation. Qualitative methods and long-term fieldwork reveal the meanings that people attach to objects and events in the world; they also clarify the relationships between what people say they do and what they actually do. Quantitative methods contribute precision to ethnographic description and provide for the testing of hypotheses.

In the next chapter, I return to the work of Peruvian shamans to explore how medical anthropology analyzes sickness and healing. What questions ought to be asked about this healing tradition? What information would be required to answer these questions? And how would one go about gathering the necessary information?

After considering these questions in relationship to Peruvian shamans, I ask them again in connection with my more recent research on organ transplantation in the United States. My objective is to show that the anthropological approach can be applied as effectively to the culture of biomedicine as to less familiar healing traditions.

SUGGESTED READINGS

A range of views on the meaning of "disease" is to be found in *Concepts of Health and Disease: Interdisciplinary Perspectives* (A. L. Caplan, H. T. Engelhardt, Jr. and J. J. McCartney, eds., 1981).

In addition to the book by Ehrenreich and English (1978), G. J. Barker-Benfield's *The Horrors of the Half-Known Life: Male Attitudes Toward Women and Sexuality in Nineteenth Century America* (1976) provides excellent historical material on the medical [mis]treatment of women.

An examination of similar issues in more recent times is to be found in Diana Scully's *Men Who Control Women's Health: The Miseducation of Obstetrician-Gynecologists* (1980).

The importance of metaphor in organizing ideas about disease is explored in Susan Sontag's classic *Illness as Metaphor* (1977) as well as in Byron Good's influential essay, "The Heart of What's the Matter: The Semantics of Illness in Iran" (1977).

David Landy's edited collection *Culture, Disease and Healing: Studies in Medical Anthropology* (1977) includes a number of important reviews of the history of medical anthropology (e.g., Edward Wellin); Thomas M. Johnson and Carolyn F. Sargent have compiled an invaluable group of essays surveying the field in *Medical Anthropology: Contemporary Theory and Method* (1990; Sargent and Johnson 1996, revised ed.).

The ecological approach is well represented by Ann McElroy and Patricia K. Townsend's *Medical Anthropology in Ecological Perspective* (1985, 2004) and the critical perspective is captured by Merrill Singer and Hans Baer's collection, *Critical Medical Anthropology* (1995).

Noel J. Chrisman and Thomas W. Maretzki's volume *Clinically Applied Anthropology: Anthropologists in Health Settings* (1982) introduces the range of applied work done by medical anthropologists.

NOTES

1. Cartwright was one among a number of white southern physicians who speculated about "Negro inferiority" (see Savitt 1978). Medical historian Harry Marks (personal communication) considers the *New Orleans Medical and Surgical Journal* the "leading southern US journal of the period" and notes that views like Cartwright's are to be found in other American and European scientific journals of the second half of the nineteenth century.

2. A randomized trial carried out by the Women's Health Initiative was halted in July 2002 when results showed that healthy women taking estrogen plus progestin had a substantial increased risk over placebos for breast cancer, heart disease, stroke, and blood clots. Women over the age of sixty-five taking the same combination had double the risk of developing dementia (Women's Health Initiative 2002). The current advice from federal health sources is for women to take replacement hormones only for severe symptoms of menopause, at the lowest dose possible, and for the shortest reasonable time.

3. Martin (1994) finds that combat metaphors that were common during the Cold War period are being replaced by the metaphor of "flexibility" that is common in the post–Cold War economic ideology (e.g., workers must be flexible to adapt to different jobs).

4. Accepting the idea that notions about disease are culturally formulated does not require us to deny that there is a biological reality to which those notions relate. As Margaret Lock put it, "There

is, of course, a biological reality, but the moment that efforts are made to explain, order, and manipulate that reality, then a process of contextualization takes place in which the dynamic relationship of biology with cultural values and the social order has to be considered" (Lock 1988:7).

It is also important to remember that the absence of a neutral/objective vantage point by which "disease" may be analyzed does not make all explanations equally useful. The advantage of the natural science model—even given its cultural content—is that it provides reasons to prefer one explanation of a disease over others (e.g., logical consistency, comprehensiveness, replicability, and potential for refutation). Ultimately, it is these standards that account for the successes of biomedicine.

5. More has been written about the concept of culture than perhaps any other term in anthropology, and no one definition is likely to win general approval. I use "culture" to refer to the shared ideas characteristic of a given social group and the patterns of behavior that result from them. For the purposes of the present discussion, the most important point about "culture" is that it is based on a biological capacity (e.g., brain size and communicative abilities) but is socially transmitted (versus genetically inherited).

6. The following description of diffusion studies does not apply to those undertaken by American anthropologists like Franz Boas, who sought to reconstruct the historical connections among circumscribed societies (e.g., Native North American Indians of the Northwest Coast) based on highly specific features of rituals, social organization, material culture products, etc.

7. The search for the origin of cultural customs and the ranking of societies along an evolutionary line from "primitive" to "civilized" was central to the anthropology of the nineteenth century. However, the development of the fieldwork tradition, with its detailed analysis of single societies, led anthropologists to favor interpretations that stressed the inner workings of discrete social systems rather than broad cross-cultural comparisons.

8. Unfortunately, Adams does not report what happened as a result of his ethnographic findings.

9. The ecological approach recognizes that human activities both affect and are affected by biological and environmental factors.

10. The political economy of health stresses the relationship between the local conditions that affect health (and access to health care) and the worldwide capitalist system. It is concerned with the mutually reinforcing relationships between medicine and structures of power (see Baer, et al. 1997).

11. Alternative names have been suggested for this branch of medical anthropology, including "clinical anthropology" and "clinically applied anthropology" (see Chrisman and Johnson 1990). I prefer "applied medical anthropology" as a general term which includes policy and planning work done by anthropologists in international and domestic health, in hospital and clinic consultations, and in the training of medical professionals. The American Anthropological Association's training manual in the field employs this term (Hill 1991).

CHAPTER 2

Anthropological Questions and Methods in the Study of Sickness and Healing

I have introduced the general perspective of medical anthropology, and I will soon consider in more detail the field's theoretical frameworks. But first, let's take a look at what a medical anthropologist considers worthy of study and how he/she goes about the research process. I use my own work on Peruvian shamanism and on organ transplantation in the United States because I want to show how these divergent topics raise surprisingly similar anthropological issues and are amenable to many of the same research strategies.

I have chosen not to structure this discussion as a review of questions and methods organized by theoretical perspective (ecological/evolutionary, interpretive, critical, applied) because in the actual context of fieldwork, areas of inquiry overlap. For example, when I was in the middle of a ritual healing session in Peru, I didn't stop to think which of the questions that came to my mind were "cultural" and which were "biological." I have occasion in the following two chapters to distinguish more clearly the theoretical issues; in this chapter, I want to give an impression of the seamlessness of fieldwork in medical anthropology.

At the same time, I do not want to give the impression that research questions are somehow independent of the researcher's own theoretical perspective, which is itself shaped by the investigator's age, gender, ethnicity, social and educational background, political views, and so on. There is no generic list of research questions that any medical anthropologist would ask. Those that I will introduce in the following sections emerge from my own training and personal history.

I have another objective for this chapter. I wish to show that fieldwork in medical anthropology is a dynamic process that is not well suited to the structured, hypothesis-testing research paradigm of the laboratory sciences. In the midst of a research project, as you are gradually becoming more sophisticated in your understanding of the social reality in which you find yourself, questions you had not even contemplated emerge as central. Sometimes, a research technique you thought would work fails miserably, or you find that the people you hoped to talk to have no interest in talking to you. At the same time, theoretical discussions in the discipline do not stand still while you carry out your fieldwork. It is not unusual to find that the direction of your research shifts in response to ongoing debates in the profession at home. The following aims to convey the fluid quality of medical anthropology fieldwork.

Studying Shamans in Peru

Research Questions

Let us return to the curing ritual that introduced the last chapter. Imagine that you have traveled to Peru to do research on this healing tradition. Imagine as well that little is known about these shamans and their practices. What questions would seem important to answer? What areas of inquiry would you wish to explore? Just as important, how would you go about organizing your research and gathering the information you consider essential?

Begin with the shaman himself. You might want to know something about his training, about what it takes to become a **curandero**, as these specialists are known in Peru. Perhaps your interest is in his curing knowledge: What distinctions does he make among types of sicknesses, and how does he determine which a given patient has?; what does he consider the source of his healing power?; what botanical knowledge does he draw upon in his curing work?; is his healing based on spiritual assumptions; and, if so, how do these relate to religious conceptions in the broader society?

There is certainly much to learn about the curing ritual as well. A good researcher would want to know what determines its scheduling and location, how the assistants are selected and trained, and what the significance is of the collection of objects in front of the shaman (the **mesa**, in Spanish). A close inspection of the latter will suggest that a good amount of time will be needed to understand fully the meanings of each individual object, as well as the cumulative import of the objects. Furthermore, how the shaman understands the mesa may be quite different from the meanings attributed to it by the patients. The organization of the ritual and the purpose and meaning of the chanting and rattling will need some attention.

Then there is the question of the use of drugs by the shaman, his assistants, and the patients. Does the San Pedro cactus, which bears mescaline at about the same concentration as peyote, trigger hallucinations for everyone who takes it? If so, how much of the content of these altered states is attributable to cultural expectations and how much to neurochemistry? If not, what other effect(s) does the drug have? (Keep in mind that it is used in combination with a liquefied tobacco juice imbibed through the nose.) Analyzing the neurochemistry of mescaline without paying attention to what the shaman tells you about his therapeutic use of San Pedro would provide an incomplete understanding of the drug's use.

So far we have barely mentioned the patients (see Photo 2.1). You might wish to learn who they are and why they have come to a shaman to be cured. What are their educational and economic/class backgrounds? What symptoms are the patients experiencing, and how have *they* interpreted them? Maybe some kind of

Photo 2.1 Jorge Merino Bravo and his patients, Lambayeque, Peru, 1988. (© 1988 R. Donald Skillman)

brief medical exam would be in order to see if their complaints match the diagnostic categories used in biomedicine. As the ritual progresses, you could try to learn how they feel and what they are thinking. Some consideration should also be given to the results of the treatment they receive from the shaman, perhaps via follow-up interviews.

Of course, all these questions apply to a single shaman and his clients—how could you be sure that the answers relate as well to other shamans and their patients? Some kind of comparative work would be in order, with a sample of other specialists sufficient to represent the full range of curing practices. It would be important to establish a clear definition of what distinguishes curanderos from others who are also engaged in healing activities, as well as to document how all varieties of curers (medical doctors included) relate to one another (e.g., do MDs refer to curanderos?). Other aspects of the general context in which shamans work might also be of concern, for example, legal statutes governing medical practices and treatment of curanderos by state officials, costs of curandero treatments compared with other types of treatments, and knowledge among the general public of shamanic healing and of the reputations of specific shamans.

There is another dimension to this healing tradition that would also merit attention: its history. How long have shamans been a part of Peruvian culture, and to what degree have their curing methods changed? Since contemporary Peru is a mix of Spanish, African, and native Andean cultures, you might even look for evidence of indigenous sources for the shaman's work. This could involve searching for parallels in current Indian communities as well as for archaeological precedents. An exploration of early colonial documents might help to define the balance between Spanish and native cultural sources for shamanic practices, as well as the potential contribution from African slaves who were imported by the Spaniards soon after conquest.

Research Methods

Consider how you would go about translating any set of the above questions into a specific research plan. You have a toolbox full of investigative techniques, from surveys to blood tests, available, but some are better suited than others to the actual circumstances under which the research would take place. For example, handing out a questionnaire to each patient as he/she arrives for a consultation with the shaman could produce suspicion and confusion. Many clients are only marginally literate, and Peruvians have not been desensitized to survey-based intrusions into private matters. You might want to run physical tests to monitor the biochemical effects of the drugs patients take. But even if permission were granted, how would you quantify the impact on your results of the testing itself? How do you balance the demands of the scientific method (e.g., testable hypotheses, replicable experiments, representative samples, and experimental controls) with the constraints and opportunities of research carried out in "natural" settings?

The solution offered by anthropologists to these methodological dilemmas is **participant observation**. The idea is that humans can best study other humans by drawing upon all the same observational and critical skills that we use unselfconsciously in ordinary social life, although applying these with greater care and rigor than we would in normal circumstances. For the Peruvian case, you would become fluent in Spanish, set up residence in a community where a shaman lives and/or practices, and begin to develop the rapport that will permit you to attend and participate in healing sessions. A central concern would be how to minimize the impact of your own presence on the ongoing work of the shaman, that is, to reconcile your wish to document what you observe with the need to be as unobtrusive as possible. As time goes on and confidence is established between you, the shaman, and his clients, you might be able to shift from unstructured conversations to more formal, tape-recorded interviews and even to multiple interviews via surveys. The guiding ethic of your research would be that those into whose lives you have intruded should be able to set whatever limits they wish on how your work proceeds, even if that means compromising your ideal research plan.

From Fieldwork to Analysis and Interpretation

Thinking about how you might proceed with research on Peruvian shamans provides a general sense of the priorities that guide anthropological research into the healing traditions of other cultures. You may have thought of questions that I did not include;

many of the questions identified and the methods described are those that structured my research with Douglas Sharon, retired Director of the Phoebe A. Hearst Museum of Anthropology (University of California, Berkeley). Our book, *Sorcery and Shamanism: Curanderos and their Clients in Northern Peru* (Joralemon and Sharon 1993), charts the lives and curing "metaphysics" of 12 shamans as well as the interactions between 4 of these shamans and a total of 129 of their patients. The text also explores pre-Hispanic and colonial sources for the symbolism of the rituals performed by shamans and the relationship between the shamans' practices and contemporary social reality.

The research for the book on Peruvian shamans was underway during the time that anthropology began a process of disciplinary self-reflection and critique. At issue were fundamental questions about the enterprise of ethnography, both as a scientific exercise and as an ethically complex undertaking. Critics challenged the assumption that anthropologists gather "facts" about other societies. They argued that ethnographic representations are texts that, as much as any narrative, reflect the cultural perspective and personal prejudices of their authors. The very presumption of ethnographic objectivity and the writing conventions (e.g., avoiding the first person) that accompany it were seen as a facade that permits academics from wealthy nations to treat persons from poorer countries as research subjects. The authority of the ethnographer as someone who claims the privilege of representing others was called into question. The ethics of fieldwork were scrutinized as never before, raising concerns about the differences in power between the researcher and the subject and about the common lack of reciprocity in the relationship between the two.

At the same time, a group of medical anthropologists was calling colleagues to account for the relative lack of attention paid to the political and economic factors that influence everything from the sicknesses people experience to the preventive and curative resources available to them. These self-styled "critical medical anthropologists" (see Chapter 4) insisted that "conventional" medical anthropologists underplayed the importance of stratified social relations as a determinant of the frequency and distribution of diseases and that they neglected the role of power and economic inequality in the practice of medicine. In a flurry of publications covering topics from AIDS to menopause (collected in Lindenbaum and Lock 1993; Singer and Baer 1995), these scholars offered samples of a more politically oriented medical anthropology.

These were some of the theoretical currents that shaped the eventual form of the book on Peruvian shamans.[1] We were encouraged by them to write about our relationships with the shamans and to consider the links between their patients' suffering and the inequalities associated with gender in Peruvian society. In a separate essay, I also reflected on the "discovery" of Peruvian shamans by New Age spiritual pilgrims and the impact it had on our research (Joralemon 1990).

I would certainly not wish to claim that in responding to the broader debates in the field, my coauthor and I resolved any of the very basic challenges they pose to ethnography in general, or to ethnomedical accounts in particular. Rather, my purpose in reviewing these theoretical controversies and how they influenced our work is to illustrate how developments in the field affect the way medical anthropologists design their research and analyze its results. Which questions are considered important and which research strategies are believed to be appropriate directly reflect broader disciplinary debates. So, too, does the responsibility assumed by the researcher in the process of writing about another culture's healing system.

Studying Medicine in the United States

Shamanism in a Third World country like Peru is a fairly standard research topic for a medical anthropologist; it is consistent with the discipline's traditional focus on non-Western cultures. However, an increasing amount of anthropological fieldwork is being carried out on sickness and healing in the United States and Europe. What happens when anthropologists turn their attention to more familiar medical practices? Do the questions they ask, the research methods they employ, or the ethical standards they follow change when the subject is **biomedicine**? In the last chapter, we saw that every medicine bears the imprint of the culture from which it emerged. Does this mean that anthropologists would approach the work of an American MD in the same way as the practice of a Peruvian shaman?

A second thought experiment will help to answer these questions. Imagine that instead of shamanic healing in Peru, the subject of your research is organ transplantation in America. Transplantation is a good example of the high-technology end of biomedicine, as clear an illustration as one might wish of the fruits of basic science and the experimental method. It has also been the focus of my research since the completion of the book on Peruvian shamans.

Organ Transplantation as an Anthropological Subject

> A blood transfusion during an appendectomy had infected Patricia (pseudonym) with hepatitis C. Over the following seventeen years, her liver progressively deteriorated, and at age forty, Patricia underwent a liver transplantation. I interviewed her in an immaculately clean, middle-class home in a city in the southwest of the United States. It had been two years since her transplant, and she had experienced only a minor rejection episode, during the first week after surgery.
>
> At one point in our conversation, Patricia retreated to her bedroom and returned with a flowery photo album. Inside were pictures taken before and after her operation. There were several that showed her swollen abdomen, the result of her diseased liver attempting to regenerate itself. Patricia remarked that she looked pregnant. Following were a set of pictures taken during a visit to the hospital one year after her surgery. Patricia and her husband are seen holding her excised liver, which was kept after removal for subsequent testing. I could not help but think how much the album looked like a baby book!

It may be hard to conceive of an anthropological angle on transplantation precisely because it seems on the face of it to be based on objective science. A good place to start is with the view of the human body on which the very idea of transplantation rests: that it is an organic system made up of replaceable parts. This is a logical extension of the mechanical model of the human body about which Osherson and AmaraSingham (1981, see Chapter 1) wrote. When the water pump in a car breaks, take it out and install a new one; when a heart no longer functions properly, do the same. After all, the heart is just an organic pump.

This mechanical understanding of the human body competes with other cultural conceptions that identify aspects of the self with various organs. For example, the heart may be a pump, but in many cultures it is also the seat of emotions, including love. What meanings will a patient attach to the experience of having a stranger's heart beating in his/her chest? How will a family whose loved one has been declared dead make sense of the request that the body, still connected to life-support machinery, be cut up for recycling? How will societies with different ideas about the self–body relationship respond to proposals to permit the selling of organs—while the seller is still alive in the case of kidneys and for other organs by contracts to be activated upon death?

The continuing shortage of organs made available for transplantation and the extraordinary expenses associated with the surgery raise another cluster of issues for a social scientist. We can gain insight into a culture's values and standards of social equality by analyzing what is considered "fair" and "just" in the way scarce organs are allocated or in the financial support provided for the operation. Should an alcoholic with cirrhosis of the liver or a lifetime cigarette smoker with lung cancer have the same status on the transplant waiting list as others whose organs have failed for reasons unrelated to their own behavior? To make transplantation available to rich and poor alike, should tax funds underwrite the costs of transplantation, which range from $25,000 to over $300,000 for the operation and as much as $1,000 per month thereafter for antirejection medications? Since health care resources are finite, how much money should be channeled into organ transplantation as opposed to other medical measures that cost less and help more people? The controversies that swirl around these issues are rich sources for information on how a given society defines personal and public responsibility.

These questions show that organ transplantation, for all its scientific content, raises many issues for an anthropologist. Let us review the researchable topics suggested for Peruvian shamanism to see how many might apply as well to organ transplantation. At the same time, we can consider which anthropological methods serve this area of investigation.

Research Questions

The training and curing knowledge of the shaman was at the top of the list of matters to explore. Unlike shamans, biomedical specialists learn their skills in a formal setting (e.g., medical and nursing schools) and the basic knowledge they acquire can be found in texts. However, an anthropological analysis of biomedical training, knowledge, and practice is still a fruitful endeavor.

There is an extensive tradition of research on the medical school experience, from the classic sociological account *Boys in White: Student Culture in Medical School* (Becker et al. 1961) to more recent research by medical anthropologist Byron Good and sociologist Mary-Jo DelVecchio Good (1993, 1995). The Goods attended classes at Harvard Medical School as part of their participant observation strategy; anthropology professor Melvin Konner took the idea a step further when he actually completed medical training and became a practicing medical doctor (Konner 1987). While not specifically focused on training in organ transplantation, this body of research does have much to say about how biomedicine's basic assumptions are conveyed to each new generation of practitioners. These assumptions include two that are central to transplantation: The mind and the body are separate aspects of human beings, and the body may be understood as an interrelated set of component parts whose functioning is mechanistic (see Gordon 1988).

Just as it was important to the research on shamans to actually observe their healing work, so would it be essential to shadow transplant specialists as they go about their daily rounds. Here is where the difference between medical theory and clinical practice comes into play. This is the arena in which surgeons, nurses, organ procurement professionals, and others translate the abstractions of the classroom into face-to-face encounters with patients and their families.

From a medical anthropological perspective, the clinic is the site where a complex of social forces intersect. In the encounters between medical specialists and patients, it is possible to see enacted the power and authority of biomedical knowledge. Also evident are the variety of alternative cultural constructions of disease held by patients from different classes and educational and ethnic backgrounds. The specialized social systems of hospitals have prestige structures and political tensions that can alternatively reinforce and clash with the hierarchies and economic divisions of the wider society.

There are important social science studies of the clinical work of a variety of biomedical practitioners. For example, Howard Waitzkin (1991) analyzes the microlevel politics of physician/patient conversations, Joan Cassell (1991) looks at the macho image of surgeons as miracle workers, and Kathryn Taylor (1988) studies the disclosure of cancer diagnoses by oncologists. Other studies have focused on cultural miscommunications between patients and psychiatrists (Kleinman 1988), nurses (Galanti 1991), and obstetricians (Singer 1987).

For organ transplantation, medical sociologist Renée C. Fox and her historian colleague Judith P. Swazey (1974, 1992) have explored the hubris of surgeons who push the boundaries of their discipline by speeding the experimental process from animal research to human trials. They had unusual access to Dr. William DeVries, the first to implant a mechanical heart into a human being (Barney Clark 1982). Their account of his character and career gives exceptional insight into responses to medical failures both on the part of the profession and of the society as a whole. They show how experimentation with artificial hearts lost medical and public support as patient after patient died, while DeVries struggled to preserve his reputation as a pioneer in medical science.

The research agenda for Peruvian shamanism included the symbolic content of the healing rituals they perform. At first, it might seem as if there would be no analogous focus for an investigation of organ transplantation, but this impression would be wrong. Like any human activity associated with matters of life and death, transplant surgery is rich in symbolic significance.

Anthropologists have long noted that life's transitions (e.g., birth, puberty, marriage, and death) are commonly marked by elaborate rituals, the purpose of which is to smooth the disruption to the social order that such status changes can cause (see Gennep 1960, Turner 1969). The body of the person(s) undergoing the transition is often the target of symbolic manipulations: special decorations (e.g., wedding gowns and burial costumes), purifications (e.g., fasting and baptismal cleansing), and even permanent physical alterations (e.g., mutilation and scarification). A particularly frequent symbolic message conveyed by these rituals is death and rebirth; the person(s) is dying from the social status previously held and being born into a new identity. How far might one get by applying this way of thinking about transition rituals, or **rites of passage**, to the experience of transplant recipients? Think of the deindividualized clothing worn by hospital patients, the strict fasting enforced before surgery, the cleansing rituals for the patient as well as surgical staff, the process by which the patient's vital signs and consciousness are taken to a death-like state, and the postsurgery sense of being reborn. The fact that all of these features have medical justifications and explanations does not diminish their potential symbolic impact. Indeed, the testimony of transplant recipients suggests that they do experience the surgery as a rebirth (e.g., Sharp 1995).

Symbolic considerations might also include, as mentioned earlier, the significance in different cultural traditions of specific internal organs and their relationship to personal identity. Even the medical literature in transplantation cites numerous cases in which recipients have been troubled by the idea that some part of the organ donor's self (e.g., personality characteristics, gender-related dispositions, and ethnicity) is still present in the kidney, liver, heart, or lung that now resides in their bodies. Transplant organizations, on the one hand, wish to dispel such ideas in order to facilitate the psychological adjustment of the recipient. On the other hand, the same organizations publicize dramatic accounts of donor families meeting recipients and describing their sense that some part of their deceased loved one survives in the transplanted organ. This is a rich area for anthropological exploration.[2]

A related research question is how cultural definitions of death, norms for the treatment of the dead, and notions of an afterlife complicate organ transplantation. In the United States, the shift from the traditional heart-based determination of death to the current dependence on evidence of brain activity began decades ago (1968), and yet next of kin and medical staff alike still voice confusion and ambivalence about "brain death" (Joralemon 1995:340). Medical anthropologists Margaret Lock and Christina Honde (1990; Lock 2002) have documented the widespread resistance in Japan to the idea of brain death and the impact this has had on the development of organ transplantation in that country. The treatment of the dead and its relationship to transplantation has been investigated as well in Germany (Hogle 1996) and Mexico (Crowley-Matoka 2001).

For Peruvian shamanism, I suggested many research topics related specifically to the patients. Fox and Swazey (1974, 1992) have made significant contributions to the analysis of the transplant patient's experience by focusing on the significance of receiving a "gift of life." They use traditional social science theory about the socio-cultural significance of gift giving (e.g., Mauss 1954) to explain the core dilemma faced by transplant recipients: The gift they receive is of inestimable value (i.e., their own survival), but it is ultimately unrepayable. Fox and Swazey coined the phrase "tyranny of the gift" to capture the impact on recipients of being on the receiving end of a nonreciprocal gift.

Lesley Sharp (1995) has studied transplant patients to see how they respond to having someone else's organ in their body. This important line of inquiry builds on the already mentioned point about the symbolism of body parts. Organ transplantation offers a unique opportunity to explore the boundaries between "self" and "body," especially when the body part being replaced carries significant cultural meanings (e.g., the heart for Americans).

There are other patient-related research issues to explore. For example, the United Network for Organ Sharing, the organization responsible for the equitable distribution of organs for transplantation in the United States, reports statistics that point to the impact of social class, gender, and ethnic divisions on everything from donation rates to the time patients spend on waiting lists. There is ample opportunity for social science analysis of these factors both at the macrolevel of national socioeconomic trends and at the microlevel of individual experiences.

Biological and cultural perspectives might be brought to bear on the question of how transplant centers match donor organs to potential recipients. Advances in antirejection drugs permit less than perfect matches between donors and recipients, but there is still evidence that shows longer graft survival when blood types and human leukocyte antigens (HLA) are matched. Segments of the population with comparatively unusual blood types and/or unlikely antigen matches spend longer on the transplant waiting list when a high priority is assigned to closer matches.

The problem has been especially acute for African Americans, who suffer at disproportionate rates from diseases for which transplantation may be the best or only treatment (e.g., cardiovascular and kidney diseases).[3] Unfortunately, African Americans also have blood types and antigens that are less common in the organ donor pool (e.g., 27 percent of African Americans have blood type B, compared with just 11 percent among Caucasians) (Kasiske et al. 1991). Relatively low organ donation rates from the African American community further reduce the likelihood of a match (Callender et al. 1995). The result is that African Americans can wait for an organ twice as long as Caucasians (Callender 1991).

The interesting issue for a medical anthropologist is how the biological notion of donor/recipient "matching" actually works in transplant allocation systems around the world. What constitutes a "good match" versus the "best match" (e.g., how many antigens should correspond) and how long are patients allowed to deteriorate on a waiting list before they are given an organ even when the match is poor? What factors other than tissue matching might account for differential graft survival? Is the reliance on strict matching evidence of racial bias in the allocation system? These questions require that attention be paid to both biological and cultural issues.

The outcome of shamanic treatment was on the agenda for research with the Peruvian patients. There is an immense amount of literature on this subject for transplant recipients, but almost all of it is based on surveys or brief, structured questionnaires. Anthropologists recognize the shortcomings of these formal research instruments, especially when the topic under consideration is as complex as the "quality of life" of persons who have undergone a medical treatment as dramatic as the removal and replacement of one or more vital organs. A supplemental approach employing qualitative methods would be a significant contribution (Joralemon and Fujinaga 1996).

Research Methods

There are certainly many other directions that anthropological research on transplantation might take, but let us turn our attention to the question of methods: How might an anthropologist investigate some of the areas already mentioned? An obvious first source of information is the mountain of professional and public relations material published each year by persons involved in transplantation. This includes research reports, ethical debates, and promotional materials (e.g., from the National Kidney Foundation). Just as Emily Martin analyzed immunology textbooks for the combat metaphors they employ (see Chapter 1), so would it be possible to do a cultural reading of publications in transplantation. Reports on the "quality of life" of organ recipients could be analyzed for what they reveal about how biomedicine defines a life worth living, as well as about the economic motivations behind and limitations of this research (Joralemon and Fujinaga 1996). Similarly, there is a multidisciplinary literature debating the merits and demerits of various approaches to organ donation that illuminates cultural assumptions about the value of the body after death (Joralemon 1995, 2001; Joralemon and Cox 2003).

Many avenues are open for research based on participant observation as well. Lesley Sharp (1995) attended the meetings of recipient support groups; she and I have both traveled to the biennial athletic competition for transplant recipients, the "Transplant Games," which is organized by the National Kidney Foundation as a part of its donor promotion campaign (see Photo 2.2). Patricia Marshall (1995) did ethnographic work in a village in India where healthy individuals are paid to donate a kidney for transplantation. And Linda Hogle (1996) has done extensive interviewing of "organ procurement" specialists in Germany.

I have found interesting differences between my present research on organ transplantation and the work I did previously with Peruvian shamans. In Peru, I negotiated the terms of my research largely on a person-by-person basis, gaining consent for participation in rituals and for individual interviews from each shaman and every patient. I was very much an outsider, and I had the distinct impression that the purpose of my presence was never entirely clear to most of those with whom I spoke. Until my work appears in Spanish and is distributed in Peru, those who cooperated with me will not see what I had to say about them or about the healing tradition of which they were a part. Our research assistants, my coauthor, and I made every effort

Photo 2.2 2008 U.S. Transplant Games Day 5 PITTSBURGH - JULY 15: Kidney Transplant athlete Holly Miyagawa participates during the volleyball competition on July 15, 2008 at National Kidney Foundation U.S. Transplant Games in Pittsburgh, Pennsylvania. (Photo by Marc Serota/Getty Images)

to proceed in an ethical fashion, but the fact is that those we interviewed gave more than they received. They also had to trust us to follow through on commitments to protect their identities when they requested that we do so.

My transplantation research presents a far more equitable relationship between "investigator" and "research subject." I am not a cultural outsider in the United States. When I interview organ recipients, they know that they will have access to whatever I publish. Furthermore, there has been organizational resistance to my research that I did not encounter in Peru. Professionals involved in transplantation are very protective of their work, and they sometimes seek to avoid granting access to researchers who they suspect might have critical agendas. For example, the National Kidney

Foundation declined to provide me with the video that they produced for participants in the 1994 Transplant Games; I was given only the very abbreviated version that was released to television stations for promotional purposes, and then only after I put in writing how I intended to use it.

There is a fascinating paradox here. The profession of transplantation medicine has precious little to fear from the work of an anthropologist; this is a prestigious and economically powerful specialty in a medical system that is itself extraordinarily well positioned in the American social fabric. A Peruvian shaman, on the other hand, risks a great deal by opening his practice to the scrutiny of an outsider. There are laws against what he does in Peru and a long history of official repression and harassment. While there are potential benefits from the notoriety a shaman gains by having international researchers present at his rituals (Joralemon 1990), there is also a serious threat posed by bringing a very discreet practice to public attention. Yet, I found far less hesitation about my research from shamans in Peru than I have encountered while working on transplantation in the United States.

This paradox relates to some of the discipline-wide debates mentioned earlier. To whom and for whom does the anthropologist write? When anthropologists investigate powerful institutions in their own countries, which Laura Nader calls "studying-up" (1969), how can they avoid accommodations that provide access at the cost of independence? What privacy rights and control over the use of research results should the anthropologist extend to persons who collaborate in research, whether they be well-connected persons at home or marginalized individuals in poor countries?

For medical anthropology, these issues have come into sharp focus as researchers have turned their attention to biomedicine. They have proven especially troubling when medical anthropologists apply their skills in clinical settings as partners to biomedical practitioners rather than as outside investigators. Critics have leveled strong charges against applied medical anthropology in biomedicine, arguing that it has the effect of promoting the already substantial control that doctors and their professional institutions have over our lives (see Chapter 7).

Summary: The Anthropological Vision

My purpose in comparing Peruvian shamanism and organ transplantation has been to give substance to the first chapter's more abstract discussion of the unique perspective of medical anthropology. These are dramatically different topics for anthropological research. However, setting them in contrast to each other shows how anthropological priorities direct us to questions and methods that have much in common regardless of the specific topic or societal setting under investigation.

This exercise illustrates anthropology's focus on the connections between medical beliefs and practices, and wider sociocultural realities. It also underscores the commitment of many medical anthropologists to integrate biological and cultural considerations in the analysis of sickness and healing.

Finally, the two research subjects indicate the central role of participant observation in the medical anthropology enterprise. Our natural science colleagues are quick to dismiss this method as "soft" and vulnerable to subjective biases. Anthropologists respond by arguing that the very distinction between "hard" and "soft" science is itself a prejudice that overstates the objectivity of the former at the same time as it underplays the sophistication of the latter. Whether it be a shaman's use of psychoactive drugs or a surgeon's declaration of brain death, qualitative research provides contextual insights that supplement and improve other methods.

Now that the special perspective and characteristic methods of medical anthropology are clear, I want to take up the field's central theoretical dilemma: the relationships between biological, political-economic, and cultural perspectives. Once again, I start with a concrete case and then develop the more abstract theoretical issues (Chapters 4 and 5). I use the 1991 outbreak of cholera in Peru as my point of departure.

SUGGESTED READINGS

The cross-cultural literature on shamanism is extensive, in part because the term is used broadly to refer to healers who employ trance states of any variety. Two review articles are a good place to start: Larry Peters and Douglas Price-Williams's "Towards an Experiential Analysis of Shamanism" (1980) and Jane Atkinson's "Shamanisms Today" (1992).

A particularly good case study of the interaction between shamans and biomedical healers is Joseph Bastien's *Drum and Stethoscope: Integrating Ethnomedicine and Biomedicine in Bolivia* (1992).

An excellent collection of medical anthropology studies of biomedicine is published in Margaret Lock and Deborah Gordon's *Biomedicine Examined* (1988).

Many books and articles are available on ethnographic methods, but a good place to start is P. J. and G. H. Pelto's *Anthropological Research: The Structure of Inquiry* (1978), H. Russell Bernard's *Research Methods in Anthropology* (1994), and Robert T. Trotter's survey essay, "Ethnographic Research Methods for Applied Medical Anthropology" (1991).

Reservations about ethnographic writing are conveyed in J. Clifford and G. Marcus's edited collection, *Writing Culture* (1986), and in G. Marcus and M. Fischer's *Anthropology as Cultural Critique: An Experimental Moment in the Human Sciences* (1986).

NOTES

1. I cannot say that the actual fieldwork was substantially changed in response to the above cited debates. Our research design reflected the training Sharon and I had at UCLA, which stressed the ethnographic exploration of shamanic symbolism. I do think that the emerging critical perspective in medical anthropology led us to pay more attention in our interviews with patients to the economic and social constraints that affected their lives. The real impact of the disciplinary debates came as we analyzed our field notes and composed the text.

2. Lesley Sharp (2006) does an excellent job exploring the complexities of donor/recipient relations.

3. This is itself a subject for combined biological and cultural research. How can one sort out the genetic contribution to these epidemiological patterns from the impact of sociocultural factors like diet, exposure to social stress associated with racial discrimination, and lack of access to treatment options (Dressler 1984, 1989)?

CHAPTER 3 Recognizing Biological, Social, and Cultural Interconnections

Evolutionary and Ecological Perspectives on a Cholera Epidemic

Medical anthropology theory is a blend of social science, epidemiological, and biological perspectives on disease. The most effective way to show how these theoretical threads come together in medical anthropology is to introduce them separately, applying each in the analysis of a concrete case of disease. This will permit us to understand what each theory does and does not explain, as well as to illustrate how they are combined. The case illustration I have chosen is a cholera epidemic in South America.

First, a word or two about the purpose of theory in social and natural sciences. A theory seeks to account for a defined set of regularities or patterns evident in a given phenomenon. For example, gravitational theory provides an explanation for the observable fact that objects, when released, fall to earth. A symbolic theory might try to explain the common association between a particular color and specific cultural meanings (e.g., red and fertility). It is not the isolated instance of a phenomenon that a theory explains (e.g., one object falling or one red symbol that stands for fertility), but the predictable repetition of the event.

Theories operate at an abstract level. They reduce the complexity of a given phenomenon to those characteristics that are considered relevant to understanding the pattern under study. Newton did not need to know the color of the apple that fell on his head in order to derive his theory of gravity. However, the color of the apple that Eve offered to Adam in the Bible's Genesis story might make a significant difference to a theory of color symbolism. Any theory must identify which characteristics are considered relevant and which evidence will be accepted.

This last point about theory is especially important because it helps us to understand the conflicts that arise over competing theoretical interpretations. Often, theoretical disagreements emerge from differences in what scholars think is relevant to an explanation of a phenomenon and what they accept as evidence. No theory can account for all aspects of a phenomenon; all theories are vulnerable to the claim that some relevant factor(s) was not included, or that evidence was missing or misconstrued.

A final observation about theory is crucial: Theories are constructed by persons whose historical and cultural situation is revealed in the sorts of phenomena they choose to theorize about, as well as by the standards of evidence they acknowledge (e.g., religious interpretations of the Black Plague during the Middle Ages, which held sufferers morally responsible for their affliction). Furthermore, theorizing does not occur in a political vacuum. Sometimes theories support the status quo in societal arrangements (e.g., gender inequities as justified by nineteenth-century medical theories), and sometimes they challenge structures of power (e.g., critiques by feminist scholars of contemporary obstetrical practices; see Chapter 6). It would take us too far afield to discuss the sociopolitical context of each of the theoretical frameworks we will be reviewing, but it is useful to keep in mind that medical anthropology is shaped as much as any field of inquiry by the constraints of the societies that support it.[1]

Thinking about Epidemics

January is midsummer in Peru. Temperatures soar, and residents of the largest coastal cities migrate to beach communities, either on day trips or for extended vacations. Huanchaco, the fishing village in which I lived during my fieldwork, is transformed on weekends to a virtual Coney Island as throngs arrive from Trujillo in overloaded buses and packed family cars. Overnight, small kiosks and seasonal restaurants spring up all along the beach; they offer every manner of refreshment, but ceviche, a raw seafood dish, features prominently on most menus. The crowds push the infrastructure of the village, including water supplies and sanitation, well beyond its capacity.

At the end of January in 1991, several years after my research on Peruvian curers had ended, there were reports of an increase in diarrheal illness in Candelaria, another coastal village just north of Peru's capital, Lima. Laboratory tests revealed the presence of the cholera bacterium. This was the twentieth century's first appearance in South America of one of history's most deadly epidemic agents. Within two weeks, 12,000 cases were recorded along the full 2,000 km of Peru's coast. The epidemic moved rapidly into the Peruvian highlands and then crossed national borders to affect Ecuador, Colombia, and Brazil. It continued to spread throughout Latin America in the following two years, making almost one million people sick and killing nearly 9,000 (Guthmann 1995). Researchers speculate that cholera may now be a permanent part of Latin America's epidemiological profile.

Epidemics offer particularly vivid demonstrations of the interconnections between biological, social, and cultural components in the human experience of disease. For many of the historically significant epidemics (e.g., smallpox, the bubonic plague, leprosy, tuberculosis, and cholera), there is substantial scientific knowledge about the organisms responsible for the diseases, about the means of transmission, and about treatment and prevention. The links between epidemics and social factors like urbanization, poverty, migration, and others are usually well known today. Finally, because epidemics can be so devastating to human communities, they provide ample opportunity for cultural interpretations as afflicted populations struggle to make sense of their suffering.

In this and the next chapter, I show how the biological, social, and cultural dimensions of the Peruvian cholera outbreak were represented in published accounts. Cholera can alternatively be understood as a well-adapted bacterium, as a symptom of societal collapse, or as a conspiracy against the poor. But first, it is necessary to know something of the history of cholera and of the investigations into its treatment and prevention.

History and Biology of Cholera

> Cholera is an acute dehydrating diarrheal disease caused by toxigenic *Vibrio cholerae* 01. Severe cases of cholera are characterized by profuse diarrhea and vomiting, muscular cramps, and collapse; the fluid loss is so dramatic that a healthy person can die within hours. Cholera is also a very contagious disease, and large epidemics with high mortality have been reported throughout historic time (Popovic et al. 1993:811).

Historical reports of epidemics likely to have been cholera date back as far as 1503. However, it was not until the early 1800s, during the first **pandemic** (prevalent throughout a country, region, or the whole world) of the disease (1817–1823),[2] that cholera spread from its home in India to Southeast Asia, the south Pacific, China, and Egypt. After a very short pause, a second pandemic (1826–1851) brought the disease to Eastern and Western Europe (1830), North America (1832), and Latin America (1833) (Kiple 1993). Within three decades, cholera became a global concern.

It was during the third cholera pandemic (1852–1859) that a breakthrough was accomplished in the scientific understanding of how the disease spreads. A London physician, John Snow, noted that the cholera cases that began to appear on August 31, 1853, in the Soho district were concentrated near a public water source on Broad Street. Closer investigation showed that, in addition to those patients who lived near the well, seven male victims who lived elsewhere had consumed its water while working in the neighborhood. By contrast, the employees of a nearby brewery, none of whom got sick, drank either free beer or brewery water while at work. Snow concluded that the Broad Street well was contaminated and, on September 7, had the pump handle removed. The outbreak subsided almost immediately. It was later discovered that a leaking cesspool had introduced cholera bacteria into the well, probably on August 28 when a baby had come down with the disease in the vicinity (Diamond 1992).

Knowing that cholera could be spread by fecal contamination of water contributed greatly to public health campaigns, but scientists still had not identified the **pathogen** (disease-causing agent). It was not until the fifth pandemic (1881–1896) that the German microbiologist Robert Koch and his colleagues isolated the comma-shaped bacterium that causes cholera. Seventy-six more years, and one more pandemic (1899–1923), passed before investigators learned how the bacterium triggers cholera's characteristic, and sometimes fatal, diarrhea. In 1959, Calcutta researcher S. N. De identified the toxin produced by the bacterium that causes the small intestine to secrete large quantities of fluids. The precise molecular-level analysis of how the toxin causes potentially fatal dehydration dates to the 1970s (Rabbani 1986).

During the first six cholera pandemics, mortality rates were extremely high: 50–70 percent of those afflicted died. Significant improvements in survival came after the development of an effective **rehydration solution** (1959–1961),[3] an orally administered fluid that replaces the water, sugar, and salts lost through diarrhea. This inexpensive treatment, commonly called Oral Rehydration Therapy (ORT), contributed to a much lower loss of life during the seventh pandemic, which began in Indonesia in 1961. The 1991 Peruvian outbreak, considered to be the "third phase" of the seventh pandemic,[4] had regional case fatality rates as low as 0.69 percent largely because of the availability of ORT (Guthmann 1995).

At about the same time that the epidemic began in Peru, there were cases reported from south Asia of a new variant, or **serotype**, of cholera, *Vibrio cholerae* 0139. Epidemiologists judge this to be the start of the eighth pandemic, the first time in history that two cholera pandemics have overlapped. This development is especially troubling because the old strain appears to offer little or no protection against infection by the new serotype. It is clear that cholera is far from being eliminated from the inventory of diseases that affect humans, even if the loss of life associated with it has been minimized as a result of ORT.

After 400 years of experience with cholera, the link between the disease and contaminated water supplies is well established. It is also clear that humans can be infected by food that has been contaminated by fecal material, as when an ill person handles or prepares food or when sewage waters are used in crop irrigation. There is evidence that cholera may survive and replicate in warm ocean waters close to locations of raw sewage releases. Shellfish taken from such waters, which form an environmental reservoir for the bacteria, may infect humans, especially if the fish is eaten raw or undercooked (Popovic et al. 1993).

Under circumstances of poor sanitation and untreated water supplies, cholera can move through a human population with impressive efficiency. During the first three days of the disease, when diarrheal flow is the greatest, the amount of bacteria released daily into the environment from a single sufferer is sufficient to infect up to ten million people (Popovic et al. 1993). On the other hand, the disease is not spread by person-to-person contact because exposure to literally billions of bacteria is required for infection to occur.

Epidemiological Accounts of Peru's Cholera Epidemic

The 1991 cholera outbreak in Peru received a great deal of attention from **epidemiologists**, who examine "the distribution of disease in large populations to isolate the risk factors that enable intervention and, ultimately, control" (Agar 1996:391). Like medical anthropologists, epidemiologists consider the "biological, social and cultural causes and ramifications of sickness" (Trostle and Sommerfeld 1996:254). However, epidemiologists are ultimately interested in social and cultural detail only as steps toward a universal explanation for what leads to a specific health problem. For most medical anthropologists, understanding the local context in which health problems arise is itself the goal of research (Hahn 1995:102–103).[5]

Epidemiological accounts of the Peruvian cholera epidemic focused on the source of the cholera bacteria and how it was transmitted. The fact that the first cases were reported from coastal communities led researchers to speculate on the possibility that contaminated seafood, especially shellfish, was responsible for the start of the epidemic. Ceviche, the uncooked seafood dish so popular in Peru, was implicated. The ocean dumping of untreated sewage from coastal cities and/or the release of contaminated ballast from ships were considered likely sources of contamination; a potential contributing factor was the summer warming of ocean currents (Crowcroft 1994).

Epidemiologists unanimously argued that, once the outbreak began, contaminated water supplies had spread the bacteria through coastal populations. Peru's inadequate and seriously deteriorated municipal water and sewage systems, always strained to the breaking point during the hot summer months when water supplies dry up, were a major culprit. For example, a 1991 study of the water system in Trujillo (Swerdlow et al. 1992), which has a population of over 300,000, showed no routine chlorination, many illegal connections to pipes with the potential of introducing contaminants, and crops irrigated with sewage water. In addition, water was available in much of the city for only one or two hours a day, which encouraged household storage in tanks that promote bacterial growth. Not surprisingly, cholera was found in 60 percent of samples taken from different locations in the water distribution system.

After identifying the source(s) of the epidemic and the means by which it was transmitted, epidemiological accounts analyzed how many people got sick (**morbidity**) and how many died (**mortality**). They also reported how many new cases were registered each month and year (**incidence**) to gauge the course of the epidemic. Calculations of the proportion of the country's population that was infected at one time (**prevalence**) indicated how much of a burden the epidemic was to medical and social services.

Comparisons of these standard epidemiological measures between different regions of the country (e.g., coast, highland, and tropical forest) suggested urban/rural differences in the risk of exposure as well as in access to effective medical care. For example, while the incidence, or "attack rate," was much lower inland than along the coast, the **case fatality ratio (CFR)** was as much as twelve times higher (WHO 1991). In other words, if you lived in a mountain community you were less likely to get sick, but more likely to die if you did, because medical services were not as available as in coastal cities.

At the national level, epidemiological statistics described a severe cholera epidemic with very low fatality due to the widespread use of intravenous and oral rehydration. In 1990, Peru's health minister ordered the distribution of 1.3 million ORT kits in anticipation of what he expected would be a bad summer season of diarrheal disease (Gall 1993). Once the epidemic began, international health organizations flew in additional supplies of the kits as well as quantities of intravenous rehydration solutions. Urgent public health warnings on television and radio were also credited with keeping mortality low in coastal cities.

In sum, investigations during the cholera outbreak followed standard epidemiological practice by focusing on the correct diagnosis of the responsible pathogen, the source(s) and mode of its transmission, and the most effective control measures (Trostle 1995). The theoretical foundation for epidemiological practice blends evolutionary theory with an ecological perspective on disease. It is to this theoretical synthesis, which has been central to epidemiology as well as to medical anthropology, that we now turn.

Evolution and the Ecological Framework

Epidemiology views disease in ecological terms as the interaction between a pathogen(s) and its **host(s)** (an organism—human or animal—that harbors the disease-causing organism), as this interaction is shaped by the conditions of a specific environment(s) (Timmreck 1993:6–9). In the case of cholera, the pathogen is the bacterium *Vibrio cholerae*, and the host is human beings. The "environment" refers to the settings in which the disease occurs, including the physical (e.g., altitude, soil, and water), biological (e.g., plants, animals, and microorganisms), sociocultural (e.g., demographic characteristics, political structures, and economic conditions), and climatic (e.g., temperature and humidity) features of these settings. The interaction between pathogen(s), host(s), and environment is represented graphically in the widely cited "epidemiological triangle" (Timmreck 1993:8).

The overarching theoretical framework for this ecological model is evolutionary theory and its central concept of **natural selection**. In brief, evolutionary theory focuses on the ability of individual organisms to reproduce in spite of the survival threats found in particular environmental contexts. Any genetically governed characteristic(s) that provides a selective advantage (i.e., increases the chances that members of a living population will survive and reproduce) will be expressed more frequently in that population over time because those with the trait(s) more often live long enough to pass their genes on to the next generation.

Variation in the genetic makeup of a population is the prerequisite for evolutionary change—if all the members of a population had exactly the same genetic material, there would be nothing to select for or against in response to environmental challenges. The ultimate source of genetic variation is **mutation**, random errors that occur as genes replicate.[6] Most mutations are disadvantageous and result in the death of the organism, during gestation or at some point in the individual's life. Spontaneous abortions are frequently caused by deleterious mutations; Cystic fibrosis and Huntington's chorea are two fatal diseases related to genetic mutations in humans. Some mutations neither benefit nor harm the individual, either because they are not expressed as a visible trait (i.e., the mutation affects the **genotype** but not the **phenotype**) or because the trait they produce is insignificant in terms of survival.

Only rarely do mutations produce traits that offer a selective advantage. A frequently cited example is the gene that codes for an abnormal blood trait, hemoglobin S

BOX 3.1
The Sickle-Cell Advantage

Investigators discovered that Hb^S frequencies are highest in areas where malaria is prevalent. Further research showed that individuals who are **heterozygous** for Hb^S (i.e., inherit one normal and one abnormal hemoglobin gene) are not only protected from developing sickle-cell anemia but also have a degree of resistance to falciparum malaria, a severe form of malaria which can cause sterility and/or death. The abnormal hemoglobin diminishes the oxygen supply needed by the malaria parasites to reproduce. Thus, persons with both the normal (Hb^A) and abnormal (Hb^S) hemoglobins have a selective advantage over those who are homozygous for either Hb^A (they are more likely to die or fail to reproduce as a result of malaria) or Hb^S (they are more likely to die from sickle-cell anemia).

Biological anthropologist Frank Livingstone (1958) added the final piece to the puzzle when he linked Hb^S and falciparum malaria to those regions where irrigation-based agriculture created new breeding opportunities for the mosquito that transports the malaria parasite to human beings. With more mosquitoes and more concentrated agricultural communities, the selective advantage of the heterozygous Bb^AHb^S was all the more powerful. The abnormal hemoglobin did not completely replace the normal hemoglobin even under these circumstances because some still inherit Hb^S from both parents and are therefore vulnerable to sickle-cell anemia. This keeps the frequency of Hb^S in check.

(Hb^S). When an individual inherits the gene from both parents (i.e., **homozygous**), it causes sickle-cell anemia, named after the sickle shape of the abnormal red blood cell. Since sickle-cell anemia causes many serious, often fatal, complications (e.g., heart failure and kidney damage) during a sufferer's pre-reproductive years, evolution would ordinarily select against the Hb^S gene. The question for researchers in the 1950s was this: Given the selective disadvantage, why do as many as 36 percent of some populations in Africa, southern Europe, and the Middle East have the trait? The evolutionary answer is summarized in Box 3.1.

Evolutionary theory employs the concept of **adaptation** to describe the continuing process by which a population adjusts to its environment in response to selective pressures. The related concept of **fitness** is a measure of how well or poorly adapted an individual or group is to a specific environment. High fertility and low mortality are the indices that indicate fitness. Thus, we would say that the abnormal hemoglobin that can cause sickle-cell anemia contributes to the fitness of human groups that live in malaria-prone regions—it is adaptive—but that it diminishes the fitness of humans in settings free from malaria. In the latter case, the trait is **maladaptive**.

Cholera and the Evolutionary Framework

How are evolutionary theory and the ecological model applied to the analysis of cholera? In a *Discover* magazine article, UCLA professor of physiology Jared Diamond gives an account of the Peruvian epidemic that draws upon evolutionary theory to explain the interaction between cholera bacteria and human hosts (Diamond 1992). He asks us to think about this interaction from the bacteria's point of view: How does an organism (the bacterium) that cannot move on its own manage to get itself spread to the greatest number of additional hosts in which it can reproduce? Diamond points to the selective advantage represented by the cholera bacteria's production of a toxin that disturbs the normal reabsorption of liquid from the small intestine back into the blood system. This produces a severe diarrhea which sends the microbes out to infect new hosts.

By casting cholera's activity in terms of a combat metaphor (see Chapter 1), Diamond notes that there is some variation in the way different strains of the bacteria accomplish this reproductive feat: "Some microbes aim for total victory, in the form of massive diarrhea that kills the patient after broadcasting billions of microbes within a few days. Others settle for a truce, whereby the host survives with chronic low-level diarrhea that sends out a small, steady stream of microbes" (p. 64).

The conditions of each new cholera outbreak, including the preventive and treatment measures available to human communities, will benefit one or the other "strategy." We might ask, for example, what conditions contributed to the dominance in recent outbreaks of the El Tor variant of the cholera bacterium. Consider the twentieth-century development of public health infrastructures and epidemic control measures in light of the following comparisons between El Tor and classic variants of cholera:

- El Tor is less virulent than classic. El Tor infection lasts longer, but there are fewer severe cases; as many as one-fourth of those affected have only moderate diarrhea, and there is a higher rate of asymptomatic carriers (i.e., the bacteria cause no discernible symptoms).

- El Tor bacteria are excreted in stools for between three and twenty days, compared with one to seven days for the classic variant. Once shed, El Tor bacteria survive longer outside the human body. They have been shown to grow to higher numbers than the classic bacteria on moderately cooked food (Popovic et al. 1993).

- Exposure to El Tor bacteria produces virtually no postinfection immunity, compared with a temporary immunity after exposure to the classic type (see Table 3.1).

We are not in a position to identify with any certainty the conditions that gave El Tor a measure of evolutionary advantage over classic variants in recent outbreaks.

TABLE 3.1 Characteristics of *V. Cholerae*, El Tor Serotype

1. Less virulent than classical: fewer severe cases (2 percent), and up to 75 percent of cases are asymptomatic.
2. Infection persists longer than classical: bacteria are present in stools for three to twenty days compared with one to seven days for classical.
3. Bacteria survive longer outside of human body.
4. No postinfection immunity: survivors can be reinfected.
5. Greater chance of transmission by food: El Tor bacteria survive and increase better than classical on even moderately cooked food.

Sources: Crowcroft 1994, Diamond 1992, and Popovic et al. 1993.

However, several changed circumstances in the twentieth century are likely to have been involved. First, the worldwide movement of human beings via systems of mass transportation certainly made the communication of cholera from one region to another far easier. Second, the increasing concentration of human populations in urban centers, especially in the Third World, has far outpaced the ability of public services to accommodate the increased numbers. For example, Lima's population rose from 645,000 in 1940 to 6.5 million in 1990 (Winn 1992:246). As a result, water and sewage systems, as well as state-sponsored regulation of hygiene in food production and sales, have been seriously compromised in countries around the world. A third factor identified by some analysts is human-induced global warming, which may contribute to larger ocean blooms of plankton on which cholera bacteria survive to be transmitted to shellfish and then to humans (Epstein 1992; Guerrant 1994).

These conditions would seem to make it far easier for cholera bacteria to reproduce, since the bacteria now have more hosts and more varied means of transmission. On the other hand, epidemic control measures work in the opposite direction, making it more difficult for cholera to take full advantage of human hosts by interrupting the cycle of infection and transmission. Is there a way for cholera to profit from the proliferation of hosts and transmission routes while avoiding the obstacles (from the bacteria's point of view) of prevention and treatment?

From the bacteria's perspective, one alternative suggests itself: Infect your host at a mild-enough level not to set off the panic buttons in the health ministries. Trigger longer-term but less severe diarrhea so that you get the same number of bacteria out in search of new hosts, but without generating human responses that put an end to the game. Prolong survival times outside of human hosts to increase the likelihood of encountering new hosts even if epidemic control measures are put in place. It would also be best if hosts do not even notice that they are infected, that is, if they have no symptoms, or symptoms so mild as to be confused with occasional diarrheas that do not call for special treatment. Doesn't it not sound a bit like the characteristics of El Tor?

Unfortunately, there is another alternative: Infect so efficiently and severely as to overwhelm any epidemic control measures. Cause the maximum diarrhea in the shortest time possible and to the largest number of humans available—even if the hosts die as a result. And, ideally, select a country that is ill prepared, logistically and/or politically, to respond to a public health emergency. The 1991 appearance in Southeast Asia of the new serotype *V. cholerae* 0139, with reported case fatalities of 5 percent and with faster transmission than El Tor (Crowcroft 1994), may represent a selection for a more virulent strain.[7] Longer experience with this variant is needed before we can speculate on its survival advantage.

The ecological/evolutionary analysis of cholera highlights the impact of changing human demographic, economic, and medical patterns on the bacteria's evolutionary trajectory. The combination of evolutionary theory with the ecological model has also provided insights into the long-term genetic implications for human hosts of exposure to other epidemic agents. An excellent example is the interdisciplinary investigation of kuru, a central nervous system disease found among the Fore people of New Guinea (see Lindenbaum 1979).

There is little doubt that the ecological/evolutionary model has made important contributions to our understanding of the dynamic interplay between disease-causing agents, human hosts, and the environments in which both seek to survive and reproduce. The model is most useful when a disease can be traced to a single agent, whose interaction with human hosts can be clearly defined. It is more difficult to apply for diseases that are multicausal, as in many chronic conditions, because with these it is more difficult to conceptualize the disease process in terms of "pathogen," "host," and "environment." For example, what is the "pathogen" behind cardiovascular disease?[8]

This shortcoming notwithstanding, the ecological/evolutionary model found an early and welcome reception in medical anthropology. It fit well with a resurgence of anthropological interest in the relationship between human societies and the environmental constraints with which they contend.[9] It also resonated with a renewed interest in the applicability of evolutionary theory to anthropological evidence.[10] For a discipline in search of a theoretical framework that transcends the particularistic studies of individual cultures, the model had great appeal.

Medical Anthropology Embraces the Ecological/Evolutionary Model

The introduction of the ecological/evolutionary model of disease into medical anthropology is traceable to an influential early textbook written by Columbia University anthropologist, Alexander Alland (1970). Alland had earlier championed an extension of the evolutionary concept of adaptation to include not just the long-term results of natural selection on gene pools but also the far more rapid processes of "cultural evolution" (Alland 1966). He argued that the uniqueness of humans is that they adapt, or fail to adapt, to the survival challenges of their environments through genetic, developmental (i.e., physiological changes during the lifespan), *and* cultural means.

Alland saw the health conditions of a human population—specifically, its disease and fertility rates—as a good measure of its environmental adaptation. A well-adapted society would, through some mix of biological (genetically governed and physiological) and cultural means, achieve low rates of disease and relatively high rates of fertility. Medical anthropology, Alland insisted, should be conceived as a part of the study of human adaptation, using the analysis of health and disease as a bridge between the discipline's biological and cultural subfields.[11]

There are three senses in which Alland applies the adaptation concept. He follows evolutionary biologists in using it to describe changes in a population's—in this case, human—gene pool that result from the pressures of natural selection. These changes in the genetic inheritance of a population are ordinarily long term, because natural selection usually takes many generations to affect a gene pool.[12] The sickle-cell example is among the most frequently cited.

This use of the adaptation concept restricts its scope to those inherited characteristics which advantage or disadvantage genetically distinct individuals in a population. Alland's second application of the concept extends it to include physiological responses that are possible for all humans because they are a part of our shared genetic constitution. The responses are triggered by aspects of the environment and are generally reversible.[13] For example, by the term "adaptive," he implies the physiological changes that result from exposure to infectious agents (e.g., short-term immunity after exposure to some cholera strains), to difficult environments (e.g., human developmental responses to high altitude settings), and to nutritional shortages (e.g., physiological changes that occur during famines). These are adaptive not in the sense that they favor the survival of some individuals over others, but that they represent capacities that improve the ability of humans in general to adjust to environmental challenges.

Alland's third use of the adaptation concept extends it even further, to refer to culturally derived activities that facilitate human adjustments to environmental challenges. The success of the human species is directly linked to the capacity to respond to survival threats via learned and shared behaviors, in addition to genetic and physiological adaptations. The capacity for culture extends the ability of humans to adapt, both in reference to the geographic settings in which they may survive and in terms of their ability to defend against dangers from other organisms. For example, Alland would point to the development of public sanitation systems and ORTs as examples of cultural adaptations that improve survival despite the presence of the cholera bacteria in the environment.

This last use of the notion of adaptation is significant because it broadens the concept to include both **somatic** (i.e., bodily or physical) and **extrasomatic** (behavioral) human characteristics. A good example of the contrast is the physical (somatic) response to extreme cold—constriction of blood vessels and shivering—versus the fabrication of clothing and shelters that protect from the cold (extrasomatic) (see Frisancho 1981:41–84). Here is how Alland explains why he uses the adaptation concept for both kinds of responses:

> It is often pointed out that the major difficulty in applying Darwinian evolution to so-called cultural adaptation is the fact that culture traits are extrasomatic and therefore not bound to genetic mechanisms. Hence it is said, quite correctly, that different rules govern their transmission. They are not only passed from generation to generation through a learning process, but may easily transgress societal boundaries without concomitant interbreeding. But how important is this difference? As I have pointed out above, adaptation is the major concern here, not the origin of traits nor the mechanisms of their transmission. The relationships between traits and environments have the same effect on adaptation whether the traits are biological or cultural, and adaptation in human groups is bound to be the result of combined biological and cultural forces (Alland, in Landy 1977:42).

Alland noted that applying the concept in medical anthropology offers the advantage of quantifying how successful or unsuccessful a social system is in meeting the goals of survival and reproduction. Rates of morbidity/mortality and fertility/fecundity are direct measures of how well a social system has adapted to its environment.[14] Thus, Alland would cite the low mortality rates in Peru's cholera epidemic as evidence of that country's successful (cultural) adaptation to the disease.

Alland's use of the adaptation concept and the evolutionary/ecological model is not unique to him or to medical anthropology. Anthropologists studying human population biology have elaborated increasingly complex models of human adaptation. Like Alland, they use the term "adaptation" to refer to the entire range of adjustments—genetic, developmental/physiological, and cultural—which aid in biological function (Baker and Weiner 1966; Frisancho 1981; Ulijaszek and Huss-Ashmore 1997).[15]

The adaptation concept has also been central to the field of **cultural ecology**, which analyzes socioeconomic arrangements in terms of the payoff they offer for human physical well-being.[16] Mark Cohen's *Health and the Rise of Civilization* (1989) is an ambitious and often-cited survey of the conclusions of this research. He summarizes the health risks and benefits of general types of human societies: hunting and gathering bands, sedentary agricultural communities, and large states. Among the health factors that Cohen considers are nutrition, exposure to infectious disease, and fertility and mortality patterns. Particularly intriguing, given stereotypes of the barely surviving hunting and gathering band, is Cohen's conclusion that many of the infectious diseases which plague settled human communities are insignificant in small-scale, nomadic societies.

Within medical anthropology, Alland's model has been elaborated by Ann McElroy and Patricia K. Townsend in their teaching text, *Medical Anthropology in Ecological Perspective* (2004). McElroy and Townsend adopt the term "**medical ecology**," which they define as "the study of health and disease in environmental context" (p. 5). Their approach is drawn directly from the synthesis of ecological and evolutionary models urged by Alland. Following Alland, they use the concept of adaptation in all three senses: genetic, physiological, and cultural.

McElroy and Townsend's work has generated a strong line of criticism from critical medical anthropologists. The ensuing debate deserves our attention. In the next chapter, we will introduce the critical and interpretive perspectives and illustrate both with further explorations into the cholera epidemic.

SUGGESTED READINGS

There are many excellent books on the historical impact of epidemic diseases: e.g., W. H. McNeill's *Plagues and Peoples* (1976), A. W. Crosby's *The Columbian Exchange: Biological and Cultural Consequences of 1492* (1972), and Christopher Wills's *Yellow Fever, Black Goddess: The Coevolution of People and Plagues* (1996).

Alexander Alland's "Looking Backward: An Autocritique" (1987) offers a useful perspective on his contribution to the ecological approach in medical anthropology. A new collection, *Evolutionary Medicine and Health* (Trevathan, Smith and McKenna 2008), expands on the application of evolutionary theory in health research.

NOTES

1. Lynn Morgan (1987) illustrates this theory/society linkage as it has shaped discussions in medical anthropology.

2. The dates of cholera pandemics are matters of some dispute. I have adopted those published in Crowcroft (1994).

3. There is some controversy over this date, based on disagreements over who deserves the credit for the discovery of oral rehydration solution (Ruxin 1994).

4. The first phase (1961–1966) carried the pandemic from Indonesia to Bangladesh, India, the former Soviet Union, Iran, and Iraq. The second phase began in 1970 with the appearance of cholera in Africa. A reduction of cases during the 1980s preceeded the start of the third phase in South America in 1991 (Crowcroft 1994:159).

5. Recent collaborative efforts between medical anthropologists and epidemiologists hold great promise for the development of theory and method in both disciplines (Trostle 2005).

6. While mutation is the only way that new genes are introduced into a species, there are three other biological forces that also contribute to genetic variation: genetic drift, nonrandom mating, and natural selection itself. Explaining these mechanisms is beyond the scope of the present discussion. A good introduction to evolutionary theory and its application to *Homo sapiens* is Jonathan Marks's *Human Biodiversity: Genes, Race and History* (1995).

7. It has long been the consensus view that most pathogens evolve toward less virulent but more persistent strains (Anderson and May 1991, cited in Crowcroft 1994). However, recent work in evolutionary biology (e.g., Ewald 1994) suggests that this may not necessarily be the case.

8. Epidemiologists have introduced a second model, the "web of causation" (see Rockett 1994:10), to capture the more complex network of contributing causes behind chronic conditions like cardiovascular disease. The scientific study of stress (e.g., Selye 1956) has also offered less reductionistic models for understanding chronic diseases.

9. The work of Julian Steward (1955) was the precursor to a developing school of "cultural ecology," which evaluates cultural practices in relationship to the contribution they make to meeting basic human survival and reproductive needs (see Moran 1990).

10. Evolutionary theory has a long history in anthropology, starting soon after Darwin's introduction of the idea of natural selection in 1859. It was applied in a naive and ethnocentric manner in the late nineteenth century, in studies which ranked human sociocultural achievements along an evolutionary ladder from "primitive" to "civilized." After a prolonged reaction against these excesses, it was reintroduced into anthropology during the 1960s and 1970s via biological studies of population genetics.

11. Alland also called for an "anthropological genetics," which would study the feedback between culturally patterned behavior and the frequency and distribution of genetic material. For example, how do marriage rules (e.g., polygamy and/or preferences for specific kin relations) influence the genetic profile of a population over time? There have been moves in this direction (see Durham 1991).

12. Bacteria and viruses have short reproductive lives (i.e., many generations in a very brief time span), and therefore evolve quickly. Humans, by contrast, do not reach reproductive age for many years and even then produce comparatively few offspring. This means that any genetic influence on the reproductive success of individuals will be slow to have a broad impact on a population. There are exceptions, however, as when a small, interbreeding population is exposed to a significant new survival threat. This can compress the effect of natural selection because the gene pool is small and the selective pressure strong.

13. Changes which occur over developmental periods—such as larger lung capacities for persons born and raised at high altitudes—may not be reversible. These produce permanent physiological changes which are not genetically inherited.

14. Other measures of adaptation, in this broader sense of the term, include the ability to work and assessments of growth and nutrition.

15. R. Brooke Thomas's (1997) review of research on human adjustments to high altitude is an excellent illustration of the way the adaptation concept has been employed in human biology studies.

16. The best known of these studies have come from decades of interdisciplinary research with the !Kung San, a society of Southern Africa (see Lee 1993). A guiding question for this work has been the following: What advantages and disadvantages for human health and nutrition are offered by a nomadic lifestyle based on hunting and gathering? The assumption is that studying contemporary societies that follow this subsistence pattern provides insights into the nature of early human adaptations, which were also based on small hunting and gathering bands.

CHAPTER

4 Expanding the Vision of Medical Anthropology

Critical and Interpretive Views of the Cholera Epidemic

Alexander Alland's vision of medical anthropology, that it should be a part of a general study of human adaptation, offered the field scientific legitimacy by grounding it in evolutionary theory and calling for a fieldwork methodology that included the collection of biological data (e.g., growth measurements, nutritional evidence, fertility records, morbidity, and mortality statistics). Like other anthropological theories promulgated during the 1960s and 1970s (e.g., **structuralism** and **cultural materialism**), it also promised a basis for the comparison of anthropological case studies.[1] In Alland's scheme, measures of fitness can be used to compare societies living in similar environments.

A countercurrent to Alland's ecological/evolutionary theory emerged in the mid-1970s (Ingman and Thomas 1975). An increased recognition of the global impact of Western economic structures (Wallerstein 1974; Wolf 1982) led a group of scholars to explore the health consequences of capitalism and of the stratification of rich and poor that accompanies capitalistic development. Following the theoretical tradition of Karl Marx and Frederick Engels, these scholars began to focus on the links between profit-driven economies, the associated push to minimize wages and human capital investments, and class-based differences in health risks and resources. Versions of this "political-economy of health" are to be found in sociology, economics, and political science.[2]

In medical anthropology, the political economy approach was named by its proponents "critical medical anthropology" (CMA) (Singer 1989a). It "emphasizes the importance of political and economic forces, including the exercise of power, in shaping health, disease, illness experience, and health care" (Singer and Baer 1995:5). In a series of programmatic articles (e.g., Morsy 1979, 1981; Baer et al. 1986; Singer 1990), CMA proponents identify what they take to be the shortcomings of "conventional" theory in medical anthropology. Their central objection to the ecological/evolutionary model is that the twin notions of "environment" and "adaptation" conceal the degree to which disease is the product not of natural processes—populations failing to adapt to challenges in the environment—but of particular socioeconomic arrangements that give advantages to some at the expense of others.

A good way to clarify the differences between CMA and the ecological/evolutionary approaches is to relate them to the cholera case I have been using as a ground for a theoretical discussion. Chapter 3 showed how an ecological/evolutionary framework can be used to explain the relationship between the cholera bacteria, human hosts, and environmental conditions of poor sanitation. The analysis interpreted changes in cholera strains as adaptive responses on the part of the bacteria to social, economic, and medical patterns of human populations. On the human side of the equation, I asked if adaptations (e.g., genetic, physiological, and cultural) have mitigated the health consequences of cholera. The answer is that aside from partial immunity after exposure to some strains of the bacteria, human adaptations to cholera have all been at the sociocultural level: improved infrastructure and ORTs.

Although this ecological/evolutionary model shows that certain socioeconomic conditions facilitate the spread of cholera, the critical model would examine why those conditions prevail in certain societies at specific points in time. It would ask who benefits and who suffers from the economic structures that provide cholera the opportunity to take hold and spread. It would subject epidemiological data to a class analysis to see how cholera differentially affects rich and poor. The critical model would ask these and related questions at several different levels of analysis, from the "macro-social" (e.g., national and international political and economic systems) to the "micro-social" and individual levels (e.g., health provider and patient interactions, sufferers' social networks, and individual psychobiology) (Singer and Baer 1995:63).

How might a critical medical anthropologist analyze the specific cholera outbreak in Peru? I have shown what insights are offered by the ecological/evolutionary framework. What additional perspective would a political-economic analysis contribute?

Political Economy of Cholera

A deteriorated public infrastructure was considered the ultimate cause of the 1991 cholera epidemic in Peru. Most epidemiological accounts of the epidemic, like the ecological/evolutionary analysis, take these conditions as a given, as the causal variables behind the origin and spread of the epidemic. A political-economic view of the epidemic, by contrast, would ask, Why were Peru's water and sanitation systems in such a state at this point in the country's history? To answer this question requires that we consider historical evidence of the relationship between economic systems, supporting political and social structures, and patterns of health and disease.[3]

Norman Gall, the executive director of a Brazilian "think tank," the Fernand Braudel Institute of World Economics, has analyzed the Peruvian cholera outbreak from this perspective (Gall 1993). He calls our attention to the expansion of Latin American economies after World War II and argues that, as elsewhere in the world, economic development brought with it shifts in epidemiological patterns that had long-term demographic consequences. In brief, populations began to increase as an improved standard of living and infrastructure development (e.g., water and sewage systems and disease prevention campaigns) reduced the impact of diseases that affected child survival and extended the average lifespan.

The "epidemiologic transition" (Omran 1971) to which Gall points has been associated with the development of industrial capitalism in many countries. It entails the following:

> (a) the replacement of the common infectious diseases by non-communicable diseases and injuries as the leading causes of death; (b) a shift in peak morbidity and mortality from the young to the elderly; (c) change from a situation in which mortality predominates the epidemiological panorama to one in which morbidity is dominant (Frenk et al., quoted in Gall 1993: 17).

The economically powerful countries of Europe, North America, and Asia were the first to go through this transition. When First World countries saw limits to capitalist expansion in the minimal public health conditions of the Third World, money began to be directed toward the development of water and sewage systems, hospitals, and disease eradication campaigns in poorer countries. Contributing to the health improvements that marked the start of the Third World's epidemiologic transition was the technical advice and direct financing provided by organizations like the Rockefeller Foundation, the World Bank, and the alphabet soup of national and international aid organizations (e.g., AID—Agency for International Development, WHO—World Health Organization, and PAHO—Pan American Health Organization).

As already mentioned, the health transition in Latin America produced significant increases in child survival and longer lifespans, which, in turn, resulted in larger populations. Higher rates of chronic conditions, like cardiovascular disease, diabetes, and cancer, also accompanied the transition. However, these did not significantly limit population growth because they tend to affect people after their reproductive years.

Gall argues that the resulting demographic pressures, coupled with urbanization and counterproductive government economic policies, contributed to a stalling of progress in public health in the poorer countries of the world. The worldwide economic downturn precipitated by the oil crisis of the 1970s and the debt crisis of the 1980s were the next blows. Together, they depleted the capital that Third World countries needed to maintain and expand the public health infrastructure. An expanded infrastructure was necessitated by a growing and increasingly older population concentrated in urban centers.

Focusing on Peru, Gall shows how the country's basic public health infrastructure, most notably its water and sewage systems, was overwhelmed between 1970 and 1990 by unprecedented growth in urban populations, chronic inflation and associated losses of capital for investment, and unsustainable public sector employment and subsidies. This, in turn, promoted a resurgence of infectious diseases, including, but not limited to, cholera. Among the specific social and economic factors Gall cites are the following:

1. In 1950, 35 percent of Peru's population lived in cities; in 1990, the figure was 70 percent. More than one-fourth of the country's population in 1991 lived in the capital, Lima (6.5 million). Roughly one-third of that city's residents lived in squatter settlements.

2. In the period 1950–1965, Peru experienced a relatively low inflation rate of 8 percent, compared to 31 percent and 25 percent for Brazil and Argentina, respectively. By about 1980, annual inflation climbed to astronomical rates, reaching an incredible 10,000 percent by the end of the decade. This contributed to increasing numbers of people living beneath the poverty line; in Lima, the poverty rate went from 17 percent of the city's population in 1986 to 44 percent in 1990.
3. Politically popular public employment (one-half of salaried workers) and subsidies for food, public transportation, and water/electrical supplies, especially during the first administration of President Alán Garcia (1985–1990), depleted the country's foreign exchange reserves and left insufficient funds for the maintenance and expansion of basic public services. Lima's water system was losing roughly 50 percent of its flow to leakage, while the rates charged to customers were well below cost. Unmetered and illegal diversions were common. The health care system suffered such severe budget cuts that hospitals lacked supplies of everything from bandages to surgical instruments; patients had to provide their own food and bed sheets.

When Alberto Fujimori became president of Peru in 1990, he initiated counterinflationary measures so severe that the plan came to be known as "Fujishock." Following the strategy imposed by the International Monetary Fund on other countries seeking credit, Fujimori's government sought to curtail subsidies and to dramatically reduce public sector employment. Overnight, fuel prices shot up by 2,000–3,000 percent. A new monetary policy resulted in immediate and drastic cuts in the spending power of both private and public sector employees; by the end of 1990, real wages for private sector employees had dropped to half their 1989 levels. Mass starvation, which might have resulted from Fujishock, was avoided by a tripling of U.S. food donations from 1989 levels.

It is important to stress Gall's point that it was not just cholera that found fertile ground in the life conditions of Peruvians during the last decades of the twentieth century. From 1975 to 1989, the annual number of reported cases of acute diarrheas and rates of acute respiratory infections rose dramatically (pp. 43–44). The country also experienced a resurgence of other infectious diseases, including malaria, dengue, yellow fever, leprosy, and tuberculosis. The relatively low mortality rates from this awesome list of diseases were due to international medical assistance, not to progress in confronting the root causes of the diseases.

Gall and others (e.g., Frenk et al. 1991) do not view the resurgence of infectious diseases in Peru and elsewhere in Third World countries as a return to pre-transition epidemiological patterns because chronic diseases associated with the post-transition state remain in evidence. Rather, they refer to an "epidemiological polarization" in which "disease and mortality patterns trace wealth/poverty differences within national economies and, on a broader canvas, in the polarization of the world economy" (Gall 1993:10). Thus, the pre-transition profile of infectious diseases, like cholera, can be found in poor countries as well as among poorer classes in wealthy nations. Post-transition diseases are found in wealthy countries and among advantaged classes in poorer nations (see Figure 4.1).

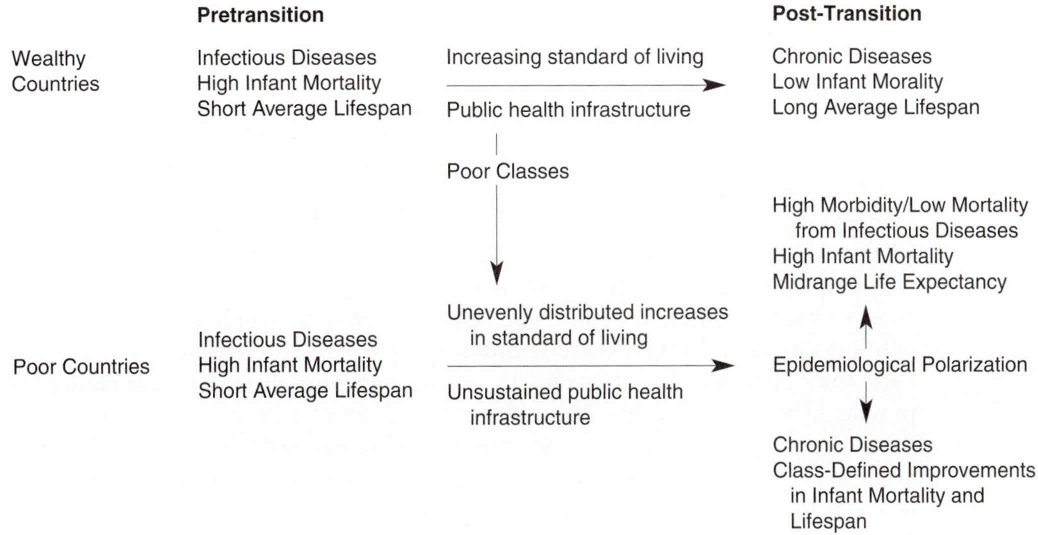

FIGURE 4.1 The Polarization of Health

Analyses like Gall's point to the interplay between disease patterns and the political-economic and class structures of human societies. They also underscore the importance of looking not just at single diseases in particular settings, but at general patterns of morbidity and mortality in a historical and comparative perspective. Notice how, although we started with the 1991 outbreak of cholera in Peru, we have found ourselves considering worldwide epidemiological patterns during the second half of the twentieth century.

Political-Economic versus Ecological/Evolutionary Perspectives

The political economy analysis reminds us that humans do not live in clearly bounded settings, where the conditions of life are shaped only, or even primarily, by local circumstances. The Peruvian cholera epidemic had its roots in worldwide developments, from the oil and credit crises of the 1970s and 1980s to human-induced global warming. This is what critical medical anthropologist Merrill Singer (1990:182) has in mind when he urges us to put "the microlevel in the macrocontext." It is also the point made by public health specialist Duncan Pedersen when he writes that the ecology model is at a crossroads:

> The large-scale structural determinants—globalization and Third-Worldization; disruptive development initiatives; increasing poverty and human rights abuses, including violence and ethnic wars; dramatic climatic changes, terrestrial and marine ecosystems under stress, population growth and massive forced migrations; trade, international travel and transportation—interacting with the micro-scale

> determinants—the living and working conditions of the local milieu, the family unit and the workplace—are all significant parts of an ensemble responsible for introducing swift changes in the ecology of disease (Pedersen 1996:756).

The recognition of the links between disease and these macro-level forces requires that we rethink two of the central concepts in the ecological/evolutionary model, "environment" and "adaptation." First, it is objectionable when, even for heuristic purposes, we describe poverty as an "environment" to which humans adapt—when the economic and political structures of other humans have created that environment (Singer and Baer 1995:46–47). The contaminated water and food supplies behind the cholera epidemic were the outcome of human behavior motivated by political interests. To treat these symptoms of poverty as "environmental" is to disguise their historical conditionality and to make it more difficult to see cholera as a product of social, rather than "natural," circumstances.

The adaptation concept, at least as applied to culturally patterned behaviors, is also challenged by the political economy analysis. Singer (1989b:228) notes that the ecological/evolutionary model never asks, "Adaptive for whom?" To decrease mortality from cholera with ORTs, without also addressing the economic divisions that were ultimately responsible for the epidemic, may only be "adaptive" in the sense that it defuses social protest and preserves the status quo of exploitative relations. I return to this point in the following section.

Advocates of the ecological/evolutionary model acknowledge that they have paid insufficient attention to the impact of political and economic forces on the environments in which human populations survive (Alland 1987:429; Armelagos et al. 1992; McElroy 1996). The term **political ecology** has been suggested as the name for a revision of the ecological/evolutionary model that incorporates political-economic forces and social relations into the analysis of human health (Baer 1996; McElroy 1996). Several case studies, including one based on archaeological material, have attempted this synthesis (Leatherman et al. 1986; Brown 1987; Thomas 1997; Goodman and Leatherman 1998).

There has been more resistance to the CMA critique of the adaptation concept on the part of those who use the ecological/evolutionary approach. Some *have* sought to restrict the idea of adaptation to the genetic changes that come about as a result of natural selection; they suggest notions like "coping" for physiological and sociocultural responses to health risks (Leatherman 1996).[4] However, other proponents of the ecological/evolutionary model argue that the adaptation concept is a useful methodological tool with which to analyze the diverse variables—biological, environmental, *and* sociocultural—that contribute to disease patterns (McElroy and Townsend 2004). They insist that social and economic arrangements have always been considered an important part of the "environment" to which humans adapt.

Supporters of the ecological/evolutionary model have not limited themselves to responding to CMA criticisms. They have also leveled attacks of their own against the CMA research agenda (McElroy 1996). The most significant point made against CMA is that by stressing political-economic forces that impinge on human health, it underplays or ignores biological and ecological factors.[5] Applied to the Peruvian cholera outbreak, the criticism would be that whatever the human contribution to the epidemic, the biological and ecological context of bacteria/human interactions is a significant part of the story. It is not enough to know why Peru was in such a dismal state in 1991—what political-economic conditions impoverished the country—to understand the full dynamic of the epidemic (e.g., the responsible organism, its mode of transmission, and the progression of the disease). Poverty plays a causal role, but the "selective agent" remains "natural."

An additional line of criticism of the CMA approach comes from different quarters, from advocates of the cultural constructivist or **interpretive** perspective. Recall that this approach to medical anthropology asks questions about the culturally derived frameworks of meaning that are brought to bear on the experience of sickness. From the interpretive perspective, CMA "depersonalize[s] the subject matter and content of medical anthropology by focusing on the analysis of social systems and things . . . neglecting the particular, the existential, the subjective content of illness, suffering, and healing as lived events and experiences" (Scheper-Hughes and Lock 1986:137).

I return once more to the cholera example to show how an interpretive approach analyzes the "subjective content of illness, suffering, and healing." Comparative material from other cholera outbreaks, as well as from analyses of different epidemics altogether, shows what an interpretive approach considers important. A constructive dialogue between advocates of the interpretive perspective and critical medical anthropologists has resulted in a synthetic, **critical-interpretive** approach (Lock and Scheper-Hughes 1990).

Interpretive View of Cholera

Medical anthropologist Byron Good and medical sociologist Mary-Jo Delvecchio Good developed a "meaning-centered approach" to illness that captures the basic assumptions of the interpretive perspective (Good 1977; Good and Good 1980, 1981, 1982). They write:

> An illness or a symptom condenses a network of meanings for the sufferer: personal trauma, life stresses, fears and expectations about the illness, social reactions of friends and authorities, and therapeutic experiences. The meaning of illness for an individual is grounded in—though not reducible to—the network of meanings an illness has in a particular culture: the metaphors associated with a disease, the ethnomedical theories, the basic values and conceptual forms, and the care patterns that shape the experience of the illness and the social reactions to the sufferer in a given society (Good and Good 1980:176).

What meanings does cholera bring with it, beyond those conveyed by the biomedical understanding of the disease? In South India, cholera, along with other epidemic diseases, is thought to be caused by goddesses as a punishment for sinful behavior (Beals 1976:187; Taylor 1976:291–292). Similar linkages between cholera, sin, and divine punishment were made in China during an outbreak in 1942; public rituals were performed to placate the angry gods (Hsu 1955). A severe cholera epidemic in Campeche, Mexico, in 1833 took 20 percent of the population, leading survivors to envy the dead: "Happy the dead, was the general remark, they had some aid during life, something like interment after death—but we must perish alone and be consumed by dogs and buzzards in our dwellings" (Shattuck 1933:40–41).

There is no interpretive analysis of the 1991 cholera outbreak in Peru to draw upon to see how the disease was perceived by those most affected. Such an analysis would document the thoughts and experiences of sufferers, their families, and others in their communities. It would explore the way ordinary people, as well as healing specialists (e.g., shamans, herbalists, and local medical personnel), accounted for the disease and how they treated it. The conceptions of cholera would be compared to those held about other diseases to derive the logic underlying local disease taxonomies and treatments.

While no interpretive account is available from the Peruvian outbreak, there are two articles that focus on the cultural dimension of the epidemic as it spread to other Latin American countries, specifically, Ecuador, Chile, and Brazil. Each asks, what meanings were attached to the epidemic, by whom, and to what end? These papers point the direction toward an interpretive approach that is simultaneously "critical" (i.e., political-economic approach).

The first essay, "Cholera in the Time of Neoliberalism: The Case of Chile and Ecuador" (Trumper and Phillips 1995), asks why the cholera outbreak got so much attention from Western experts and media sources when far greater loss of life from many other diseases, even other enteric (intestinal) diseases, had long been a fact of life in Latin America. The authors argue that we need to focus on the match between the "discourse on cholera" and the First World's view of Third World countries as "nonwhite, nonmodern, poor, and most importantly, sick" (p. 169). Cholera, cast as a nineteenth-century horror returning to ravage the "backward and undeveloped world," became a warning of the price to be paid by failing to embrace "modern" economic (i.e., capitalist) and political arrangements. In short, a public health menace is transformed into a punitive action against countries that have yet to adopt fully Western institutions.[6]

Trumper and Phillips show how the ruling classes of Ecuador and Chile gave this Western-derived message local accent by talking about the epidemic in terms of their own modernizing myths. In Ecuador, the anti-cholera campaign took on the tone of a patriotic battle in the country's struggle to develop, in which backward parts of the population—paternalistically referred to *nuestras indígenas* (e.g., "our" Indians and poor coastal blacks)—were threatening the country's progress. The public health message was that the poor owed it to their country's future to improve their hygiene and cure themselves.

Ecuador's government was concerned to protect national industries, especially seafood exports and tourism, from the bad press of a cholera epidemic.[7] This meant that the significance of the epidemic had to be diminished. For example, a press release in the important newspaper *El Comercio* reassuringly noted that tourists had nothing to worry about because cholera, "regrettably," was a "disease of poverty" (p. 179). The president of Ecuador, Rodrigo Borja, counseled against unnecessary panic and criticized those who thought "every little upset stomach" might be cholera (p. 178). According to Trumper and Phillips, political pressure caused the Ecuadorian media to drop sensational headlines about cholera well before the epidemic subsided.

Trumper and Phillips suggest that Chilean officials' response to the spread of cholera reflects the country's nationalist rhetoric. The notion of a "Chilean miracle" of recovery and development under Pinochet's dictatorship (1973–1989) supports Chilean claims to being different from their Latin American neighbors, an argument that has historical roots in racist ideas of an upper class that is "white" (i.e., not Indian or black)—"the English of South America" (p. 180). Trumper and Phillips summarize this ideology of racial superiority:

> In Chile the population is cleaner and healthier than the inhabitants of the tropics because it is white, or given the ambiguities of the discourse, at least whiter. That is to say that the Chile that really counts, the dominant class, is white. The majority, nonwhite and nonmodern, working class or marginal or peasant, only count occasionally, mainly when there is a need for labor power; it is this Chile that is seen as susceptible to a cholera epidemic (p. 181).

Chilean officials initially denied that cholera could become a problem in their country; it was a foreign disease that one would expect to plague the poorer, tropical/darker countries to the north. But, when import restrictions failed to block the spread of the disease into Chile, the official construction of the disease shifted. It was now to be viewed as a test of Chile's ability to preserve its development gains. On the line was a substantially privatized medical system, a major feature of Chile's neoliberal government reform program. Another significant component of the anti-cholera campaign in Chile, as in Ecuador, was the idea that a disciplined population could overcome the disease.

Chilean discourse on cholera, Trumper and Phillips argue, transformed the disease from a threatening epidemic to just another enteric (intestinal) disease, one of the everyday aggravations that are kept under control by a modern state. In their words, "Cholera is only one among many nuisances that can be forgotten, like the smog that covers Santiago, like the foul smell of port cities, like the atrocities of the military regime, like the children's detention centers where the abused and street children are kept out of sight, like the millions marginalized" (p. 187).

Trumper and Phillips's reading of the way cholera was interpreted in line with nationalist myths of modernization finds an interesting counterpoint in an article about the response of poor Brazilians to cholera control campaigns (Nations and Monte 1996). As in Ecuador and Chile, the official public health message about cholera in Brazil was that it thrives on conditions of poverty, ignorance, and filth. The anti-cholera campaign drew upon powerful combat metaphors and images to rally public support for the eradication effort. How these messages were interpreted by those most at risk is the focus of Nations and Monte's analysis.

In the impoverished northeast of the country, where 87 percent of Brazil's cholera cases occurred, the anti-cholera campaign had unexpected consequences: Poor residents began openly resisting the efforts of public health workers. To understand why, Nations and Monte ask us to "see cholera through the eyes of poor Brazilians who suffer most its consequences" (p. 1012). Using a research technique called "Rapid Ethnographic Assessment,"[8] they explored what cholera meant in the lives of eighty persons residing or working in one of two poor communities. Using an abbreviated and directed form of traditional anthropological research was a part of an effort to overcome local resistance to the anti-cholera campaign. In other words, it is an example of "applied medical anthropology."

The researchers discovered that many poor people interpreted the "War Against Cholera" in terms of the hostility and neglect they experience from public officials and from the wealthier communities in whose homes and businesses they work. Cholera, in popular parlance, the "dog's disease," became an accusation against the poor for the conditions in which they are forced to live. The campaign's military metaphors, for people who are daily on the receiving end of state violence and repression, suggested removal/eradication not of the disease but of the *diseased.* "We ARE the cholera," declared an eighteen-year-old woman (p. 1017).

These associations in the minds of the poor transformed a public health program into a genocidal conspiracy of the rich to isolate and eliminate unwanted people. In defiance, prevention and treatment efforts were refused and ridiculed. People spat out pills and dumped water-purifying chemicals. They hid symptoms to avoid being labeled "infected." Health care workers came to be seen as the enemy.

This interpretation of cholera in terms of class divisions in Northeast Brazil recalls similar historical examples during previous cholera outbreaks as well as in epidemics of other diseases. For example, there were riots throughout England during a cholera outbreak in 1832 because poor people doubted the existence of the disease. They believed that public health measures were a pretext to coerce the poor "into hospitals for use in vivisection experiments, for dissection after death, or to keep down the population" (Richardson 1989:226).

Nations and Monte cite as a similar case the accusatory language used during the early stages of the AIDS epidemic, when Americans blamed the poor of Haiti for the introduction of the disease into the United States (see Farmer 1992). They might also have mentioned the false linkages drawn in the United States during the nineteenth century between leprosy outbreaks and Chinese immigrants. The idea that leprosy was the "Chinamen's Disease" resonated so well with anti-immigrant sentiments that few noticed how rarely Chinese were actually affected by the illness. But even a symbolic association between the dreaded disease and recent arrivals from China was sufficient to encourage passage of the Chinese Exclusion Act (1882), which severely restricted immigration from Asia for years (Gussow 1989).

The way cholera was interpreted in different countries and by different classes illustrates how ideas about disease can have strategic purposes that serve political and economic interests. This is what Margaret Lock and Nancy Scheper-Hughes (1990) have in mind when they call for a synthesis of cultural and political economy approaches to medical anthropology. Their **critical-interpretive** method, first "describes(s) the variety of metaphorical conceptions (conscious and unconscious) about the body and associated narratives and then show(s) the social, political, and individual uses to which these conceptions are applied in practice" (ibid., p. 50).

On the one hand, illness metaphors and narratives reflect and reproduce core values, many of which support a society's social and economic structures. I illustrated this in Chapter 1 by showing how racial and gender categories were reinforced by disease beliefs in nineteenth- and twentieth-century America; recall as well the link between the mechanical model of the body and the rise of industrial capitalism. The use of nationalist ideology in Ecuadorian and Chilean accounts of the cholera epidemic are further examples of how disease interpretations may be used to perpetuate a society's power structures—by projecting onto the sufferer's experience the legitimizing myths of exploitative relations.

On the other hand, the interpretation of illness experiences may also play more subversive roles in society. Sickness can be a way to protest against inequality, and demands for better health can be a politically useful avenue for reform. The individual experience of suffering, far from mechanically reproducing existing power structures, may challenge the sickness-producing conditions to which individuals are exposed. The rejection and/or reinterpretation of dominant conceptions of cholera in Brazil illustrates how individuals, singly and collectively, can contest underlying political-economic interests. If we accept that the way we think about disease actually shapes the way we experience it, then the struggle over whose conceptions of a disease win becomes far more than a battle of interpretations. Think of the Brazilian woman who identified her community with cholera: How would she experience the onset of severe diarrhea?

Taking a Broader, Inclusive Perspective

The cholera accounts reviewed in this and the last chapter show how different theoretical lenses—epidemiological, ecological/evolutionary, political-economic, and interpretive—bring to light different facets of the human experience of this disease. At the microscopic level, cholera can be seen as a bacterium capable of releasing a toxin that disrupts the reabsorption of liquids in the human small intestine. Cholera can be conceived epidemiologically in terms of its source(s), means of transmission, and the numbers of people who suffer from its effects. Cholera may also be understood in the context of the economic and political systems that leave segments of the world's population vulnerable to its repeated assaults. And consideration should also be given to how we and others *think about* cholera and how our ideas about the disease relate to the assumptions and interpretations by which we make sense of other parts of our world as well.

The theoretical perspectives brought to bear on cholera are linked to different academic disciplines or to different subfields within disciplines. As an unfortunate result, they have been developed, applied, and defended without sufficient opportunity for cross-fertilization and constructive critique. Medical anthropology has begun to offer that opportunity by bringing its dual vision—biological and cultural—to bear on analyses of health and disease.

There is, as yet, no single, comprehensive theoretical agreement in medical anthropology, no consensus model to which most would give their assent. However, there have been significant improvements and revisions in competing models precisely as a result of the critical application of each perspective to the frameworks and findings of others. For example, epidemiologists are developing increasingly sophisticated disease causation models that pay explicit attention to the health consequences of racial, gender, and class divisions (Krieger 1994; Marmot 1994; Krieger and Sidney 1996). There are ecologically minded medical anthropologists responding constructively to the critique of the concepts of "environment" and "adaptation" (Armelagos et al. 1990; Thomas 1997; Goodman and Leatherman 1998). Even critical medical anthropologists, who are more often in the position of hurling bombs at other models, have accepted that they need to pay more attention to the individual level of suffering and to the cultural frameworks by which disease is constructed (Singer 1990).

Let me end this theoretical exploration with some of the priorities that I think ought to be a part of medical anthropology research. First, medical anthropology ought to move away from the disease-by-disease focus of biomedicine and concentrate instead on the range of health risks to which a specified human community is exposed. This is important for several reasons, but most significantly because it facilitates an analysis of the patterns of disease that accompany particular socioeconomic and political systems. It has already produced important insights in epidemiology—as evidenced in the revisions to the health transition model reviewed earlier—as well as in several historical/evolutionary surveys of human health (e.g., Cohen 1989—see Chapter 3; Fábrega 1997).

A second and related priority must be to assess the array of health-promoting resources that are, or are not, available to a specific human community. I have in mind far more than access to biomedical services, such as family and social support systems, functioning public health infrastructures, workplace safety regulations and enforcement, culturally appropriate treatment and prevention (and financing), adequate nutrition, and so on. These need to be understood in a context that includes general social structures as well as the intimate world of a sufferer's experience.[9]

My third priority involves a fuller application of the interpretive perspective. This may be accomplished by exploring health risks and resources in reference to what medical anthropologists Margaret Lock and Nancy Scheper-Hughes call "the three bodies" (1990): the individual body, the body social, and the body politic. The individual body refers to "the lived experience of the body-self" (p. 50)—the individual's immediate sense of self as an embodied entity. The cultural shaping of even this most direct sense of self (e.g., cultural variation in the experience of pain; Zborowski 1969; Good et al. 1992) influences what people consider evidence of sickness (i.e., health risks) as well as what responses are deemed appropriate (i.e., health resources).

The social body points to "the representational uses of the body as a natural symbol with which to think about nature, society and culture" (ibid., referencing

Mary Douglas). The cholera sufferer as a symbol of poverty and filth and the leper as social outcast are examples of how the sick body is put to symbolic use. In the case of AIDS, early stereotypes of victims as homosexual men dramatically affected how Americans evaluated the risk of getting the disease, as well as the level of funding for AIDS research.

As Lock and Scheper-Hughes point out, the fact that the body is "good to think with" is confirmed by ethnographic examples of body symbolism from around the world (ibid., 60–65).

The body politic refers to "the regulation, surveillance, and control of bodies (individual and collective) in reproduction and sexuality, work, leisure, and sickness" (ibid., p. 51). We have already introduced examples of the politics of the sick body: medicine as social control for African Americans and women (Chapter 1), the denial of cholera in Ecuador and Chile for nationalistic purposes, the immigration restrictions in the United States based on the claim that the Chinese brought leprosy, and the isolation of Haitians as alleged AIDS carriers. What constitutes a health risk and what is done about it confirms physician/anthropologist Rudolf Virchow's (1821–1902) observation that "medicine is a social science and politics nothing but medicine on a grand scale."

In addition to these general priorities, I am persuaded by parts of the critique of the ecological/evolutionary model.[10] We must reconceptualize the "environment" variable in a way that more accurately reflects the pervasive impact of humans on each other and on the physical and biological world. The notion of "political ecology" helps in this regard; it calls our attention to the degree to which the "environment" is a product of "the dialectical interaction of natural and sociocultural forces" (Baer 1996:453).

I also agree with critical medical anthropologists that the notion of adaptation lacks conceptual clarity and disguises as "natural" the threats to health faced by human communities as a result of political-economic structures. I think we can avoid confusion by conceptually distinguishing the following: (1) long-term changes in gene pools that result from the processes of natural selection; (2) developmental and physiological adjustments to bio-environmental stressors (e.g., altitude, climate, and disease-causing organisms) that are made during an organism's lifespan; and (3) culturally patterned "coping processes in which the goals, needs, options, and constraints shaping human actions are contingent on changing historical conditions" (Leatherman 1996:479).

I find great promise for a synthetic view of medical anthropology—one that is "equally sensitive to bio-environmental factors in health, the experience of suffering among those are ill, and the primacy of political economy in shaping the impact of bio-environmental factors on disease, sufferer experience, and the character of the health care system deployed in response to disease and illness" (Singer and Baer 1995:50). I think there may already be bridges in place between the ecological/evolutionary, critical, and interpretive models (e.g., political ecology and critical-interpretive approaches). Exploring the 1991 cholera outbreak has shown just how important is each perspective in a holistic understanding of a human health problem.[11]

SUGGESTED READINGS

In addition to the sources cited in the text on the "epidemiologic transition," see also S. J. Olshansky and B. A. Ault's "The Fourth Stage of the Epidemiologic Transition: The Age of Delayed Degenerative Diseases" (1986).

Nancy Scheper-Hughes's *Death Without Weeping: The Violence of Everyday Life in Brazil* (1992) is a powerful ethnography of the health conditions in a poor community in Northeast Brazil, especially as these affect mothers and their children. An equally compelling account of the relationship between individual suffering and national/international politics focuses on HIV-AIDS in Brazil: *Will to Live: AIDS Therapies and the Politics of Survival* by João Biehl (2007).

Arthur Kleinman's *Patients and Healers in the Context of Culture* (1980) provides many of the basic concepts used in interpretive approaches to medical anthropology.

NOTES

1. Anthropology has long struggled with the problem of comparison. For a discipline committed to the detailed analysis of human behavior in specific settings, it is difficult to accept the decontextualization that is required for comparisons between societies.

2. This is an abbreviated treatment of the critical perspective's central assumptions, which is designed primarily to contrast it to the ecological/evolutionary approach. Merrill Singer and Hans Baer (1995, Chapter 2) have written an especially clear overview of the critical model and its central concepts.

3. This relationship has been the subject of a great deal of attention, from Engels' (1969) classic study of industrial life in England to anthropologist Mark Cohen's (1989) survey of the health implications of major changes in human subsistence activities and settlement patterns. I return to these theoretical discussions in the next chapter.

4. An alternative term will have to be defined in a way that distinguishes it from "adaptation." Otherwise, no real conceptual improvement is made.

5. Note that this is essentially the inverse of CMA's criticism of the ecological/evolutionary model. CMA proponents agree that they have neglected ecological factors (Baer 1996:452) and have also promoted the adoption of a "political ecology" approach.

6. Gall (1993) is subject to this criticism, especially to the degree that his analysis seems to blame Peru and other Third World countries for creating the conditions in which epidemics thrive. This is perhaps most evident in the concluding lines of his study: "They [Third World countries] also face new challenges of regeneration posed by the decapitalization of complex societies. Their fate is in their own hands" (p. 104).

7. This was not an idle worry. The epidemic in Peru is said to have cost the country almost $170 million in lost tourism and export revenues (Trostle 1995).

8. This research technique emerged in the context of development projects for which anthropologists were asked to provide focused ethnographic studies. Building on prior knowledge of a community, the technique uses sampling methods, survey instruments, and carefully circumscribed interviewing to give a deeper understanding of a problem than would otherwise be possible (see Trotter 1991). The method attempts to give ethnographic detail without requiring long-term participant observation.

9. A particularly moving example of this comprehensive exploration of health resources is Laurie Abraham's *Mama Might Be Better Off Dead* (1993), which documents health care structures in Chicago through the experience of a poor African American family.

10. I think the critique has been overstated at points (e.g., Singer 1996), but that, in general, it has had a positive effect.

11. Lest we think of cholera only in historical terms, it is worth remembering that natural and human-caused disasters, from the tsunami that struck Indonesia in 2004 to the horrendous social upheaval in Zimbabwe in 2008–2009, continue to offer opportunities to this dreadful disease.

CHAPTER 5

The Global Petri Dish

I made the mistake of reading Richard Preston's *The Hot Zone* (1994) on a cross-country flight. His vivid description of an airline passenger infected with the Ebola virus, complete with medical details of liquefying organs and decomposing blood vessels, made me want to request a parachute. In the mid-1990s, we were just beginning to realize how devastating the AIDS epidemic would become, but I didn't know at the time how many other novel diseases would be added to my medical vocabulary in the following years: severe acute respiratory syndrome (SARS), bovine spongiform encephalopathy (mad cow disease), hantavirus (hantavirus pulmonary syndrome or HPS), West Nile virus, and monkeypox. These are some of the so-called "**emerging infections**":

> Emerging infections are clinically distinct conditions whose incidence in humans has increased. Emergence may be due to the introduction of a new agent, to the recognition of an existing disease that has gone undetected, or to a change in the environment that provides an epidemiologic "bridge" [from another species to humans] (Lederberg et al. 1992:34).

Less sensational but potentially more devastating than these dramatic new diseases are those that are said to be "**reemerging**," among them many pathogens that a triumphant twentieth-century biomedicine had declared under control.[1] In some cases, such as tuberculosis, a steady decline in incidence in affluent countries has been reversed by the development of drug-resistant variants and cutbacks in public health prevention programs. In others, including the mosquito-transmitted dengue fever, a resurgence of disease has accompanied the expansion of impoverished sectors of urban centers in poor countries, with a corresponding increase in the breeding opportunities for disease vectors.

The Centers for Disease Control and Prevention (CDCP) tallies forty-nine emerging and reemerging infections (http://www.cdc.gov/ncidod/diseases/eid/disease_sites.htm), a daunting collection of pathogens that may make the future look like the past, when acute infections dominated mortality statistics for both wealthy and poor populations.

Exacerbating the situation are two characteristics of modern life. First, the rapid air transportation of large numbers of people over great distances accelerates the spread of infectious agents. Second, the massive concentration and industrialization of food production techniques (e.g., huge poultry farms, centralized cattle feeding lots, and slaughterhouses) increase the geographic scope of any food-borne infection, as contaminated products from one site are shipped to distant distributors.

The repeated cases of *E. coli* infections and the spread of mad cow disease in Great Britain in 1993 illustrate this danger.[2] Taken together with other forces that move microbes ever more efficiently across regional and national boundaries (e.g., migration patterns, civil strife, and natural disasters), these features of our current world create a global petri dish populated by pathogens that recognize no nationality (see McNeill 1976).

The question for this chapter is what modifications in the theoretical models presented in the analysis of the cholera epidemic are required to make sense of this evolving situation? In particular, can the epidemiological transition model (Chapter 4) be reconstructed to account for the way emerging and reemerging diseases obliterate geo-political boundaries and threaten to reverse medical accomplishments? Do ecological, interpretive, and political-economic perspectives sharpen our understanding of contemporary disease patterns, or do we need to augment these frameworks to take into account the changing picture of world health?

Transitions

The epidemiological transition model, described in Chapter 4, focused on two significant developments in the history of human disease: the rise in infectious diseases that accompanied the industrial revolution and the shift from infectious diseases to chronic conditions that occurred in wealthy countries during the twentieth century as public health, living standards, and medical science improved. As originally conceived, the model was overly optimistic about the progressive direction of disease patterns. It pointed to a lineal evolution from short lives ended by infectious diseases to long lifespans complicated by chronic conditions. What to do when the very diseases that the second epidemiological transition was supposed to have left in the dustbin of history reassert themselves, sometimes in multidrug-resistant strains and in the middle of affluent communities? The model also overplayed the significance of national-level trends, missing variations in smaller population segments (e.g., by class, ethnicity, and sexual preference), and failed to account for epidemiological patterns that do not respect territorial boundaries. For example, the original model would have difficulty explaining the HIV/AIDS epidemic, which tracks along different subsectors of affected societies and which moves across borders as fast as a sex tourist returns home or an infected long-distance trucker hauls cargo between nations, visiting prostitutes along the way.

Several scientists from the Department of Anthropology at Emory University (Barrett et al. 1998) suggest a solution to these shortcomings. They recommend extending the time frame covered by the model to include a much wider sweep of human evolutionary history, pushing the first epidemiological transition back to the rise in infectious diseases that accompanied the Neolithic Revolution.[3] The second transition would still be linked to the shift from infectious to chronic diseases that accompanied the era of industrialization from the mid-nineteenth to twentieth century, but a third transition would be posited to account for the changes in disease patterns that intensive globalization has brought over the past decades. This third transition would be defined by three major trends: (1) "an unprecedented number of new diseases;" (2) "increased incidence and prevalence of preexisting infectious diseases;" and (3) "re-emerging pathogens generating antimicrobial-resistant strains" (p. 256).[4]

The primary factors behind the present problem of re/emerging diseases are directly related to human actions.[5] For example, ecological changes associated with global warming, deforestation, colonization, and hydroelectric dam projects all have consequences for the nexus between humans and disease vectors, often creating new opportunities for pathogens to reproduce and spread. Demographic changes, including historically unprecedented concentrations of population in mega-urban centers, produce conditions ripe for disease transmission. We have already mentioned the impact of international travel and commerce on the global spread of pathogens and of the industrialization of food production and distribution. The development of drug-resistant strains of old diseases is directly tied to the inappropriate use of antibacterial agents (e.g., prescribed for nonbacterial diseases, used for shorter than stipulated periods of time) and to failed or abandoned public health programs. The case of malaria is particularly instructive (see Box 5.1).

BOX 5.1
Malaria and the Evil Pesticide

One of the world's greatest killers, malaria, is staging a comeback in the United States. Spraying with the insecticide DDT (dichlorodiphenyl trichloroethylene) had effectively eliminated the disease by the early 1950s, but laws prohibiting the pesticide have allowed the anopheles mosquito that transmits the malaria parasite (*Plasmodium falciparum* and *P. vivax*) to rebound. In 2002, there were 1,337 U.S. cases of malaria and eight deaths (http://www.cdc.gov/malaria/facts.htm). Although these are minor casualties compared to rates in countries where malaria was never close to being eradicated—worldwide there are 300 million cases of malaria and 3 million deaths per year (Desowitz 2002:75)—public health officials worry that they may signal a return to earlier times, when malaria was endemic to many parts of the United States.

Malaria specialists argue that bans on the use of DDT, which were inspired by Rachel Carson's (1962) account of environmental damage due to overuse of the pesticide, represent a tragic miscalculation, a classic case of the baby being tossed out with the bathwater. They point out that strategic spraying of house walls in malarial zones immediately diminishes infection rates without harm to humans and with a negligible impact on the environment.

The only alternative, synthetic pyrethroid deltamethrin, is far more costly and significantly less effective. Calls for resurrecting DDT come from notable scientists, including three Nobel laureates, and a growing number of physicians and public health workers.

There is much in the malaria case to interest medical anthropologists: the evolution of pesticide-resistant mosquitoes and drug-resistant parasites due to inconsistent or incorrect applications of chemicals and medications, the contribution of human-induced climate change and environmental damage to the proliferation of mosquito breeding opportunities, the socioeconomic impact of rising rates of infection, and the international politics of disease eradication programs. A particularly interesting line of research would focus on the attempted rehabilitation of DDT's reputation: from the archetypical environmental toxin to an "instrument of salvation" (Rosenberg 2004:43) in the war against child-killing, predatory parasites.

Barrett et al. (1998) note that the anthropologist's holistic framework and understanding of socio-behavioral dynamics can advance our understanding of the epidemiological reality of the twenty-first century, precisely because so many of the underlying factors promoting re/emerging diseases are linked to social patterns. What requires more attention is how well our traditional models fit with the circumstances of a world where social patterns can be shaped not only by local culture but also by global currents. As in the previous two chapters, I use a single case to highlight the challenges of this "new world order" to each major perspective in medical anthropology. The outbreak of SARS during the winter and spring of 2003 serves this purpose because of how quickly it moved from local to global and because it triggered some unprecedented responses.[6] My objective is not to provide a complete analysis of SARS, but rather to point to the sorts of questions that it raises for each medical anthropology model.

SARS: The First Global Epidemic of the Twenty-First Century

A disease of unknown origin, apparently highly infectious and potentially deadly, was reported in southern China as early as November 2002. The symptoms included high fever, nonproductive cough, shortness of breath, malaise, diarrhea, chest pain, headache, sore throat, and vomiting. For many victims, the symptoms worsened quickly and resulted in a deadly pneumonia. In the absence of scientific identification, the disease came to be known by its general presentation: severe acute respiratory syndrome (SARS). By the time the resulting epidemic was over (July 2003), there were 8,427 cases in more than 30 countries, with 916 reported deaths (Person et al. 2004). By far the largest numbers of cases were in China, Hong Kong, and Taiwan, but people were infected in places as far away as Germany and Brazil.

Scientists attribute the disease to a coronavirus that jumped species (i.e., a zoonosis), from the wild civet cat (*Paguma larvata*) in the Guangdong province in southern China to the humans who sell them for medicinal uses in "wet markets," that is, where live animals are sold. It became clear that the virus was transmitted through the air, when close person-to-person contact permitted respiratory droplets in coughs and sneezes to carry the virus from infected to healthy persons. Large numbers of health care workers and their family and friends were also infected before proper isolation procedures were initiated and protective face masks were required. An initial effort on the part of Chinese public health officials and politicians to avoid reporting the disease contributed to its rapid spread. Extraordinary measures were taken internationally to put an end to the epidemic, including the quarantine of 131,132 patients and close contacts in Taiwan.

One Health Ecology

Challenges to the Ecological/Evolutionary Perspective

The classic cases cited by proponents of the ecological/evolutionary perspective in medical anthropology—kuru in New Guinea, malaria among African peoples who adopted irrigation-based agriculture, and high-altitude adaptations in Andean South

Germany and Japan experimented on prisoners with biological agents during World War II; and Russia and the United States both developed stockpiles of biological weapons during the Cold War. We have vivid memories of the letters carrying anthrax powder that were sent to various sites, including the Senate Office Building in Washington, DC, in September and October 2001,[11] but there were earlier attempts to use biological agents by home-grown terrorists (i.e., neo-Nazi groups, antitax militias, and religious cults).

The murderous attacks of September 11, 2001, and the anthrax letters later that month gave new urgency to state and federal planning for bioterrorist attacks. Congress boosted the budget of the CDCP for research and planning related to bioterrorism, from $49.9 million in 2001 to $870 million in 2003 (Glasser 2004). The newly constituted Department for Homeland Security made funds available to the states to improve emergency response preparations. Frontline responders in the health care and public safety systems (e.g., emergency room staff, fire personnel, and police), as well as members of the military, are being vaccinated against some of the more serious infectious agents, even when the vaccine itself carries serious risks of complications. The vaccine against smallpox, for example, kills one to two people for every million inoculated, but this did not stop the government from attempting—unsuccessfully in the end—to administer it to 500,000 troops and 440,000 public health care workers and medical staff.

There is a sad irony in the attention being given to bioterrorism: While money to support this work flows in, proven public health prevention measures against "ordinary" diseases are taking budgetary hits. Ronald Glasser, M.D., a pediatric physician and author, points out that thirty-two states cut their public health allocations, sometimes by as much as 24 percent (Michigan), between fiscal years 2002 and 2003 (Glasser 2004). AIDS prevention and flu vaccination programs are among the casualties. Even the federal funds designated for bioterrorism preparations end up being used just to minimize the impact of cuts in public health budgets at the state level. Glasser uses the SARS epidemic as a case in point, showing that even though we ought to have learned that preparation, surveillance, and decisive action can prevent the spread of diseases, "we are no better prepared for a SARS epidemic than we were last year [2003]. *Homeland security*, curiously interpreted to exclude the most plausible and deadly threats facing our population, has remained the priority" (Glasser 2004:42).[12]

Does medical anthropology have anything to contribute to these efforts? Monica Schoch-Spana, an anthropologist (PhD Johns Hopkins University 1998) and Senior Fellow at the Center for Biosecurity of the University of Pittsburgh Medical Center (UPMC), believes it does. She explains (telephone interview, March 2, 2004) that state and federal planners were developing worst-case scenarios for a bioterrorist attack that presumed the public would respond in a lawless and chaotic Darwinian struggle for self-survival. The image came close to the Hollywood disaster movies in which crowds of panicked citizens trample each other and destroy property in a desperate effort to flee from the menace or to secure scarce remedies. Operating under the assumption that this was what could be expected in the aftermath of a bioterrorist attack, planners gave military/police control measures paramount consideration in preparedness guidelines and paid little to no attention to measures designed to inform the affected population or to solicit its cooperation.

Schoch-Spana knew from prior research that this was a dangerous misreading of how people actually behave in large-scale emergencies. Documenting positive public responses to the influenza pandemic of 1918, to the outbreak of West Nile virus in 1999, and to the World Trade Center and anthrax attacks of 2001, she has argued to local and national officials that the public should be treated "as an asset, not a problem."[13] She stresses the importance of timely, honest, and consistent information sharing, limits to interventions that infringe on civil liberties, and the engagement of volunteers in humanitarian responses.

Schoch-Spana describes her role as a "midwife to constructive public policies" and as a "burr under the saddle of government." To those who might suggest that she has sold out by participating in an enterprise that threatens to limit civil liberties in the name of national security, Schoch-Spana replies that the stakes are simply too high not to give decision makers the benefit of the social scientist's knowledge of public behavior. She says she cannot abandon the idea of public service; if we resist the militarization of emergency planning, she argues, it is incumbent upon us to propose an alternative model based on what we know about human responses to crises. A good social critic, she explains, makes a good applied anthropologist.

In Chapter 7, I return to the ethical implications of applied medical anthropology and to the question of how one can be an "insider" and a critic at the same time. For the moment, I want to underscore that Schoch-Spana's work in bioterrorism is solidly grounded in the medical anthropology of epidemics, just as it is inspired by the anthropology and sociology of group behavior. There is an urgent need for this knowledge, not just for the possibility of bioterrorist attacks but also for a better-informed public health response to all the re/emerging diseases that this chapter has considered.

SUGGESTED READINGS

Robert S. Desowitz's *Federal Bodysnatchers and the New Guinea Virus: People, Parasites, Politics* (2002) is an insider's irreverent look at the biology and politics of epidemic control, focusing on malaria, West Nile virus, trypanosomiasis, and retroviruses.

Mary Ellen Snodgrass' *World Epidemics: A Cultural Chronology of Disease from Prehistory to the Era of SARS* (2004) provides an encyclopedic review of major epidemics throughout human history.

Felissa R. Lashley and Jerry D. Durham's collection *Emerging Infectious Diseases: Trends and Issues* (2003) has excellent essays on seventeen diseases, as well as general chapters on related issues (including bioterrorism).

Laurie Garrett's *Betrayal of Trust: The Collapse of Global Public Health* (2000) is an excellent source on the failure of governments to take disease prevention seriously.

The web site for the Centers for Disease Control and Prevention (http://www.cdc.gov) is an invaluable resource for research on infectious diseases. It also includes reports on the many prevention programs and emergency planning activities of the Centers. The University of Pittsburgh's Center for Biosecurity, where Monica Schoch-Spana is a Senior Fellow, has a useful web site for work on bioterrorism: http://www.upmc-biosecurity.org

NOTES

1. Many of the infections in this category are reappearing only in the sense that affluent populations are newly threatened by pathogens long considered defeated, but which had never disappeared from poor countries or from impoverished sectors of rich countries. It should also be noted that the appearance of "new" diseases has been a constant in human history, rather than a unique feature of the past decades.

2. An outbreak of *Escherichia coli* infection in Colorado between June and July 2002 was traced to ground beef produced by the ConAgra Beef Company. Only a nationwide recall of 354,200 pounds of beef limited the infection to eighteen persons in Colorado and eight in six other states (http://www.cdc.gov/mmwr, July 26, 2002/51(29); 637–639). At the peak of the "mad cow" or bovine *spongiform encephalopathy* (BSE) epidemic in England in January 2003, there were almost 1,000 new cases per week. It is thought that the "new variant Creutzfeldt–Jakob disease" (vCJD) among humans is linked to consumption of BSE-contaminated products. By December 2003, there was a total of 153 cases of vCJD in the world, most (143) from Britain and associated with exposure to BSE (www.cdc.gov.ncidod/diseases/cjd/cjd_fact_sheet.html).

3. The Neolithic Revolution refers to the period about 10,000 years ago when humans began to domesticate animals and engage in intensive agriculture. The resulting increased exposure to animal-derived diseases and to diseases that thrive in permanently settled communities is thought to have increased the incidence of acute infections for human populations. Barrett et al. (1998) argue that this is the proper starting point for the first epidemiological transition, not the much later Industrial Revolution.

4. A critical aspect in this third transition is that the reemergence/emergence of infectious diseases can have the effect of leveling epidemiological patterns across socioeconomic groups—poor and rich alike are vulnerable to many of the new/returning infectious agents. While there will still be many class-related risk factors for specific diseases, money alone will not protect from the new epidemics.

5. The authors cite factors described in a report of the U.S. Institute of Medicine (Lederberg et al. 1992).

6. There are other diseases I could have chosen, including some that carry higher mortality rates and that are likely to persist longer. However, the conditions that created SARS and the national and international responses to it are likely to be involved in many of the emerging infections of the twenty-first century. SARS also brings into sharp relief some of the problems medical anthropological models will have to resolve to adapt to the new epidemiological reality.

7. We should remember that face masks are routinely worn in public in some Asian countries to prevent the spread of even the common cold, while they are strongly associated in Western countries with medical settings and major health crises.

8. Some have pointed out that the effort to protect against stigmatizing of whole populations risks producing an "authorized" version of an epidemic that may actually hinder the rational targeting of groups that present the greatest risk. An interpretive account of the CDCP's efforts would compare the message being promoted to the public with the health priorities that scientific understandings of the epidemic alone would dictate.

9. Critical medical anthropologists have analyzed health constraints in socialist countries as well as in capitalist economies. It is the evolving mix of the two in the case of China that poses a special challenge.

10. While I focus on the responses to the epidemic here, it is clear that both the ecological and critical perspectives would analyze what biological, economic, and social conditions in this province favor the emergence of zoonotic diseases.

11. A total of five persons died from anthrax exposure during the attacks, and 10,000 more took the two-month course of antibiotics because of potential exposure. Bruce Edwards Ivins, a researcher at a government biodefense lab, was the only person charged in the attacks by authorities (in 2008), and that was after his death by a drug overdose.

12. It is crucial that we not assign exclusive blame to bioterrorism initiatives for shortcomings in public health funding in the United States. Neither the federal government nor the states have ever provided adequate funds for public health programs, despite massive documentation of cost savings associated with prevention of disease. Unfortunately, departments of public health were second-class citizens in the world of health care well before 9/11.

13. This was also the title of a 2003 national leadership summit organized by Schoch-Spana.

CHAPTER

6 Healers and the Healing Professions

At the start of my Peruvian fieldwork, I undertook a search for curanderos who would be willing to participate in my research. I visited and spoke with many individuals who considered themselves "healers," but who did not practice in the shamanic tradition I had come to Peru to study. There were herbalists, Tarot card readers, spiritists, pulse readers, and even a man who cured with the power of a small pyramid he had constructed in his backyard. Of course, this variety of healers was in addition to the full complement of biomedical practitioners who operated from local hospitals, clinics, and private offices.

Not all of the societies studied by anthropologists have as many different kinds of healers as I encountered in Peru.[1] In small-scale, hunting and gathering bands, the common pattern puts curing knowledge and therapeutic practice in the hands of most of the adults in the group (e.g., Lee 1993). Among village-based horticulturalists,[2] some individuals may be known for special curing skills, but rarely are these persons more than part-time healers. Typically, they carry on the activities appropriate to their age and gender and engage in the work of healing only in their spare time (e.g., Ackerknecht 1963:621–633)

Healing roles proliferate in societies that have wider political integration (e.g., multi-village federations or "chiefdoms") and more highly stratified social systems. It is not uncommon in these societies for there to be a mix of healing roles based on the kinds of health problems for which each is judged effective: bone setters, midwives, herbalists, healers who hold religious office, and so on. In the even more integrated state societies of the past (e.g., early Greek and Arab societies and the Harappa culture of northwestern India), some healing roles were full-time professions.

Medical anthropologists have used the term **plural medical systems** to refer to societies that have many distinct healing roles (see Leslie 1977). In addition to studying individual healers in such systems to document the curing traditions they represent—as Sharon and I did with Peruvian curanderos—medical anthropologists and other social scientists have also analyzed how healing roles relate to one another in plural medical systems. My purpose in this chapter is to introduce concepts that facilitate the comparison of healing roles and then to apply them to the two kinds of healers with which I am best acquainted: Peruvian curanderos and biomedical practitioners.

Healing Roles: Organizing the Diversity

Health Care Sectors

Arthur Kleinman (1980) provides a classification for healing activities in plural medical systems. He first distinguishes a **popular health care sector** within which healing acts depend upon a general body of knowledge available to the populace as a whole. He notes that in all societies the majority of sickness episodes are managed entirely within this sector, often at the household level and under the supervision of mothers or other adult females. In this sector, healing is not the privileged activity of select practitioners.

At the opposite extreme, in the **professional health care sector**, healing is carried out by persons with specialized training and knowledge. Elaborating on Kleinman's discussion of this sector, some of the defining features of a **healing profession** are (1) standardized and formal training based on an organized body of knowledge; (2) credentials or licenses required to practice; (3) structured relationships among those in the profession (e.g., mutual referrals, specializations, and prestige/experience rankings); and (4) organizations which enforce standards of practice, share knowledge, and protect the profession from competitors.[3]

Biomedical physicians and nurses come to mind when the notion of a healing profession is raised, but there are many other medical systems with healing professions in the above sense of the word. Ayurvedic medicine in India, for example, pre-dates biomedicine by centuries as a professionalized healing system. Its practitioners are licensed after studying in approved Ayurvedic schools; they constitute an important segment of contemporary India's medical establishment (Leslie 1968). Other examples of professional healers are Chinese and Japanese traditional herbal specialists and acupuncturists (Leslie 1976; Unschuld 1985), and, in the United States, chiropractors (Wardwell 1988). This list could easily be amplified, especially if healing professions of the past were included.

In an intermediate position between the popular and professional sectors, Kleinman identifies a **folk sector**,[4] in which healing is done by "non-professional, non-bureaucratic, specialists" (Kleinman 1980:59). Folk healers typically undergo a nonformal education, often by apprenticeship, to learn their curing art. While the populace as a whole may not be fully aware of the subtleties of the folk healer's practice, the overlap between popular and folk concepts of disease is greater than that between the popular and the professional sectors. Healing roles in the folk sector lack the defining features of a healing profession.

The Peruvian curanderos with whom I worked are a good example of healers in the folk sector. Their healing practices were learned informally, by assisting other curers, and they had no professional organization to represent their interests or to enforce standards. Furthermore, the curanderos shared conceptions of disease (e.g., daño) with their patients, and even employed a similar metaphorical language when talking about the causes and treatment of disease (Joralemon and Sharon 1993).

Healers' Relationships between and within Health Care Sectors

Kleinman acknowledges that the boundaries between these three sectors are fluid and contested. Knowledge and practice from the professional sector can be adopted by the folk and/or popular sectors. For example, some curanderos prescribe pharmaceutical products for their patients and employ biomedical as well as traditional disease concepts. The curandero with whom Douglas Sharon originally worked, Eduardo Calderon, blended the information he gained from biomedical texts with what he had been taught by his curandero mentor. My first research subject, José Paz Chapoñan, had a consulting room modeled after a doctor's consulting office, complete with framed certificates and a steel desk.

There is also movement between health care sectors, as when folk healers who practice without formal training and certification initiate a process of professionalization so as to increase their status and protect their interests. For example, the involvement of curanderos in an international conference on traditional medicine held in Peru in 1979 was part of an effort to gain public recognition and to promote collaboration between medical professionals and curers. In neighboring Bolivia, physician Walter Alvarez led a drive to gain official recognition for herbal healers among the Kallawaya, a Quechua/Aymara ethnic group; he even set up "herbal colleges" in several communities (Bastien 1992:62). Closer to home, the movement to professionalize midwifery is another case of healers attempting to cross health care sectors (Davis-Floyd 1992).

It is also important to recognize that relationships among healers within a given health care sector can be highly competitive. Peruvian curanderos are quick to dismiss each other's work, or even to assign bad motives to their competitors. José Paz regularly regaled me with stories of how incompetent were the curanderos whom his patients had consulted before coming to him for help.

Professional sector healers can also attempt to discredit the practices of their competitors by calling into question the quality of the training and/or knowledge on which their claim to professional status depends. A good example is the rivalry during the nineteenth and early twentieth centuries between biomedical healers and those professionally trained in **homeopathy**, a healing tradition premised on the theory that a substance known to cause a disease can, in very small doses, also cure it (Anderson 1996:380–385). The American Medical Association, soon after its founding in 1847, began to censure member physicians who had dealings with homeopaths. In 1878, a Connecticut doctor who consulted with his homeopathy-trained wife suffered sanctions from his local medical society (Freund and McGuire 1995:208).

Klienman's classification of health care sectors helps to organize the diversity of healing roles into a comparative framework. It also underscores the importance of specialized knowledge and professionalization to the social status of healers. More needs to be said, however, about the foundation on which healers' authority rests.

Authority of Healers

Social and Cultural Dimensions: General Concepts

Sociologist Paul Starr, author of the influential *The Social Transformation of American Medicine* (1982), reminds us that healing roles do not necessarily come with high social status. He notes that the Romans considered medicine a lowly profession, mostly for slaves, freedmen, and foreigners (p. 6). As recently as 1869, an American journal characterized medicine as "the most despised of all the professions which liberally-educated men are expected to enter" (p. 7). Starr argues that a healing profession gains power and prestige when it acquires social and cultural authority and converts that authority into economic and political control over the medical domain.[5]

Starr's notions of social and cultural authority are useful concepts for the comparison of healing roles, within as well as between the healing sectors that Kleinman identifies. Starr defines authority in general as "the possession of some status, quality, or claim that compels trust or obedience" (p. 9). Authority may be grounded in the threat of physical coercion (e.g., violence and imprisonment) or persuasion (e.g., indoctrination), but the most successful form of authority is that which rests on the willing consent of those under its domain.

The willing consent of subordinates is guaranteed when two conditions prevail. Subordinates must depend upon those who have authority over them—as a sick person depends on the skill of the healer—*and* the superior social role must be culturally legitimated by shared values and interpretations of reality—as when a sick person shares with a healer views of the body and of the meanings of illness. Starr calls the first condition **social authority** and the second **cultural authority**:

> Social and cultural authority differ in several basic ways. Social authority involves the control of action through the giving of commands, while cultural authority entails the construction of reality through definitions of fact and value. Whereas social authority belongs only to social actors, cultural authority may also reside in cultural objects, including products of past intellectual activity, such as religious texts, recognized standards of reference (dictionaries, maps, mathematical tables), scholarly or scientific works, or the law (Starr 1982:13).

Starr goes on to explain that these two kinds of authority are not always combined. Social authority may compel obedience in the absence of cultural authority, for example, when citizens obey laws even when they have lost confidence in the government. Likewise, cultural authority may not be accompanied by social authority, as when respected figures speak on matters over which they have no formal jurisdiction. However, social actors who are able to draw upon both kinds of authority hold powerful social positions.

Therapy Outcome and Healer Authority

In theory, a solid foundation for the social and cultural authority of healers would be a record of successful outcomes. The ability to cure would support a healer's claims to superiority over others and could be used to promote professionalization (i.e., increasing social authority). Such success would contribute to the respect and faith that patients bring to their encounters with healers (i.e., increasing cultural authority). Certainly, the expectation of a successful outcome can itself improve the likelihood of positive results, as the extensive literature in psychosomatic medicine amply demonstrates.[6] Thus, faith and outcome can have a mutually reinforcing relationship that improves the social and cultural authority of a healing role.

But, having noted the positive effect of successful outcomes on the authority of a healing role, I must add that the evaluation of a therapy's efficacy is a very complicated matter. The factors which make it hard to assess therapeutic results include the following: (1) Many sicknesses are self-limiting, and therefore "cures" may be incorrectly attributed to a healer's intervention; (2) patients do not necessarily apply the same criteria as healers or investigators in assessing the results of the therapy they receive; (3) an individual case of sickness may have social significance that a successful "cure" would have to address, in addition to mitigating physical symptoms (e.g., sicknesses believed to be caused by sorcery may require retribution); and (4) chronic conditions may have no clear point at which a therapy may be said to have ended and its results achieved (see Kleinman and Gale 1982:406).

The social and cultural authority of a healer is supported by anything that appears to his/her clients to be a cure, but when the results are ambiguous or negative, the healer's authority can suffer. For example, when a new disease appears, for which existing therapies are ineffective, the cultural authority of healers may be challenged. If other healers, representing a different medical system, have greater success, there may also arise a contest over social authority.

A good illustration of the cultural and social authority of healers being challenged by new diseases is the experience of Amerindian shamans during the Spanish conquest of the New World in the early 1500s. European explorers and colonists brought with them an array of epidemic agents to which indigenous populations had not previously been exposed, including smallpox, measles, mumps, yellow fever, and bubonic plague (Crosby 1972; McNeill 1976). The resulting demographic disaster was of stunning proportions, producing dramatic population losses for many decades (Joralemon 1982). Shamans and other indigenous healers were impotent in the face of these devastating new diseases, and they quickly lost credibility in their communities. This represented a significant loss of social and cultural authority, one which undermined existing religious beliefs with a corresponding decay in the entire social fabric.

Authority in the Folk Health Sector: Position of Peruvian Curanderos

Social Authority of Peruvian Curanderos

Peruvian curanderos are not part of a recognized profession and therefore operate in legal and social marginality. Many curanderos experience harassment from local police, who use rarely enforced legal restrictions on nonlicensed medical practices to extort protection payments. Church and civic officials have also been party to repressive measures against curanderos (Sharon 1978). In Starr's terms, this is to say that curanderos have little social authority.

Curanderos certainly recognize the tenuous position they occupy in the Peruvian medical system. Some prefer to maintain a very low profile to avoid the notice of local officials, for example, by performing their ritual sessions in remote agricultural fields. Other curanderos bank on the support of well-connected clients to keep them out of trouble. José Paz responded to my question about difficulties with legal authorities by listing the highly placed individuals he had cured, including the mayor of his small town. Foreign anthropologists who study curanderos can also provide a degree of protection (see Chapter 7).

Outcome of Curandero Therapy

I noted above the complications that make it hard for researchers to determine the outcome of a therapy. Sharon and I attempted to do so for curandero treatments, following the example of Kaja Finkler's (1985) outcome study of Mexican spiritualist healers,[7] but we found the methodological difficulties nearly insurmountable. For example, how do you manage follow-up interviews with patients who travel to get treatment from mountain hamlets six hours away, who have no telephone or other means to be contacted, and who do not want relatives or neighbors to know that they attribute their sickness to sorcery and have consulted a curandero? The interviews we were able to carry out were informative, especially in the detail they provided about patients' life circumstances, but we were not able to exercise sufficient control over the timing and structure of interviews to assess outcome in a scientifically reliable manner.

In addition to the practical difficulties we encountered, there was also a definitional problem that made assessing the impact of curandero therapy problematic. What constitutes a "cure" when the patient and curandero attribute physical symptoms to conflicts in social relationships? Is it the alleviation of symptoms or the repair of interpersonal relations that marks a successful treatment? Arthur Kleinman and James Gale (1982) discovered a similar limitation in their study of the results of Taiwanese folk healing, leaving them with "serious reservations as to whether [their] study provides a culturally appropriate and psychosocially complete account of outcome" (p. 422).[8]

Cultural Authority of Curanderos

Curanderos may have relatively low social authority, and it may be difficult to establish scientifically that their treatments are effective, but many Peruvians, from diverse social classes, seek their help. Clients of the healers that Sharon and I interviewed included business owners, political officeholders, educators, military officers, and even a few medical professionals. These persons were willing to spend significant amounts of money and to subject themselves to physically exhausting ritual treatments because they shared with curanderos the belief that sorcery can be the cause of sickness.

The combination of pharmacological and symbolic therapies that curanderos employ is part of Peru's cultural heritage. There is archaeological evidence suggesting that the curandero's cactus, San Pedro, had ritual and medicinal use at least as early as the pre-Hispanic Chavin culture (1500–500 B.C.; Joralemon and Sharon 1993:182–187). The synthesis of indigenous and Catholic images on the curandero's altar, or mesa, speaks to the capacity of this healing tradition to adapt to changing social circumstances. As I mentioned above, there is further indication of the tradition's cultural vitality in the disease conceptions and sickness metaphors that curanderos and their patients share. In sum, curanderos have substantial cultural authority, even in the context of competition with biomedical healers.

The status of Peruvian curanderos, with relatively low social authority but a solid reservoir of cultural authority, is not uncommon for folk healers in plural medical systems. Some predict that the mixed status of curanderos and other folk healers indicates that, sooner or later, they will lose out to biomedical practitioners, who have greater authority because their treatments are more effective (e.g., Foster and Anderson 1978:252–253). A close look at the authority of biomedicine—how it developed and what challenges it faces—suggests that the future for folk healers may not be so bleak. At the very least, folk healers are not alone in having their social and cultural authority questioned.

Authority in the Professional Health Care Sector: Case of Biomedicine

What Sets Biomedicine Apart?

Biomedicine deserves special attention because its social and cultural authority extends across the globe. There are other healing professions that cover wide regions—I mentioned India's Ayurvedic medicine and China's acupuncture when I introduced the notion of a healing profession—but none that has the worldwide acceptance of biomedicine or its international clout in the development of health policies. For example, the United Nations' World Health Organization is a biomedical institution, even though it sometimes seeks to incorporate other medical traditions (see Chapter 7).

The fact that biomedicine's authority transcends cultural boundaries requires explanation. It seems to run counter to the argument of medical anthropologists and other social scientists that biomedicine is "culturally and historically specific and far from universal," that it is "a product of western culture and society" (Gordon 1988:20; and see Chapter 1).[9] How could a healing system so intricately embedded in a particular cultural tradition gain global authority?

To answer this question, it is necessary to review, however briefly, the history of biomedicine. As in the above discussion of Peruvian curanderos, the focus is on the social and cultural authority of biomedicine and its practitioners. I pay special attention to the rise of biomedicine in the United States, and then identify some of the factors that account for its expansion around the world. I also review some of the threats to biomedicine's authority.

Social Authority of Biomedical Healers

In the nineteenth century, the medical profession was generally weak, divided, insecure in its status and income, unable to control entry into practice or to raise the standards of medical education. In the twentieth century, not only did physicians become a powerful, prestigious, and wealthy profession, but they succeeded in shaping the basic organization and financial structure of American medicine (Starr 1982:7–8).

The solidification of power on the part of biomedicine in the United States during the twentieth century was the result of a variety of factors, some initiated by the profession itself and others related to broad sociocultural developments. Doctors were successful in standardizing medical education, improving the structure and functioning of hospitals, and lobbying for legislation against the healing practices of competitors (e.g., homeopathic physicians; see the preceding section). Taken together, these structural changes in biomedical training and practice created a new social authority and a resulting economic monopoly for the profession (see Freidson 1970; Starr 1982).

On the international scene, biomedicine developed a close association with Euro-American colonial administrations, and therefore with the development and global spread of capitalism. The biomedical practitioners who worked in British, French, and American colonial administrations, as well as for overseas religious missions, were instrumental in the expansion of biomedicine. Also important were the efforts of biomedical healers and researchers who worked in other countries during wars (e.g., malaria control in the Pacific and Southeast Asia during World War II) and on large scale development projects (e.g., the Panama Canal and yellow fever eradication efforts, 1900–1914).

Some scholars who have studied the history of biomedicine's global expansion suggest that the singular purpose of providing biomedical care in colonial settings was to keep the requisite workforce healthy and to diffuse potential sources of resistance to colonial domination (Brown 1979). The linkage between biomedicine and Western political-economic goals—domestically and internationally—leads analysts like Vicente Navarro (1976) to argue that a more accurate term of reference for biomedicine would be "capitalist medicine." These views may understate the humanitarian motive behind international disease prevention and control measures, but there can be no doubt that biomedicine's association with colonial administrations contributed to its growing social authority abroad.

Outcome of Biomedical Healing

In the United States, as well as abroad, the social and cultural authority of biomedicine increased as a result of improved therapeutic outcomes, which resulted from developments in the scientific and technical knowledge about disease and human physiology. Especially notable developments were a better understanding of bacterial infection and the development of antibiotics (e.g., sulfa drugs after 1935 and penicillin after 1944), refinements in surgery techniques associated with the development of the modern hospital in the 1920s, and the discoveries of vaccines (e.g., a vaccine for whooping cough in the 1930s and for influenza in the 1940s). The often-repeated testimonials to the "miracles of modern medicine" were largely based on the dramatic evidence of biomedicine's mastery of epidemics that had long afflicted human populations (e.g., smallpox and polio). "Medicine will find a cure," became Western culture's article of faith in its healers.

There **were** significant improvements in health measures for biomedicine to point to as proof that it was delivering its share of a better world. In the early 1900s, the average lifespan for Americans was about forty-six. There were over eighty infant deaths for every 1,000 births, and major infectious diseases (e.g., pneumonia, influenza, and tuberculosis) accounted for fully forty percent of deaths (Freund and McGuire 1995:17–19). By 2005, life expectancy in the United States had risen to an average of 77.8 years, 6.8 infants died for every 1,000 born, and infectious diseases caused less than 10 percent of deaths (CDC "National Vital Statistics Reports," Vol. 56, No. 10, 2008).

There is contention about how many of these statistics are properly attributed to the impact of biomedical interventions, versus the health benefits of rising standards of living and the construction of public health infrastructures (see the following section). However, there is no doubt that biomedicine has received much of the credit for improved health and longer lifespans, nor that biomedicine's authority among competing medical systems has long been based on the claim of better outcomes.

Cultural Authority of Biomedicine

In Chapter 1, I illustrated how closely biomedicine mirrors and reinforces cultural conceptions and social values, this by way of making the point that, like all medicines, it constitutes a "cultural system" which offers "a way of perceiving and thinking about health and illness [which is] coded in the traditions of a society" (Leslie 1977:512; see also Rhodes 1990). The many correspondences that anthropologists and sociologists have found between biomedicine and Western culture (e.g., Wright and Treacher 1982; Hahn and Gaines 1985; Martin 1987, 1994; Lock and Gordon 1988; Lindenbaum and Lock 1993; Good 1994, 1995) help to explain the substantial cultural authority that biomedicine has enjoyed in the United States and western Europe for much of the twentieth century.

Still unexplained, however, is how a medical system embedded in the traditions of the cultures in which it developed managed to gain cultural authority in other societies. Certainly, part of the answer lies in the already mentioned association between biomedicine and powerful colonial administrations. A record of therapeutic success, especially in epidemic control, was an additional factor supporting the international reputation of biomedicine.

Biomedicine's cultural authority in non-Western societies was further promoted when it was bundled together in international development projects with other products of Western science and technology. The assumption behind these projects was that "progress" meant highways, dams, tractors, and communication systems, *as well as* physicians, hospitals, clinics, and disease eradication campaigns. The "discourse of development" (Escobar 1993) conveyed to Third World countries the unmistakable message that the future lay in emulating Western science, technology, medicine, and economics. The cultural authority of biomedicine on the world stage was advanced as a part of a package called "modernization."

Challenges to Biomedical Authority

By the second half of the twentieth century, there were problems looming for the authority of the biomedical profession. As early as 1968, the phrase "crisis in American medicine" began to appear in print (Battistella and Southby 1968); by the mid-1970s, references to a health care crisis were ubiquitous. At first, the concern focused on how much medical care cost, and how many were unable to afford it, but soon the medical profession found itself under attack for questionable ethics, impersonal treatment of patients, and unjustified claims of effectiveness.

Before reviewing the major lines of criticism of biomedicine, I want to make clear that my objective is not to question the skill or motives of individual physicians or the merits of biomedical treatments. This is not an exercise in "doctor bashing," but a demonstration that even a powerful medical profession can find its social and cultural authority questioned. Furthermore, it is important to understand the challenges to biomedical authority during the later part of the twentieth century because these challenges are directly related to the involvement of medical anthropologists in efforts to improve medical services in the United States and abroad (see Chapter 7).

Economic Critique and Biomedicine's Social Authority

The most direct assault on biomedicine's authority came in response to its out-of-control costs. In 1970, Americans spent $6.9 billion on health services. Ten years later, the annual price tag had risen to $230 billion. By 2002, Americans were spending $1.5 trillion ($5,440 per person) on health services; this represented roughly 15 percent of the country's Gross Domestic Product (GDP) (Pear 2004). By comparison, European nations spend an average of 8.5 percent of their GDP on health (http://www.oecd.org).

The American medical profession had successfully resisted every proposal for national health insurance since the 1920s and fought other reforms that it perceived to threaten the autonomy of the individual doctor. Meanwhile, the cost of diagnosis and treatment spiraled upward, partly because of the expense of technological innovations and partly because of the inflationary pressures built into a "fee for service" system in which third parties (i.e., insurance companies) pay medical bills (Starr 1982:384–385).[10] Thus, the medical profession was struggling against cost containment measures that it viewed as external interference, while larger and larger numbers of Americans found health care of any kind entirely unaffordable.[11]

Although the economic crisis in biomedicine was treated as a systemwide issue by experts in public policy, it had special significance for the disadvantaged classes and ethnic populations (e.g., African, Hispanic, and Native Americans) that lost access to basic medical care because of its cost. The economics of medical care contributes to significant differences in health indices between classes and ethnic groups. For example, in 2005 African American males lived, on average, six years fewer than Caucasian males; more than twice as many African American babies died per 1,000 live births as infants born to non-Hispanic white mothers (CDC "National Vital Statistics Reports," Vol. 57, No. 2, 2008).

Clinical Critique and Biomedicine's Cultural Authority

Questioning the cost of medical services represented the first and most serious challenge to biomedicine's social authority, but there were attacks on the medical profession's cultural authority as well. Many of these focused on the relationship between the patient and physician in a medical system increasingly devoted to technology and highly specialized experts. Among the accusations were that doctors were losing any personal connection to their patients, that they displayed gender and racial prejudices (96 percent of MDs were white males in 1974), and that they practiced professional collusion to avoid accountability for treatment errors.

Feminist scholars and activists produced some of the most influential critiques of biomedicine. A flurry of publications during the 1970s and 1980s documented the relationship between the social and "medical" control of women, from the outrage of ovariotomies at the turn of the twentieth century (see Chapter 1) to the questionable medical management of pregnancy, childbirth, and menopause (e.g., Arms 1975; Scully 1980; Martin 1987).[12] Feminists also drew attention to the underrepresentation of women's health concerns in biomedical research and to the tendency of the profession to adopt male physiology as the standard by which principles of care are set (Hubbard et al. 1979; Gee and Krieger 1994; Laurence and Weinhouse 1994; Rosser 1994).

It was not just women who judged doctors harshly for perceived clinical prejudices. African Americans added their voice to the critical chorus, especially after the revelations of the infamous Tuskegee research project, in which 399 poor, rural black men who suffered from syphilis were left uninformed about their disease and untreated for four decades. Public health researchers wished to document the progressive course of the disease (Jones 1993). When the project came to light, it resonated with the experience of many African Americans, who had long been subject to racist treatment from doctors and public health officials. The problem of unequal treatment is exacerbated by the fact that just 4 percent of physicians are African Americans, despite the fact that they make up 13 percent of the population (Association of American Medical Colleges, 2007).

Outcome Critique

I argued above that the social *and* cultural authority of biomedicine expanded in large part as a result of improved outcomes. An influential group of historians, epidemiologists, and social scientists claim that biomedicine was not, in fact, responsible for many of the health improvements for which it has taken credit. An even more radical claim is that medical care has an overall negative impact on health as a result of **iatrogenic** diseases, those caused by the very process of treatment (e.g., hospital-related infections, the side effects of drugs, and unnecessary treatments) (Illich 1975).

The assertion that biomedicine has been wrongly credited with some major health improvements is based on historical analysis of epidemiological data. This analysis shows that the general rise in the living standards of developing economies, including improved nutrition, water purification, and sewage disposal, was the primary factor responsible for longer lifespans and reduced infectious disease rates (McKeown 1976). Most persuasively, the decline of eight major infectious diseases (e.g., measles, scarlet fever, tuberculosis, typhoid, pneumonia, influenza, whooping cough, and diphtheria) occurred well before the discovery of vaccines and antibiotic treatments for those diseases (McKinlay and McKinlay 1977; Friedman 1987).

The argument about iatrogenic diseases was initially made by social critic Ivan Illich in a polemical book titled *Medical Nemesis* (Illich 1975). Some have dismissed his claims as overstated, but there are good reasons to take seriously the health risks posed by biomedical practice. There are the notorious cases that gain national attention—such as the devastating impact of thalidomide on thousands of infants during the 1960s[13]—but there are also less well-publicized instances in which treatment induces sickness. For example, there are complications that result from cesarean sections (e.g., surgical wound infections) that make the unjustifiably high rate of such procedures in the United States (about 23 percent) all the more troublesome (Davis-Floyd 1992). Insufficient attention to the interactive effect of multiple prescriptions, and the overuse of psychoactive drugs to treat less severe mental illnesses are additional illustrations.

Impact of the Critiques

A measure of the decline in biomedicine's social authority in the United States is the emergence of medical corporations that impose budgetary oversight on diagnostic and therapeutic decisions (e.g., for profit hospitals, health maintenance organizations [HMOs], and "managed care"). Another sign of diminished social authority is the proliferation of malpractice lawsuits—roughly 20,000 claims per year—and of hospital ethics committees partially staffed by nonmedical community members. All of these developments undermine the power of physicians to control their own professional activities, which is a mark of a profession's social authority.

It is harder to assess the net impact of these critiques on biomedicine's cultural authority. One indication may be the proliferation of competing healing alternatives, some of which have had enough success in the medical marketplace to have won coverage under insurance plans (e.g., chiropractic and acupuncture treatments). A review of non-biomedical healing options in the United States notes the resurgence of alternative healing activity: "ethnic groups have begun to celebrate their cultural heritage and promote a strong ethnic identity and the conservation or reclamation of traditional values and practices; many religious groups have increasingly focused attention on healing; and the middle class generally has fueled a massive self-care and alternative care movement" (O'Connor 1995:32).[14]

There is, as well, a general sense in which Americans seem more prepared than in the past to believe the worst about medical doctors. Stories contributing to a growing mistrust of biomedical practitioners appear routinely in newspapers and television programs: the Medicaid-scamming clinic, the incompetent physician who manages to keep on practicing, the unanticipated cancer-causing properties of drugs, and so on. Taken together, these media accounts exacerbate the decline in the cultural and social authority of biomedical practitioners in the United States.

Authority of Biomedicine in Non-Western Countries

Good News, Bad News

Biomedicine in other countries, especially in the Third World, has been subject to a mix of positive and negative appraisals. On the positive side, biomedical care is given credit for an increased lifespan in many countries (e.g., from forty to sixty-six in India and Egypt), for the complete eradication of one major epidemic disease, smallpox, and for effective treatments and inoculations for many other common diseases (e.g., ORT for diarrhea and vaccinations against polio, diphtheria, tetanus, measles, and yellow fever). According to UNICEF's 2000 "Progress of Nations" report, inoculations against polio have dropped cases from 35,000 worldwide in 1988 to just 7,000 at the turn of the century.

On the negative side, there is abundant evidence that biomedicine has had little impact on many of the health problems that afflict the majority of the world's population. In developing countries, access to biomedical care is extremely limited, due, in part, to the scarcity of doctors and nurses and to severe constraints on public health budgets. Immunizations and inexpensive disease prevention programs do not reach the majority of people at risk in some of the poorest countries. Compelling evidence of continuing health disparities across the globe is provided in the World Health Organization report "The Global Burden of Disease: 2004 Update" (http://www.who.int/en/). Among its conclusions is that "South-East Asia and Africa together bore 54 percent of the total global burden of disease in 2004, although they account for only about 40 percent of the world's population (Part 4, page 40)."[15]

Now, biomedicine cannot be blamed for the pernicious health effects of socioeconomic systems that leave large parts of the world's population without enough food to eat, clean water to drink, or sufficient protection from preventable diseases. At the same time, biomedicine's focus on expensive, hospital-based services and on curative over preventive measures has had the effect of directing scarce financial resources in developing countries toward priorities that do not match well with the actual health problems of local populations. Targeted public health campaigns for water treatment, sanitation, vaccinations, and improved nutrition are more difficult to fund when health budgets are spent on hospital construction and advanced medical training for physicians.

The recognition that medical care in the Third World had to be redirected toward public health and disease prevention motivated the World Health Organization's 1978 conference in the former Soviet Union city of Alma Ata (WHO 1978). Representatives from sixty international organizations and 134 countries promoted the ambitious goal of "health for all," which they acknowledged would require social and economic development as much as medical services. Doctors might not be responsible for reversing the poverty and injustices that are at the root of many diseases, but, the World Health Organization believes, their work should be part of a collaborative movement in that direction.

Participants in the Alma Ata Conference recognized two essential facts about the provision of medical care in poor countries. First, there are too few doctors, and those that there are tend to be concentrated in wealthier and more urban settings. For example, in 1964 there were just 5,235 MDs in all of Peru, and 65 percent of those practiced in the capital city of Lima. In rural areas of the country, there was one doctor for every 26,500 people.

The second observation about medical services in poor countries is that training more doctors and building more hospitals is not the solution. The majority of health risks faced by people who live in poverty are not complex medical problems for which expensively educated physicians are required. Much can be done to lower mortality and morbidity by straightforward public health measures and basic prevention techniques. These can be learned quickly and without advanced medical knowledge or technology.

Importance of Primary Health Care

The concept of **primary health care** (PHC) is central to the Alma Ata plan of action. It is based on the principles (1) that health services should be designed to address specific community needs; (2) that the community should participate fully in the identification of its needs, as well as in the design, implementation, and evaluation of health initiatives; (3) that access to services should be guaranteed for all; (4) that the local cultural context should be respected (including the contribution of traditional healers); and (5) that there should be full integration of health planning into the overall social and economic development of countries (see Macdonald 1993).

The Alma Ata Conference's concluding declaration stresses the importance of designing health programs to meet the particular needs of individual countries, regions, and/or communities. However, it also cites some priorities that all PHC plans should include, such as the following:

- basic nutrition and adequate food supplies
- sanitation and safe water
- maternal and child health care (including family planning)
- immunization against major infectious diseases
- prevention and control of locally endemic diseases
- culturally appropriate treatment of injuries and diseases
- essential drugs at low cost

The Alma Ata Conference's promotion of primary health care has been of special interest to medical anthropologists. It stimulated a wide range of projects to which medical anthropologists have contributed: in program design, implementation, and evaluation (Coreil and Mull 1990). In the next chapter, I give several examples to show how anthropology has been applied to the challenge of meeting the above-cited goals.

Alma Ata and PHC in Question: Biomedicine Reasserts Its Authority

The Alma Ata Declaration and the concept of primary health care it articulated called for a radical departure from business as usual for biomedicine in developing countries. Not only did it broaden the scope of "health care" to include social and economic development, it also challenged biomedicine to adopt more of a public health and prevention orientation. Furthermore, it championed a culturally sensitive approach that required doctors to consider working side by side with shamans, midwives, and herbalists, even if they were dubious about the effectiveness of alternative treatments.

Predictably, criticisms soon emerged, as did efforts to water down the PHC agenda. From the medical community came the argument that the Alma Ata Declaration was idealistic, naive, and impractical. A distinction was made between "comprehensive primary health care"—essentially the holistic vision embodied in the Declaration—and "selective primary health care"—medical responses to the most important diseases (Mull 1990). The former would have to remain a long-term goal, while the latter was urgently required. "Until primary health care can be made available to all, services targeted to the few most important diseases may be the most effective means of improving the health of the greatest number of people" (Walsh and Warren, cited in Macdonald 1993:77).

John Macdonald, author of *Primary Health Care: Medicine in Its Place* (1993), points out that while the logic behind a selective approach to PHC is appealing, the net effect is that medico-technical interventions are perpetuated without addressing the underlying social causes of disease. He illustrates this with an experience in Bangladesh, where health workers sought to demonstrate to him the success of a diarrheal disease (DD) campaign based on the social marketing of ORT.

> I was led to a family house and after introductions the topic of DD and ORT was raised. The atmosphere suddenly became charged, with the grandfather of the house gesticulating excitedly and leading me by the hand out of the door and round to the backyard with the ORT workers in tow. He pointed to the water pumps, the source of water supply for several families. The pumps were submerged in foul water. The man continued his explanation: the whole family knew how to make up a home-based oral rehydration solution and they used it frequently in the home. But the cause of the problem remained the water supply and it was with that that they needed help. The social marketing of the "appropriate" technology, the medico-technical intervention of oral rehydration, was addressing the symptoms of the problem and ignoring the cause (Macdonald 1993:83).[16]

This debate about "selective" versus "comprehensive" primary health care may be viewed as an international manifestation of the same professional conflict in which biomedicine is engaged in the United States. Medical specialists working in international health, like their American colleagues, work to protect their social and cultural authority over the provision of health care. Alma Ata's Declaration potentially threatened that authority, just as the criticisms of American medicine challenged its position. By recasting conventional medical interventions as "selective primary health care," international biomedicine preserves its privileged position while appearing to accept reform. Its focus hasn't changed—only its terminology. A second line of criticism has been directed at the concept of primary health care. From this perspective, even the original idea of PHC embodied unacceptable compromises on the health of the poor. Dr. Paul Farmer is the most passionate advocate of this argument (see Box 6.1).

BOX 6.1

Primary Health or "Preferential Treatment for the Poor"?

Physician and medical anthropologist Paul Farmer has made a career of challenging the assumption that health care for the poor has to involve utilitarian compromises of the sort embodied by the concept of primary health care. He argues that insufficient political will, not inadequate wealth, creates the double standard of full care for richer nations (or, at least, for the rich in those countries) and "essential" care for the poor. If we turn the table and assume that, if anything, the poor deserve "preferential treatment" precisely because they are the most in need, then the logic driving primary health care initiatives would no longer seem so compelling (see Farmer 2003).

One would be hard-pressed to imagine a place more in need than rural Haiti, the location of Farmer's first major project. In the town of Cange he built a hospital, Zanmi Lasante (Partners in Health), capable of far more than primary health care, with sophisticated diagnostic equipment, a well-stocked pharmacy, and trained medical staff. Farmer's anthropological training encouraged a respectful treatment of his clients' knowledge of and responses to disease, even when it came to the much-maligned practices of the Haitian religion, voodoo. During dictatorial regimes and extreme civil strife, Farmer and his colleagues continued to deliver first-world medicine to the poorest of the poor.

But it was in the slums of Lima, Peru, and prisons of Russia that Farmer mounted his most successful challenge to the status quo of world health specialists. The core problem in both places was the evolution of multi-drug resistant tuberculosis (MDRT), which resulted from crowded and unhygienic living conditions, poor nutrition, and inconsistently administered drug therapies. Farmer's challenge was to convince public health officials in each country and in international health organizations that the long course of treatment required for MDRT—as much as two years—was feasible even in these difficult situations. He demonstrated that "directly observed treatments" (DOTs) could be accomplished with modest investments among highly mobile urban poor and in understaffed and overpopulated prisons. To everyone who would listen, and to some who wouldn't, he has made the case that the world cannot afford to let MDRT incubate in slums and prisons, if only because it will quickly find its way into every other community and afflict persons from all classes. Sometimes, advocating for the poor requires making arguments that appeal to the wealthy.

Conclusion

It is no clearer on the international stage than in the domestic context how biomedicine will come out of this struggle for authority. In both arenas, biomedicine is well positioned to influence the centers of power, whether it be by lobbying the U.S. Congress or by occupying administrative positions in international health-funding organizations. However, the pressure for improvements in health and greater control of costs is also a powerful political force.

One thing is certain: Many of the issues raised at the international level have increasing import within the United States. Health statistics for poor segments of the U.S. population look more and more like those from Third World countries; uninsured Americans have as little access to primary health care as rural populations in some poor countries; and infectious diseases (e.g., tuberculosis) are staging a domestic comeback due, in part, to deteriorating living conditions. The priorities of primary health care—community participation, collaboration, and equity—might well be on the medical reform agenda in the United States as well.

What role do medical anthropologists play in the struggle to improve the health of people at home and abroad? Some have documented the successes and failures of biomedicine in the United States. Others have assessed the effectiveness of international health projects. In the following chapter, I take a closer look at medical anthropologists who apply their skills in the training of doctors and in the design, implementation, and evaluation of health projects. I also consider objections to this applied work, which include the claim that it serves only to reassert biomedicine's social and cultural authority.

SUGGESTED READINGS

Medical anthropology has produced a wealth of ethnographic material on healers and healing practices in societies around the world; Arthur Rubel and Michael Hass review this literature in their essay "Ethnomedicine" (1990).

Mark Nichter, in "Ethnomedicine: Diverse Trends, Common Linkages" (1991b), offers some general comments on the anthropological study of healers.

Recent anthropological studies of alternative healers in the United States include Csordas (1994), O'Connor (1995), M. Brown (1997), and Hess (1997a).

Medical anthropology research on biomedical healers includes studies of medical school socialization (e.g., Konner 1987; Good 1995) and ethnographic accounts of physician behavior (e.g. Stein 1990; Cassell 1991; Kaufman 1993).

The link between biomedicine and the international expansion of capitalism is illustrated in E. Richard Brown's "Public Health in Imperialism: Early Rockefeller Programs at Home and Abroad" (1976).

In addition to Paul Starr's history of American medicine, E. Freidson's *The Profession of Medicine: A Study of the Sociology of Applied Knowledge* (1970) and J. Ehrenreich's collection *The Cultural Crisis of Modern Medicine* (1978) should be consulted.

The classic *Our Bodies Ourselves* (Boston Women's Health Book Collective 1971) was a landmark text in the feminist critique of biomedicine.

There are online reports on the world's health from the World Health Organization (http://www.who.org) and UNICEF (http://www.unicef.org/).

Also important is the World Bank's *1993 World Development Report: Investing in Health* (1993).

For information on Alma Ata–inspired programs related to the creation of community-based health workers, there is the WHO's *Traditional Birth Attendants: A Field Guide to Their Training, Utilization and Evaluation* (1981) and Barbara Pillsbury's "Policy and Evaluation Perspectives on Traditional Health Practitioners in National Health Care Systems" (1982).

Judith Justice's *Policies, Plans and People: Foreign Aid and Health Development* (1986) is a useful case study of how development projects operate in Nepal.

Jeannine Coreil and J. Dennis Mull published a very useful collection *Anthropology and Primary Health Care* (1990).

Laurie Kaye Abraham's *Mama Might Be Better Off Dead* (1993) is a powerful account of the health experience of poor Americans.

Tracy Kidder's *Mountains Beyond Mountains* (2003) tells the remarkable story of Dr. Paul Farmer's work in Haiti, Peru, and Russia.

NOTES

1. Horacio Fábrega's *Evolution of Sickness and Healing* (1977) provides some of the framework for the following discussion of healing roles in different kinds of societies.

2. This term refers to sedentary or semisedentary villages that grow food crops primarily for subsistence use (i.e., not for sale or trade) and which are politically independent from one another. Typical examples are found among Native South Americans in the Amazon basin.

3. This list of attributes for a medical profession is adapted from sociological and anthropological sources (Freidson 1970; Leslie 1977).

4. The term "folk" may not be ideal—it is imprecise and suffers from romantic connotations—but I have not seen a preferable alternative. The term has wide currency in medical anthropology.

5. The success of therapies certainly contributes to healers' authority, but there are too many complications involved in how patients and their communities assess treatment outcomes to suggest that positive results alone determine how much authority a class of healers is able to claim. This point is discussed further in the sections on "therapy outcome."

6. The journal *Psychosomatic Medicine* publishes research on the impact of faith and expectation on therapy outcome. Anthropologists Robert Hahn and Arthur Kleinman, in their article "Belief as Pathogen, Belief as Medicine" (Hahn and Kleinman 1983), considered the harmful as well as curative effects of belief.

7. Finkler (1985) used a general health questionnaire, the Cornell Medical Index, in interviews with patients before and after their consultations with healers at Spiritualist temples in Hidalgo, Mexico. She found that, in general, symptoms declined after spiritualist treatment.

8. Robert Anderson (1991) reviews the full range of methodological difficulties in outcome studies of ethnomedical treatments and makes the point that many of the same problems are also encountered in biomedical research. He concludes that, despite the obstacles, anthropologists should still strive to document in biomedical terms the effects of ethnomedicine.

9. Analysts point to the linkages between biomedical concepts and such Western philosophical distinctions as mind/body dualism, and the separation of nature from the supernatural (Gordon 1988; Good 1995).

10. There is little incentive for cost cutting when providers are free to set their own fees and when those who receive medical services are not directly billed.

11. The U.S. Census Bureau reports that in 2002 43.6 million Americans had no health insurance. This was 15 percent of the population, compared with 14.6 percent in 2001 (http://www.census.gov).

12. Among the concerns raised regarding the medical management of pregnancy and childbirth were that physicians make use of monitoring devices (e.g., ultrasound and fetal monitoring instruments) and delivery procedures (e.g., the woman in a prone position and routine episiotomy) to exercise control over pregnant women and that cesarean sections are performed more for the convenience of the doctor than as a matter of medical need. The principal issue regarding medical responses to menopause, as suggested in Chapter 1, was that a natural transition in a woman's life is being medicalized and treated with potentially dangerous drugs.

13. Thalidomide, a tranquilizer, was given to pregnant women to reduce the effects of morning sickness. It caused babies to be born with missing limbs (phocomelia).

14. The variety of alternative healing options in the United States is staggering, from those that are linked to specific ethnic groups (e.g., Puerto Rican spiritists, Mexican curanderas, and African American "rootworkers") to those identified under the umbrella of "New Age Healing" (e.g., neoshamanism, channeling, and polarity therapy). Among the anthropological sources on these alternative therapies are Harwood (1977), Trotter and Chavira (1981), Snow (1993), and Brown (1997).

15. The WHO report uses the concept "DALY" (disability-adjusted life year) to measure the burden of disease. This metric calculates the number of years lost from premature death and years of life lived in less than full health.

16. This example should remind us of the previous chapter's discussion of the cholera epidemic, especially the critical view of Trumper and Phillips (1995).

CHAPTER

7 Applying Medical Anthropology

I recall vividly the first nighttime ritual I attended with a *curandero* named Victor Flores (Photo 7.1). Some twenty patients, my colleague Douglas Sharon, and I had been transported from Victor's home in the city of Trujillo to a walled enclosure in the middle of agricultural fields about five miles out of town. There were no lights, except for the flashlight held by Victor's assistant as she helped set up the ritual altar. No one spoke above a whisper.

Photo 7.1 Victor Flores and assistant, Moche, Peru, 1986. (Courtesy of Donald Joralemon)

As Victor took his place, seated with the altar before him, he began his opening chant, first with rhythmic rattling and then with an almost inaudible lyric. The assembled group fell silent. Before long, we were called to stand in a half-circle in front of the altar, as Victor proceeded with his introductory invocations. Unexpectedly, he included the visiting anthropologists in his declarations. Present, he said, were "doctors from the great universities of the world."

The title "*doctor*" in Spanish, as in English, can refer to university professors with a PhD as well as to medical doctors. The ambiguity of the term permitted Victor a strategic stretching of the truth. By calling us "*doctores*" rather than "*antropologos*" (anthropologists), which would have been more accurate, Victor created the impression in the minds of his patients that medical specialists had come to learn how he cures. Even better, they had traveled to Peru from the "great universities of the world"; in other words, Victor's skills were internationally renowned.

This was neither the first nor the last time that our presence was used by curanderos to promote their practice. In another case, we had seen the number of patients of a curer increase dramatically as word got out that "even foreigners" attended his rituals. Peruvians commonly grant special prestige to outsiders, especially from developed countries. By association, those aspects of Peruvian culture that outsiders hold in high esteem gain local status as well. Thus, we were good for business.

My fellow researcher, Douglas Sharon, had taken his role as a promoter of traditional medicine a step further even before we began to work together. He had used the novelty of an American investigating *curanderismo* as an entree to the local medical school, where he taught a course on Peruvian traditional medicine to fledgling doctors. At the time, there was a public service requirement that placed medical school graduates in rural areas for a year before they could get their final license to practice. The faculty of the medical school thought that an anthropologist might be able to teach their students enough about popular health beliefs to improve communication and understanding between patients and doctors during this mandatory year.

A particularly well-received part of Sharon's course was a field trip to the home of a very well-known curer, Eduardo Calderon, for a demonstration of diagnostic and curative procedures. The medical students stood in rapt attention as Eduardo performed the traditional *limpia con cuy*, in which a live guinea pig is rubbed over a patient's body and then cut open to divine the source of his/her symptoms (see Photo 7.2).

After my fieldwork ended, I had occasion to reflect on the impact of our presence on the practices of the curers with whom we worked (Joralemon 1990). According to scientific methodology, we were interfering with the phenomena we were studying, which taints the "data" we collected. But, from the point of view of the curers, the public relations boon that our presence represented was a good reason to participate in our research project. Because we wished to see Peru's curing traditions survive, we were happy to be of some small service.

Should we have become involved in this way? Or should we have sought to minimize the effect we had on those we studied? Was Sharon actually improving relations between doctors and local curers, or was he arming new physicians with the knowledge they would need to subvert their competitors? Is it any of our business whether or not curanderos continue to flourish in Peru?

Photo 7.2 Eduardo Calderon, Las Delicias, Peru. Performing a guinea pig cleansing ritual (limpia con cuy) for medical students from the University of Trujillo. (Courtesy of Douglas Sharon)

Sharon and I were not engaged in an explicit intervention project in Peru; we did not consider ourselves "applied medical anthropologists," even though a part of what we did was directed at improving the social recognition of curanderos. Nevertheless, we were forced by circumstances to confront some of the thorny issues that accompany applied work. These begin with the basic question of whether anthropologists in general, and medical anthropologists in particular, should (or ought, or must) work to improve the life circumstances of those they study and, if so, under what conditions and toward what end?

Compared with the experiences of other anthropologists who have faced this question, our dilemma will seem trivial. Nancy Scheper-Hughes (1992), for example, had to decide whether to try to save the life of a baby whose mother had effectively abandoned it to die of starvation because she was unable to care for it any longer. Ralph Bolton (1992), personally affected by the loss of friends to AIDS, chose to redirect his professional work to support AIDS research and prevention. Many other medical anthropologists have dedicated their energies to diminishing the toll of other diseases (see Hill 1991), as well as to improving the cultural sensitivity of physicians (e.g., Chrisman and Maretzki 1982).

The stakes were certainly lower for Sharon and me in Peru, but having had to think about our responsibility to the curanderos and patients from whom we learned influenced my own thinking about applied medical anthropology. In this chapter, I sketch the history of such work, give some contemporary illustrations, and discuss the critical commentaries to which it has been subject. My ultimate question is this: Do anthropologists have something to offer to the resolution of health and health care problems?

Medical Anthropology in International Development: A Brief History

Throughout the history of anthropology, there have been efforts on the part of individual anthropologists to use their research skills and ethnographic knowledge to practical ends. The founding figure of American anthropology, Franz Boas, for example, applied his skills in **anthropometry** (the measurement of the size and proportions of the human body) to counter anti-immigrant politics in the 1920s. He demonstrated that there was no scientific foundation for the claim that immigrants had smaller brains, which, through intermarriage, would weaken the average intelligence of American citizens.

During World War II, a generation of psychological anthropologists, including Ruth Benedict and Margaret Mead, worked for the Defense Department. They researched the cultures of U.S. allies and enemies to provide military planners a greater understanding of the motivations of soldiers, citizens, and political leaders. For example, in *The Chrysanthemum and the Sword*, Ruth Benedict (1946) explored the importance of Japan's emperor to that country's "national character" and argued that the U.S. terms of surrender should permit the emperor to remain as a symbolic figurehead for the sake of postwar reconstruction (see also Gorer and Rickman 1949).

After World War II, a discrete career path began to develop in anthropology for those who wished to work on the resolution of health problems. A foreign assistance priority in the U.S. government, prompted by the success of the reconstruction of Europe under the Marshall Plan, spurred a proliferation of international development projects. This, in turn, stimulated the emergence of applied anthropology. Since many of these development projects had health components, they attracted those whom we would now label medical anthropologists.

Anthropological Troubleshooters, 1945–1973

In the early years of international development, the role of anthropologists was largely limited to troubleshooting problems that arose as projects were implemented. Development experts operated under the assumption that their task was to modernize the economies and health care systems of poor countries. Prevalent in their thinking was the idea that traditional practices are obstacles in the way of "progress," a concept that was defined according to a thoroughly Western model (e.g., mechanization and industrialization). When local populations, the "recipient people" in the development language of the day, resisted development projects, the experts turned to anthropologists to identify and remove the cultural obstacles that frustrated their innovations.

A classic example of the work of anthropologists as troubleshooters is Edward Wellin's (1955) research on the south coast of Peru. The Rockefeller Foundation's Division of Medicine and Public Health had supported the creation of a regional health organization, the Ica Departmental Health Service, within Peru's Ministry of Public Health and Social Welfare. One of its objectives was to encourage the household boiling of water to prevent typhoid, cholera, and other waterborne diseases. This was to be accomplished by a community hygiene worker, who was provided basic information about environmental sanitation and communicable diseases.

In the small town of Los Molinos, only 26 of 200 families were routinely boiling their drinking water after two years of household visits and public lectures by the hygiene worker and public health doctors. Wellin was asked to find out why so few were following what seemed to the health workers a simple and straightforward technique to prevent disease. He interviewed women household heads who had adopted the practice and others who had not; he also completed a brief ethnographic survey of the community's health beliefs, social structure, and views of the hygiene worker.

Wellin found many reasons behind the community's resistance to water boiling. For some, it was hard to reconcile the idea that boiled water was "good for one's health" with local beliefs about the cause of diseases. As in many parts of Latin America, community members believed that foods and natural forces (e.g., winds) are either "hot" or "cold"—not in the literal thermal sense, but as an essential quality of the substance or force. When exposed to too much of either hot or cold elements, a person's internal equilibrium is upset, and disease can result. According to local ideas, water has an essential "cold" quality until it is cooked, when it becomes "hot" (even after it has cooled) and potentially harmful. Then it may only be used to counter an illness caused by exposure to "cold" forces. One might drink boiled water during an illness, but never as a general practice.

In addition to the conflict between local disease beliefs and the public health program, Wellin discovered that class barriers inhibited the efforts of the hygiene worker, a twenty-five-year-old married woman from another town in the region. Wellin concluded that she was most successful with persons from her own middle-class background, and far less so with either the poor or more prosperous segments of the town. He also found that there was some confusion about a "health worker" who brought no medicine and did no diagnoses, but who wanted to snoop into the daily activities of families.

It is significant that in this case, as in many others, the anthropologist was called in only after a project encountered difficulties. Benjamin Paul, a Harvard anthropologist and editor of an influential early collection of social science essays in public health (Paul 1955), made the case for ethnographic information in the earlier stages of development planning: "*Before* asking a group of people to assume new health habits, it is wise to ascertain the existing habits, how these habits are linked to one another, what functions they perform, and what they mean to those who practice them" (p. 1; emphasis added).

Notice that neither Wellin nor Paul challenged the conventional wisdom of the period, that the implementation of development projects is difficult because of the culture of the "recipient peoples." These anthropologists argued that ethnography is required for successful projects because it enables planners to pinpoint potential sources of resistance in the target community. Medical anthropologist George Foster, whose consulting in international health began in the early 1950s, observes that an equally important question—rarely asked—is how the bureaucratic behavior of the planners and the institutional culture of the development organization can also contribute to program failures (Foster 1982:193; see also Justice 1986).

Disenchantment and Disengagement

It did not take long for a mutual disregard to emerge between development experts and anthropologists. From the point of view of the development organizations (e.g., Agency for International Development), anthropologists seemed more likely to complicate matters than to contribute the anticipated quick fixes. Instead of returning from a fast trip to a project site with a useful solution, anthropological consultants were likely to send word from the field that an additional period of months would be required to understand fully what was at issue. Even if a report were forthcoming, it would often as not cite insufficiencies in the project design as the problem, rather than local cultural obstacles. Development experts asked, "Whose side are these anthropologists on, anyway?"

Anthropologists, on the other hand, grew more and more frustrated with the lack of input in the initial project planning process. They were disdainful of the cultural ignorance of development experts and of the patronizing of local communities with a "we know best" attitude. In the 1960s, the widespread opposition to the U.S. involvement in the Vietnam War further alienated anthropologists from government employment of any sort.[1] It was easy to take a principled stand against such work because there were ample job opportunities in colleges and universities—anthropologists could make a living teaching without accepting morally questionable work for the government, especially since the U.S. government was out of favor in some academic circles anyway (Hoben 1982:54–55; Morgan 1990).

The growing disenchantment between development organizations and anthropologists reduced the number of the latter hired by the former. By 1974, only one anthropologist was working full time for the Agency for International Development (Hoben 1982:359). Some applied work continued to be done by anthropologists under the umbrella of private foundations and United Nations-sponsored organizations, but there were also strong currents in opposition to the use of anthropology in development projects of any variety.

Social Soundness Guidelines and the Return of Applied Anthropology, 1973–1980

The record of failed development projects and a shift in Washington politics eventually led to a call for a new approach to foreign aid. The U.S. Congress responded with the Foreign Assistance Act (1973–1974), which mandated a change in the guiding priorities for the Agency for International Development (AID). AID was now to fund projects which (1) promote a more equitable income distribution; (2) improve agricultural production with the use of appropriate technology; (3) involve the poor in decisions that affect their lives; and (4) attend to the "interrelationships among technology, institutions, and economic, social, environmental and cultural factors" (Foreign Assistant Act 1979).

In response to this legislation, AID administrators developed the "Social Soundness Guidelines" (1975), which required that research be carried out in communities prior to project planning so that interventions would match local needs and potential problems could be prevented. It took thirty years for development experts to recognize the need to learn about the local context before designing projects because they operated under the assumption that "the west is the best"; they believed they already had the ideal blueprint for a better tomorrow (Foster 1987; Pillsbury 1991:66). The Social Soundness Guidelines seemed, at least initially, to mark a philosophical shift in the development profession toward smaller projects that were better adapted to the "felt needs" of local communities.

The almost immediate impact of AID's new approach was the creation of jobs for which anthropologists were well trained. Who better to do the baseline research in local communities? For the first time, there was a role for anthropologists in the early stages of development planning. And it could not have come at a better time, since shrinking college/university budgets and an overproduction of PhDs left many anthropologists searching for employment outside the academy. By 1977, twenty-two anthropologists had found full-time work at AID; three years later, the number was up to at least fifty, with an additional hundred on short-term contracts (Hoben 1982:359). Apparently, it was acceptable once again to work for the government; applied anthropology was back.

At the same time that the policies at AID were being redefined, other international development organizations were also taking new directions. As we saw in the previous chapter, the United Nation's World Health Organization (WHO) began in the 1970s to promote primary health care, community participation, and "sustainable development" as key priorities. Other organizations, such as the Pan American Health Organization (PAHO), the United Nations Children Fund (UNICEF), and the Food and Agriculture Organization (FAO), also shifted their orientation toward more grass-roots planning. Like the Social Soundness Guidelines, these changes encouraged the involvement of anthropologists in development projects, although more often as short-term consultants than as permanent employees.

There was also a proliferation during the 1970s of anthropologists working for private, nonprofit organizations and foundations that promote health initiatives in the United States and abroad (e.g., Save the Children, CARE, and Ford and Rockefeller Foundations). Many of these organizations focus on small projects that depend upon mutual planning between technical experts and local community members. Anthropologists with fieldwork experience in targeted areas were obvious candidates for work as facilitators in this process.

The Reagan/Bush Years (1981–1993) and Beyond

Development work that depends either directly or indirectly on funding from the government of the United States is always vulnerable to the changing currents of presidential and congressional politics. This was especially notable when Ronald Reagan defeated Jimmy Carter in the 1980 presidential election. Carter's administration had supported foreign assistance and had been instrumental in the implementation of a more context-sensitive approach to development planning. Reagan's team sought to replace government-to-government aid with support for private organizations and industries. They also reintroduced a Cold War philosophy that saw development as a means to combat the spread of communism.

A practical result of the Reagan agenda was the evaporation of government employment for applied anthropologists. Many left their positions voluntarily, recognizing that their contribution was not likely to be appreciated, and others were marginalized in institutions that found it difficult to fire them due to public employment regulations. Those who worked on short-term contracts for government organizations like AID found they had less success in the competition with other development experts for work on new projects.

However, applied anthropologists continued to find work in "nongovernmental organizations" (NGO; e.g., private and nonprofit) and "multilateral" institutions (e.g., U.N. agencies, the World Bank, and regional development organizations). In some cases, they set up their own foundations and consulting firms, such as Cultural Survival and the Institute for Development Anthropology. They also joined organizations that other social scientists and policy experts had established, for example, Harvard's Institute for International Development and the International Center for Research on Women. In addition, applied medical anthropologists turned to the domestic context to work on health projects funded by states, cities, private foundations, and community-based health organizations.

The political shift that accompanied William Clinton's terms (1993–2001) had an effect on international health programs, especially in that family planning funds were disconnected from antiabortion politics, but a Republican-controlled Congress restricted the options for a democratic administration. George W. Bush's (2001–2009) approach reasserted priorities from his father's term, but with some new support for HIV-AIDS programs. Applied medical anthropologists continue to work on government-supported projects, but NGOs and multilateral organizations play an increasingly important role in creating employment opportunities for social scientists.

Work of Applied Medical Anthropologists in International Contexts

It is impossible to convey the full range of applied medical anthropology projects in international health, but the following two examples illustrate important differences in how such work is conceived. In the first example, the anthropologist is employed by a governmental organization and contributes methodological techniques and cultural expertise to the design and implementation of a health education campaign. The second project showcases the medical anthropologist as social activist, one who analyzes the socioeconomic conditions behind health problems and designs an intervention with social reforms in mind.

Growth and Nutrition: An Educational Project in Indonesia

When the notion of primary health care was translated into specific prevention programs, a great deal of attention was paid to the nutrition of children under the age of five. UNICEF reports that "about half of all child deaths are associated with malnutrition" and that "three quarters of all these malnutrition-related deaths are linked not to severe malnutrition but to mild and moderate forms" (UNICEF 1996).[2] Some diseases are directly caused by poor nutrition (e.g., kwashiorkor)[3], and many others are made far more severe—potentially fatal—for the malnourished child (e.g., gastrointestinal infections, measles, and chicken pox).

In the late 1970s, Indonesia, with support from the World Bank, initiated a "Nutrition Improvement Project," which trained volunteer nutrition workers from rural communities to monitor child growth and promote nutritional education. Medical anthropologist Marcia Griffiths participated in the pilot investigation for this project, which sought "to identify positive changes mothers might make in feeding practices, to analyze mothers' possible resistance to making these changes, and to highlight their motivations for changing" (Griffiths 1990:157).

A total of ten villages were selected to help in the design of the program. Each conducted "self-surveys" to assess the nutritional status of children in their community.[4] Community meetings were held to discuss the results of the surveys and to solicit solutions directly from the mothers who had participated. From these discussions, project staff developed "question guides"—a less formal interview instrument than a preset questionnaire—which were used by women chosen from communities in subsequent educational visits to families. The eventual goal was for mothers to develop with the nutritional volunteer plans for healthier feeding practices targeted to their particular circumstances and needs.

Griffiths underscores the importance of the anthropological research methods that were used in the project. Nutrition volunteers were trained in the techniques of participant-observation and open-ended interviewing, which helped them to discover behaviors that formal surveys would have missed. For example, observation and leisurely conversations with mothers revealed that while children were typically breastfed for two years, they were permitted to nurse only from one breast (left in Java, right in South Sumatra). As a result, infants would cry from hunger, and the mothers would give them liquids and solid foods that were either contaminated or nutritionally inadequate. Several explanations were advanced for the favoring of one breast, but, more importantly, the discovery of the practice encouraged a modification of the educational message: "Each time you breastfeed, use both the right and left breasts; be sure your child is satisfied" (Griffiths 1990:161).

In addition to the family visits, the project also designed a media program that included short radio dramas (e.g., a conversation between two mothers about their babies) scripted around points of potential resistance and delivered by the nutrition volunteers. Anthropological insights helped to make the dialogue in these dramas culturally appropriate; feedback from village women as the scripts were written was also crucial.

The project was evaluated after a year and a half. One thousand households were assessed, 600 in the project areas and 400 in comparison districts.

> Evaluators looked at the mothers' participation in nutrition activities, their nutrition knowledge scores, the mothers' and children's consumption of key foods, their dietary intake of calories and protein, and the infants' nutritional status as measured by weight-for-age, height-for-age, and weight-for height. [Project] household scores for each of these indicators were significantly better than those of comparison households (Griffiths 1990:166).

According to Griffiths, the experience in Indonesia confirms the value of anthropology in the design, implementation, and evaluation of primary health care initiatives. She encourages social scientists to be involved from the beginning to the end of projects, to balance qualitative and quantitative methods, and to focus research on the areas of concern to program managers. She warns anthropologists against writing general ethnographies, which "are seldom useful in program planning" (ibid., p. 168). The product of research must be limited to what planners need to know.

Medical Anthropology and HIV/AIDS Prevention: Sex Workers in Congo (Formerly Zaire)

In November 1997, the United Nations agency UNAIDS released a report in which it declared that the number of HIV-infected persons had reached 30 million worldwide—which was one-third more than had previously been estimated. The news was particularly bleak for sub-Saharan Africa, where 7.4 percent of people aged 15–49 are infected. In Botswana, close to 30 percent of the total population is HIV-positive, and similarly devastating rates are found in Zambia and Zimbabwe.

Anthropologist Brooke Schoepf and her colleagues (Schoepf et al. 1991) have worked since 1985 on AIDS prevention in the central African country of Zaire. The primary transmission of AIDS in this region is by heterosexual intercourse with an infected partner. Prevention requires that the general population be educated and motivated to alter sexual behavior. This is an extraordinarily difficult challenge, given cultural norms about sexual relations (e.g., male prerogatives for multiple partners), economic conditions that leave women vulnerable to male dominance, and the symbolic significance of blood, semen, and vaginal secretions (p. 189).

One of the initiatives on which Schoepf et al., worked was a series of "risk-reduction workshops" for female sex workers, who are at the highest risk for HIV infection.[5] The workshops included role-playing the situations in which these women would have to ask clients to use condoms. They also provided crucial information about HIV transmission from mother to infant and about how to sterilize needles and syringes to minimize the risk of infection for drug users. Remarkably, a local women's church group, after learning of the workshops, requested that the team come to do sessions for them as well. An additional role-play was added: a wife persuading a husband to stay home instead of going with friends to bars for extramarital sexual relations.

The researchers did follow-up assessments with the participants to determine whether the workshops had an impact on behavior and, if not, why (Schoepf et al. 1991). At six months, the indications were positive: All but one of the sex workers who had participated in the workshops reported that they were requiring clients to use condoms. However, at nine months the use of condoms was down, largely because clients—especially high-status students—were insisting that condoms do not stop HIV infection. The source of this erroneous conclusion was a published interview with a U.S. sex researcher, who had been quoted as saying that condoms provide only incomplete protection (p. 198).

This AIDS prevention project drew explicitly from an anthropological analysis of social and economic relations. Schoepf and her colleagues show how sexual negotiations between women and men are tied to Congo's postcolonial, socioeconomic turmoil. They characterize AIDS as "a disease of development and underdevelopment" (Schoepf et al. 1991:201):

> The rapid spread of AIDS in the region results from the gendered structure of inequality within a stagnant economy in which accumulation by international capital and a local ruling class leaves the majority pauperized. Within the poor majority, as within the privileged and middle classes, most women are economically and politically subordinated, their autonomy restricted, and their choices circumscribed (Schoepf et al. 1991:203).

This approach to applied medical anthropology differs from that illustrated by the Indonesian example. The latter is in the tradition of Edward Wellin's work in Peru, according to which the anthropologist's job is to serve as a cultural expert and mediator—a "culture broker"—between development planners and community members.[6] In the AIDS prevention program in Zaire, the anthropologist was a social activist who helped to reveal and challenge the conditions that put women at risk for infection in the first place.

Applying Medical Anthropology in the United States

There is an instructive parallel between the increasing engagement of medical anthropologists in international health and the gradual introduction of anthropological experts into health care settings and programs in the United States. In both cases, anthropology appeared to address the complex sociocultural factors that get in the way of successful public health interventions and effective patient/physician relationships. Failed projects opened the door to anthropologists in international development organizations; a medical profession under broad attack (see Chapter 6) has had the same effect in the United States.

Medical anthropologists contribute to health care in the United States in many ways. They work on public and community health projects (O'Reilly 1991; Whiteford 1991), consult for hospitals and clinics (Chrisman and Maretzki 1982; Chrisman and Johnson 1990), and participate in the training of medical professionals (Dougherty

1991; Johnson 1991). As the presumptive cultural expert in all of these arenas, the medical anthropologist is most often called upon to apply ethnographic knowledge to the assessment of health needs, the planning of culturally acceptable interventions, and the resolution of communication difficulties between health workers and patients.

It is tempting to match the international case examples with several illustrative applied projects in the United States. There are certainly many excellent candidates. But it may be more valuable to spend some time on a concept that has become central to the role medical anthropologists play in a variety of domestic health care settings: **cultural competency**. Whether called upon to teach it or to apply it, medical anthropologists have gained entrance into biomedicine on the basis of the claim that introducing cultural competency into clinical care improves patient/physician interaction and treatment outcomes.

Cultural Competency: Whose Culture, Whose Responsibility?

What it means to be culturally competent is often best understood by negative example, that is, by seeing what happens when culture is not sufficiently factored into the relationship between doctors and their patients. Although there are innumerable cases of "cultural incompetence" in the literature (see Galanti 1991), essayist Ann Fadiman's (1997) account of the awful circumstances surrounding the care of a Hmong child, Lia Lee, in Merced, California, has become the standard reference in anthropology and biomedicine alike.[7] It is, without question, a powerful story beautifully told, but it leaves a critical question largely unanswered: If failure to communicate across cultural divides is the problem, what's the solution?

The Health Resources and Services Administration's Bureau of Primary Health Care (BPHC) believes it has the answer: Assimilate and implement "a set of attitudes, skills, behaviors, and policies that enable organizations and staff to work effectively in cross-cultural situations . . . acquire and use knowledge of health-related beliefs, attitudes, practices, and communication patterns of clients and their families to improve services, strengthen programs, increase community participation, and close the gaps in health status among diverse population groups" (United States, HRSA, BPHC 2000).

The glossy brochure in which this definition of cultural competency appears describes projects supported by the BPHC, from Brooklyn, New York, to the Hawaiian Islands. There are smiling pictures of Hispanic children, an Asian woman reading a prescription, a Buddhist looking contemplative, and any number of other ethnically distinct individuals. The projects include referral systems for traditional healers, audio cassettes on health issues recorded by community members in appropriate languages, community health educator programs, interpreter services, and diversity in hiring practices.

There is much in the BPHS' initiatives to applaud, but there is also a major shortcoming: "Culture" is confused with "ethnicity" and essentially treated as a characteristic of the patient that threatens to impede communication. This should sound familiar. It is the same error that plagued early international development projects, which treated the culture of the "recipient people" as an obstacle to overcome and left unexamined the culturally laden presuppositions of the planners. Applied medical anthropologists struggle to remind health care workers that culture is not coterminous with ethnicity, that the shared patterns of thought and behavior that define cultures are also characteristic of groups distinguished by gender, age, religion, occupation, and others. Indeed, cultural competency can usefully begin with the recognition that biomedicine is itself a foreign culture,[8] and that the assumptions that underlie its practice are as much in need of attention as are the beliefs of patients.

Conflating culture with ethnicity encourages medical staff to develop a cookie-cutter approach to cultural competency, using oversimplified and stereotypical synopses of beliefs and practices of each ethnic group. A recent textbook designed to promote a "culturally competent approach" (Purnell and Paulanka 1998) could lead to just this problem. It offers structured overviews of sixteen ethnic groups, with sections on "12 domains of culture" (i.e., inhabited localities, communication, family roles/organization, workforce issues, nutrition, pregnancy and childbearing practices, death rituals, spirituality, and health care practices and practitioners). The editors stress the risk that generalizations can lead to stereotyping (p. 3), but this is exactly what such handbooks are likely to produce in the rushed context of a public health clinic or hospital emergency room. And there is no chapter offering insight into the oddest culture of all, biomedicine!

Applied medical anthropologists work on cultural competency in a variety of U.S. health care contexts. Elisa J. Sobo was employed by the Center for Child Health Outcomes at the Children's Hospital and Health Center in San Diego, California. She and her colleagues worked on a measure of "functional biomedical acculturation" to assess how much of the culture of biomedicine is familiar to families (Sobo and Seid 2003). Ruthbeth Finerman and her colleagues at the University of Memphis used standard anthropological interviewing techniques to explore the challenges and frustrations of those who are employed as medical interpreters for Latino patients. They found a conflict between medical staff who treats interpreters as "just a translation device" and the interpreters' own view of their role as cultural brokers who try to mediate between sometimes-hostile staff and overwhelmed migrant workers (Finerman et al. 2003).

These anthropologists, like their international counterparts, assume that "cultural competency" extends to an understanding of the social and cultural structures that underpin biomedicine. Improving communication between health care workers and the people they serve requires all parties to the interaction to explore the assumptions that go into their "explanatory models" of disease (Kleinman 1980). The challenge of this work is to push a medical profession not known for self-reflection and criticism to respond positively to the suggestion that it is part of the problem. In this regard, applied medical anthropologists face a dilemma similar to those who work internationally: How to function within a system while simultaneously critiquing it.

Between a Rock and a Hard Place: Applied Medical Anthropology under Attack

Applied medical anthropologists—whether they work on international or domestic health projects, teach in medical schools, or consult in U.S. hospitals—report that they are in the position of having to continually justify their presence to sometimes-hostile technical experts, scientists, physicians, administrators, medical students, and even patients. The tenuous position of these anthropologists makes them vulnerable to everything from political swings in Washington to budget pressures in hospitals and medical schools. They frequently work without the benefit of collegial support because it is rare for more than one anthropologist to be included on development teams, teaching faculty, or hospital/clinic staff (Alexander 1977). They usually occupy marginal, ill-defined roles in organizations ruled by rigid professional hierarchies (Chrisman and Maretzki 1982).

At the same time, applied medical anthropologists have also found their work questioned within their own discipline. Replaying issues raised during the 1960s and early 1970s about applied anthropology in general, critics ask how to draw the line between practical accommodation to the demands of an employing organization and being co-opted to an agenda incompatible with anthropological principles.[9] The most thoroughgoing questioning of applied medical anthropology has come from critical medical anthropologists.

Critical Medical Anthropology Assault on Applied Medical Anthropology

The Mexican anthropologist Guillermo Bonfil Batalla (1966) attacked what he called the "conservatism" of applied anthropologists, who, by working within the system, manage only "to change what is necessary so that things remain the same" (p. 92). Critical medical anthropologists Merrill Singer (1989a), Nancy Scheper-Hughes (1990), Hans Baer (1993), and others have made the same point about applied medical anthropology. They ridicule the "timid anthropologist" (Scheper-Hughes 1990:191) who is so afraid of offending medical colleagues that he/she becomes a handmaiden to biomedicine (Greenwood et al. 1988). They warn that the applied medical anthropologist merely helps to extend the physician's ability to control his/her patients and to depoliticize health problems by treating them as individual rather than social problems (see Singer 1989a:1195).

Critical scholars acknowledge that their analysis of the class interests behind health care systems can lead to a "politics of despair" (Scheper-Hughes 1990:189): Why try to do anything if you believe that it is the entire social/economic structure that is at the root of the problem? If "tinkering with the system" only serves to maintain its oppressive characteristics, is the only option an unlikely social revolution?

Singer (1995) answers that there is room for a "system-challenging praxis," a "critically applied medical anthropology" which unapologetically confronts medical teachers, researchers, and practitioners with evidence of the political and economic interests in biomedicine. The approach would adopt an explicit advocacy role for patients and would bring to bear a wider social analysis to disease. Critically applied anthropologists would work with "labor unions, women's health collectives, ethnic community organizations, gays and others victimized by the stigma of AIDS, health consumer groups, self-help and self-care groups" (Baer 1993:311). They would help to document and work to reverse the health problems associated with environmental pollution, occupational hazards, and poor living conditions. And they would join in the campaign in the United States for a national health insurance system.

Singer (1995) offers his own experience as the Director for Research at the Hispanic Health Council, a community-based organization in Hartford, Connecticut, as an example of "system challenging praxis." He employs anthropological research methods to assess the health needs of the local Puerto Rican population and designs programs that address problems like alcoholism, substance abuse among children and adolescents, drug treatment for pregnant women, and AIDS prevention for intravenous drug users. Standard medical responses to these health issues would tend to be at the individual treatment level; the Council attacks them as socially embedded and poverty-related problems that require community-wide responses.

Singer's work, together with other Council staff and community volunteers, extends to aggressive lobbying at the local, state, and national levels for project funding and health services. For example, the Council was instrumental in the state approval—the first in the nation—of a sterile needle exchange program as an AIDS prevention measure (Singer 1995). Similarly, when research revealed unacceptable levels of hunger among children from low-income families, the Council initiated a campaign in local media to encourage changes in local, state, and federal programs. These two projects illustrate the Council's commitment to empowerment and community education as core aspects of its mission (Singer 1995).

Response from Applied Medical Anthropologists

The critical commentary on applied work in health settings has generated predictable responses from those who are engaged in this work. To the judgmental tone and rhetorical excesses of the critique, applied medical anthropologists have countered with equally harsh attacks. Several have pointed to the "pre-made antagonism to biomedicine" (Csordas 1988:417) that seems to drive the agenda of critical scholars. Sue Estroff, an anthropologist working in the Department of Social Medicine at the University of North Carolina, characterizes the critique as "a sort of Star Wars quest to identify and document the evil presence of Darth Vader in yet another form—Western, capitalistic biomedicine" (Estroff 1988:421). Thomas Johnson (1995:108) bemoans the "acrimonious confrontations" brought on by the writings of critical medical anthropologists.

Among the points made in response to the critical appraisal of applied work are the following:

- Linking biomedicine to the dominating structures of capitalism does not take us very far toward an understanding of the microlevel context of patient/physician interactions. "*All* institutions in *all* societies replicate the basic values and social structure of the society in which they function" (Press 1990:1002). We must focus "upon the particular manifestations of these values within the clinical encounter, rather than upon their existence, per se, within the clinical setting" (ibid.).

- Drawing black-and-white distinctions between a dominating biomedicine and oppressed patients obscures the constraints under which doctors and other health professionals themselves operate, especially those associated with the corporatization of health care in the United States (Stein 1995:116). Just who is the victim of capitalist forces in medicine and who is the beneficiary?

- Health care institutions, even in capitalistic societies, are not monolithic or all powerful. There are chinks in the armor where an applied medical anthropologist, working within the system, can help to produce systemic change. "There is direct confrontation of a system, and there is also subversion" (Heurtin-Roberts 1995:111).[9]

There have also been efforts on the part of applied medical anthropologists to get beyond the sometimes-strident attack of their critical colleagues to reexamine what it is that they are doing and to ask if they should be doing something differently (e.g., Wright and Johnson 1990). Thomas Johnson finds common ground in two principles underpinning the critical approach to applied work in health: "enhancing democratization and eliminating mystification" (Johnson 1995:110). In other words, all applied medical anthropologists should ask themselves these questions: Does their contribution improve access to the resources (including knowledge) of biomedicine? Do they help to reveal whose interests are served by disguising the ultimate reasons that those resources are not made accessible?

Personal Reflections

In 1996, I was invited to speak at a national conference of organ transplantation specialists in Washington, DC. The meeting was organized by the federal agency responsible for coordinating the acquisition and distribution of organs for transplantation (Health Resources and Services Administration, Division of Transplantation). The conference goal was to consider how to increase the supply of organs in light of the failure of past initiatives to stimulate donation rates enough to keep pace with the national waiting list. I was asked to talk about cultural obstacles to donation and to suggest ways around them.

I was immediately reminded of the role of early applied anthropologists in international development, who were called in to identify and remove cultural obstacles that were thought to be inhibiting the acceptance of projects. The message I delivered was also reminiscent of the conclusions these applied anthropologists often brought back to the organizations that hired them: The obstacles are those of your own "culture," not of the "target population." My presentation asked my largely medical audience to think more critically about the distance between its rather instrumental understanding of a deceased's body—as a collection of reusable parts—and the views of the general public. I suggested that nonmedical conceptions do not so quickly separate the individual from his or her physical form.

I had disposed of several drafts of my paper because the argument seemed too blunt—even confrontational—and I feared that my medical audience would simply tune me out. If I lost them by the tone of my presentation, I reasoned, then my talk would have little impact. I was the only anthropologist brought to speak at the conference, and I thought I should make every effort to convey my ideas in the most effective way. Quite honestly, I pulled some punches.

I might have delivered a talk that asked how many of those in the audience stood to gain financially were donation rates increased (e.g., more surgeries and more income). I could have challenged the transplantation specialists to explain how the general public should be expected to donate organs when access to most transplant surgeries is limited by the "green screen" (i.e., the ability of a prospective patient to pay for the transplantation). If I was a truly critical medical anthropologist, I would have pointed to the prominence at the conference of representatives from the pharmaceutical companies that produce antirejection medications, and asked if increasing donation is about saving lives or making money.

It is not likely that such a speech would have won many friends, nor even encouraged much intellectual reflection. I doubt I would have received another invitation to speak had I been so explicitly confrontational. But then, at least I would have been the anthropologist that Nancy Scheper-Hughes recommends: "the court jester, that small, sometimes mocking, sometimes ironic, but always mischievous voice from the sidelines . . . afflicting the comfortable, living anthropology as the *uncomfortable science*" (Scheper-Hughes 1990:195).[10]

I chose a less adversarial approach on this occasion and for this audience because I thought I would otherwise simply be dismissed; it is hard to "afflict the comfortable" if they are not listening. I prodded my conference audience to think about their own "culture of the body"—how different it is from the general public's view—but I did not level any accusations. I believe I came across as a questioning colleague rather than as a court jester. Each anthropologist has to determine the strategy that best fits his/her circumstances and long-term objectives.

I see little to be gained by the internecine conflicts sparked by medical anthropologists accusing each other of being either too radical or not radical enough. There are many ways to engage biomedicine and its practitioners in a dialogue informed by anthropological insights, and there are just as many avenues to pursue social and political reforms that would democratize and demystify medicine. Public health projects—domestic and international—medical care, and medical training can be improved by both the annoying activist and the marginal insider.

This said, I also think that the exchange between applied and critical medical anthropologists has had a salutary effect on all parties to the debate. It has stimulated greater reflection on the relationship between anthropology and biomedicine, and has encouraged a clarification of purpose for those who wish to engage in the work of promoting health. The debate has also helped medical anthropologists to imagine entirely new ways to be involved in health care, including some that replace "culture brokering" in patient/physician interactions with "community organizing" around health issues (e.g., see Singer 1995).

Conclusion

In Chapter 6, I took a historical look at the rise of biomedicine in the United States, Europe, and through the rest of the world. I paid special attention to the forces that have come to challenge the social and cultural authority of this powerful profession. In this chapter, I considered the contribution of applied medical anthropologists who work to deepen the cultural understanding of technical experts and medical practitioners. I have also introduced the perspective of other medical anthropologists who see their role as that of a social activist.

There is one more arena of medical anthropology *in* medicine that deserves treatment, and that is the anthropological analysis of medical ethics. What do medical anthropologists have to say about such issues as female genital mutilation in some African societies, the market in kidneys for transplantation in southern India, abortion, the right to die, informed consent, and so on? This is the focus of the next chapter.

SUGGESTED READINGS

A good overview of applied medical anthropology is found in Carole E. Hill's edited collection, *Training Manual in Applied Medical Anthropology* (1991).

Good case studies and interesting commentaries on the subject of applied medical anthropology are found in theme issues of *Social Science and Medicine* ("Toward a Critical Medical Anthropology," H. Baer, M. Singer and J. Johnsen, Guest Editors, 1986) and *Medical Anthropology Quarterly* ("Knowledge and Practice in International Health," P. Stanley Yoder, Guest Editor, 1997).

Mark and Mimi Nicter's *Anthropology and International Health: Asian Case Studies* (1996) is another important source.

N. J. Chrisman and T. M. Johnson review the work of medical anthropologists in medical schools and clinical settings in *Clinically Applied Anthropology* (1990).

For information on cultural competency, see the web site for the National Center for Cultural Competency (http://www.dml.georgetown.edu/depts/pediatrics/gucdc/cultural/html).

NOTES

1. The resistance of anthropologists to government work intensified when it was revealed in the mid-1960s that ethnographers had been on the payroll of the Central Intelligence Agency, doing research on village politics in Southeast Asia to facilitate military planning. The incident sparked a very difficult debate about professional ethics in the American Anthropological Association, and further discouraged anthropologists from accepting government employment.

2. UNICEF has championed a set of child survival programs which are grouped under the acronym GOBI-FF: **G**rowth monitoring, **O**ral rehydration therapy, **B**reastfeeding, **I**mmunization, **F**amily planning, and **F**ood supplements (some add another **F** for female literacy). Measuring a child's growth, encouraging breastfeeding, and adding food supplements during weaning are interventions directly related to the problem of childhood malnutrition.

3. Kwashiorkor is a protein-deficiency disease associated with poverty, occurring when a child is weaned without access to adequately nutritious solid foods. The characteristic symptoms of the disease are swelling ("moon face"), retarded growth, mental apathy and withdrawal, appetite loss, and skin discoloration and rashes.

4. Nutritional status was determined by comparing the children's age and weight to international growth standards.

5. Schoepf et al., report that in several cities in Central and East Africa 90 percent of poor prostitutes are HIV-positive (1991:190).

6. Although the aim of the Indonesian project was to build an educational program from "the bottom up" (i.e., beginning with the ideas of community members)—and was thus more participatory than the earlier Peruvian research—it still employed the idea that anthropologists help to identify and overcome local "resistance" and cultural obstacles.

7. A three-month-old child with medically unexplained seizures encounters a medical system ill equipped to understand the language and culture of her family. A sad litany of miscommunications and failed interventions over the following years ends in a catastrophic loss that the doctors and family blame on each other.

8. Janelle S. Taylor (2003) makes this point about Fadiman's book, which explains the Lee family's behavior by way of an exploration of Hmong history and culture, but traces the behavior of the doctors who cared for Lia Lee to characteristics of their individual personalities. Taylor asks, isn't there a "culture of biomedicine" on the other side of the equation, shaping the medical staff's response no less than Hmong culture influences the Lees'?

9. Patricia Marshall (1991) reviews many of the issues of research ethics as they apply to medical anthropology. She references the American Anthropological Association's "Principles of Professional Responsibility" and the National Association for the Practice of Anthropology's "Ethical Guidelines for Practitioners."

10. I have not seen good examples to bolster the assertion that incremental changes have resulted from medical anthropologists working within the system. I suspect this is because the impact is more likely to occur at the level of attitudes and general clinical practice; changes at this level would be hard to document.

11. The reference to anthropology as the "uncomfortable science" comes from British anthropologist Sir Raymond Firth, who said that it is the role of the discipline in the policy arena to "question established positions and proclaimed values" (Firth 1981:200).

CHAPTER

8 Anthropology and Medical Ethics

The 1996 conference organized by the Division of Transplantation (see Chapter 7) encouraged speakers and participants to "push the limits" of current organ procurement strategies in light of the growing gap between supply and demand. Cadaveric donation rates had stalled at about 4,500–5,000 per year, while the number of patients on national transplantation waiting lists had grown dramatically—to over 44,000 at the time of the conference. Physician Michael Rohr, Director of Transplantation Services at the Bowman Gray School of Medicine at Duke University, declared that the "tragedy of lives lost due to organ scarcity" required a reconsideration of ethical objections and "legal impediments" to the acquisition of organs by means other than altruistic donations. He was referring to proposals that would allow organs to be taken unless the deceased had registered an objection ("presumed consent"), and to other plans that encourage financial incentives for permission to take organs.

The second of these procurement strategies—cash for organs—was promoted during an afternoon session at the conference by Lloyd Cohen, who holds advanced degrees in law and economics and teaches at George Mason University. Cohen is a long-term advocate of a market approach to the problem of organ shortages. He proposes a "futures market" in which a per-organ fee of $5,000 would be paid to the estate of those who agree to sign contracts for the removal of their organs, should they die in a fashion that permits transplantation (Cohen 1995). Cohen defended his proposal and urged that it be given a "fair test" to see if the profit motive might not solve the shortage.

An elderly, Southern woman in the audience rose to ask a question. She and her husband had consented to the donation of their daughter's organs after a fatal traffic accident. The woman reflected on how this altruistic act had helped to reduce the pain she and her husband felt at their loss. She asked Cohen why he insisted on using crass terms like *salvage* and *harvest* instead of *donation* and *gift* when the act of consent has this kind of emotional meaning to the surviving family. Cohen was blunt in response: The use of romantic terms for organ procurement obscures the fact that everyone but the "supplier" is profiting from the transaction. The woman, stunned by Cohen's dismissive tone, promptly left the room.

I had previously written about the debate over organ procurement strategies (Joralemon 1995) and was familiar with Cohen's proposal—which is actually among the less extreme of those offered by advocates of market solutions to the organ shortage.

I had tried to describe the conflict between gift and market approaches to organ procurement with the same anthropological detachment that I used in my ethnographic writings on Peruvian shamans. I cast the dispute in terms of competing cultural values in American society, especially as regards the relationship between the "self" and the "body" at the point of death: When is the individual's identity no longer connected to his/her physical self?

As I listened to the exchange between Cohen and the woman who had donated her daughter's organs, I found myself having a hard time maintaining that sense of anthropological distance. On the one hand, the interaction was a dramatic illustration of alternative views of the meaning of death and the proper treatment of the dead. But it was also an interaction that I found personally disturbing because my own views were closer to the woman who had lost a daughter than to Cohen's. I was repelled by the idea that *my* society might be willing to put a price tag on kidneys, hearts, livers, lungs, and so on.

After the conference, I continued to ponder my reaction to the exchange. I wanted to make a reasoned ethical argument against the commercialization of body parts because I don't want to live in a society that encourages people to think of their anatomy as a collection of retail goods. Was there a way for me to frame an argument against marketing organs by drawing upon my anthropological knowledge? Or would I have to separate my views as a citizen of the United States from my academic analysis of an ethical debate in the field of transplantation medicine?

To understand how anthropology might engage in debates about ethics in medicine, we have to take a look at the general field of medical ethics. How have scholars studied ethical issues related to health and disease, and what contribution have social scientists made to this field of inquiry? How have anthropologists, in particular, dealt with the ethical priorities that govern healing activities in different societies? With this overview, I can return to my dilemma as an anthropologist: Do I have any business justifying a position about financial incentives for organs on the basis of my disciplinary knowledge?

Medical Ethics: A Comparative Framework

Terminological Concerns

The notion of **medical ethics** is sometimes used to refer only to the standards of conduct, and the associated values, which should ideally govern the relationship between biomedical practitioners and their patients. The concept of **bioethics** partially overlaps with this narrow definition, but includes the values and standards that ought to guide the conduct of scientific research in health (e.g., human experimentation) as well as the activities of doctors, nurses, and others.[1] The aim of bioethics, according to an influential view, is "to decide how humankind ought to act in the biomedical realm affecting birth, death, human nature, and the quality of life" (Clouser 1978:126).

It should be apparent that the terms "medical ethics" and "bioethics" can be applied only to the contexts in which biomedicine is practiced. But aren't there ethical considerations in other healing systems? Shouldn't there be a term that does not give special priority to the ethics that operate in a single tradition and embraces all healing processes?

For some commentators, it is enough to broaden the scope of "medical ethics" to include "the cultural values and norms which guide healing-related behavior" in any given society (Weisz 1990:7). Anthropologist Richard Lieban (1990:236) offers an alternative general term, **medical ethnoethics**, to refer to the "moral tenets and problems of health care as they are conceived and reacted to by members of a society." In this more comparative framework, bioethics (or biomedical ethics) would be one ethnoethical system among many.[2]

An alternative would be to use the existing terms, but to correct for their ethnocentric connotations. Here, I use "medical ethics" as a cross-cultural concept that refers to the rules of conduct and underlying values that guide healing activities in each society. Bioethics is a shorthand reference to "biomedical ethics" and encompasses the rules and values that apply to health-related research and clinical practice in the profession of biomedicine. I understand bioethics to apply as well to the academic discipline which studies ethical issues in biomedicine and attempts to resolve ethical disputes at the clinical level (e.g., on hospital ethics committees) as well as in the realm of public policy (e.g., as consultants to national ethics commissions).[3]

Question of Ethical Universals

The terminological issue of what ethics in healing should be called is not just about conceptual precision and clarity. It also highlights the question of how universal are the principles and values on which ethical standards in biomedicine are based. An important line of thinking in the academic field of bioethics argues that the ultimate moral precepts from which specific ethical rules are derived are "applicable to all people, at all times and places, equally" (Clouser 1978:116, citing Bernard Gert).

Some bioethicists distinguish "basic" moral rules (*not* culturally relative) from "derived" moral rules (context-specific). For example, a basic moral rule warning doctors against harming their patients is considered universal. But what constitutes "harm" in specific situations (e.g., euthanasia) will be determined by beliefs and expectations that may be particular to the culture in which the basic rule is applied. The task of bioethics, in this formulation, is to identify the universal precepts and to apply them rationally in specific contexts.

The most commonly cited "basic" principles that ought to guide healing activities are **autonomy**, **beneficence**, **nonmaleficence**, and **justice** (Beauchamp and Childress 1994; see Muller 1994:451). The principle of autonomy is that each person has the right to make medical decisions for himself or herself. Beneficence describes the requirement of a healer to act in the best interest of the patient. Nonmaleficence, or "do no harm," has a venerable history in biomedicine and is incorporated into the Hippocratic Oath. The principle of justice speaks to the importance of a fair distribution of the benefits of healing in the context of finite resources.

Renée Fox (1990) has noted that these purported universal principles are actually linked to the American "value-complex of individualism, underscoring the principles of individual rights, autonomy, self-determination, and their legal expression in the jurisprudential notion of justice" (p. 206). She points out that the emphasis on individualism in bioethics comes at the expense of the socially oriented values of responsibility, obligation, duty, kindness, empathy, caring, altruism, and so on (p. 207). She concludes that bioethics has paid insufficient attention to its "American-ness" by assuming that its views are *trans*cultural. "American bioethics has been more intellectually provincial and chauvinistic than it has recognized" (p. 208.)

Several bioethicists have made similar criticisms of the "four-principle" approach (e.g., Callahan 1984; Veatch 1989; Hoffmaster 1990), and several collections of essays have sought to bring an international perspective to medical ethics (e.g., Crigger et al. 1988; Pellegrino et al. 1992). However, even the ethicists who recognize the cultural relativity of medical ethics nevertheless argue that the global reach of biomedical technology requires that we aim for an ethical code that transcends societal boundaries. They search for a "metaethics" that provides a "foundation for a common morality by which different ethical systems may be judged and through which transcultural cooperative efforts can be transacted" (Pellegrino 1992:15).[4] Predictably, some would reinsert the four principles of traditional bioethics as the foundation for even this worldwide code.[5]

Social scientists take an empirical approach to the question of what is and is not universal about bioethics. They urge a comparative study of medical ethics that starts with ethics-focused case studies in distinct healing traditions and diverse cultures. These studies would analyze the context and content of ethical judgments related to health and disease. With this baseline, comparisons are possible between ethical systems in different societies. Horacio Fábrega (1990) suggests that these comparisons should focus on the precepts and standards by which health practitioners relate to their patients, to each other, and to political actors and institutions.

Jessica Muller (1994:453) argues that the primary assumption that should guide a comparative medical ethics is that, "Moral decision making is contextual. . . . Moral dilemmas and the means to resolve them cannot be separated from the institutional, political, economic, social and cultural contexts in which they are embedded" (p. 453). Medical ethics should examine "how people actually behave in problematic situations and the reasons or justifications they give for their behavior" (p. 454). It also should analyze "the political, institutional, and sociocultural factors that lead to the conditions in which ethical dilemmas appear" (p. 454).

We are a long way from achieving the goals of a comparative medical ethics, and therefore from knowing what commonalities there might be among various cultures' ethical systems. This is in large part due to the fact that social scientists have been slow to focus their research on the ethical underpinnings of medical practices. The study of ethics—or "moral philosophy"—in healing has been dominated by philosophers, theologians (especially Catholic and Protestant), legal experts, physicians, and biologists (Fox and Swazey 1997:244). Social scientists have been reluctant recruits to the study of bioethics, and their entrance into the field has not always been welcomed.[6]

It is, however, possible to make some provisional observations about the ethical priorities in healing activities in different kinds of societies. In doing so, I follow Horacio Fábrega's (1990) review, which identifies patterns in medical ethics among societies with similar social-structural organizations. Keep in mind that I am painting with broad strokes; there will inevitably be a great deal of variation beneath my generalizations.

Medical Ethics beyond Biomedicine

Medical Ethics in Small-Scale Societies

There is probably no culture in which the activities of healers are not guided by either formal or informal rules of conduct. In the small-scale societies that generations of anthropologists have studied, the healing role is often a temporary occupation of individuals whose own experience of being healed imposes a moral obligation to heal others. Ethical conduct is defined as conformity to the demands of supernatural forces and/or entities whose power can either cause or cure illness.

In these societies, healers are in a mediating position between their own community and the spirits or gods. They can be required to balance the general well-being of the group against the individual's health when sickness is caused by the violation of sacred rules, even if, in the process, the patient ends up suffering more. Healers in small-scale societies may also be expected to inflict harm on others—as a defensive measure or revenge—when sickness is sent by enemies in other villages.[7]

Native South American societies provide excellent illustrations of how medical ethics in small-scale communities reflect ideas about human/supernatural relations and intervillage politics. It is not unusual to find shamans in village-based societies who are called to their vocation, willingly or not, by spirits who demand a permanent relationship with individuals the spirits heal. The relationship typically entails a reciprocal obligation between shaman and spirit: the shaman guarantees compliance with responsibilities to the spirit (e.g., for feeding) in exchange for the power to heal and/or harm.

In the particularly dramatic case of the Warao of Venezuela, one group of shamans protects the health of the community as a whole by magically killing children for the cannibalistic God of the West (Wilbert 1993). This is part of a quid-pro-quo arrangement between humans and the gods, which requires the former to feed the latter in exchange for benevolent treatment. Shaman priests among the Kogi of Colombia link sicknesses to ritual transgressions and make punishment a part of the therapeutic process (Reichel-Dolmatoff 1950). Shamans among the Yanomamo of Venezuela and Brazil aim to cause sickness when they turn their powers against enemy villages (Chagnon 1997; see also M. Brown 1988).

Ethics and Folk Healers

When healing traditions with roots in small-scale communities are carried into larger social settings, the medical ethics that guide the healer's conduct can be transformed by encounters with other medicines and by new sociopolitical contexts. Greater competition among healers produces what Fábrega (1990:600) calls an "ideology of consumerism," in which practitioners try to discredit each other's practices, and patients seek to protect themselves from the misuse of healing powers. Urban environments with mobile populations can limit the amount of time spent with patients as well as the knowledge that healers have of their clients' lives (Press 1971; Finkler 1985). When patients are strangers who have no ongoing relationship with the healer, the ethical responsibility that goes along with their relationship can be minimal.

The shamans of north coastal Peru—a region of large towns and cities with a primarily mestizo population—illustrate how medical ethics among folk healers can be affected by the context in which they practice. Although Peruvian **curanderismo** is rooted in the shamanism of Andean and Amazonian native cultures, it also embraces folk Catholicism. The shaman with whom I worked in 1980, José Paz, defended the ethical standards of his practice by repeatedly declaring, "*Soy un hombre de Dios*" (I am a man of God). His ritual chants invoked Catholic saints, Jesus Christ, and the Virgin Mary, while associating his patients' enemies with the Devil. He claimed that his healing capacity was a "gift from God" but that it came with the obligation to act morally at all times.

Like their counterparts in village-based traditions, coastal shamans attribute many sicknesses to the aggressive attacks of their patients' enemies. However, in the largely urban environments from which the shamans' clients are drawn, it is person-to-person rather than intergroup hostilities (i.e., village versus village) to which illnesses are attributed. For example, the shaman's most frequent diagnosis, **daño** (harm caused by sorcery), links symptoms to trouble between spouses, neighbors, business competitors, and others. As a result, the shaman's healing work is grounded in an ethic of protection and revenge in which harming and healing are two sides of the same coin.

Ethics in the Great Traditions of Medicine

In state societies, healing roles become full-time occupations with standardized training and professional organizations. Medical ethics are correspondingly elaborated into more formal codes of conduct. Fábrega (1990, 1997) reviews the ethical guidelines of the ancient states in which a literate medical profession produced comprehensive accounts of health and sickness. These are the "Great Medical Traditions" of Greco-Roman, Islamic, Chinese, and Indian civilizations.

> Medical ethics is a paramount concern of practitioners of the "great" traditions, which suggests that issues of competition, authenticity, commercialization, frank quackery, and the like were not only prevalent but also of considerable concern in many civilizations and empires, not just the European. . . . This emphasis on morality and invidious comparison of the reputable to "quacks" and "unorthodox" practitioners clearly suggests a sense of humanitarian concern and ethical responsibility, but also, it needs to be recognized, a concern with economic rewards and competition (Fábrega 1997:118–119).

In addition to profession-protecting ethics, these medical traditions also stipulated ideals by which healers ought to abide in their relationships with the sick. As

Richard Lieban (1990:233–235) notes, some of these ideals are strikingly similar to the earlier-mentioned basic principles of bioethics. For example, the seventh-century Chinese essay, "On the Absolute Sincerity of Great Physicians," written by Sun Szu-miao (581–682?), "requires the physician to develop first a sense of compassion and piety, and then to make a commitment to try to save every living creature, to treat every patient on equal grounds, and to avoid seeking wealth because of his expertise" (Qui 1992:155). One could find each of the four basic principles in this ethical code.

However, the ethical guidelines promoted in the great medical traditions—like those in smaller-scale societies—are also deeply embedded in each culture's views of personhood, of responsibility to self and others, and of human destiny.[8] For example, the Indian tradition of Ayurvedic healing draws its ethical guidelines from the Vedas, which see "self" and "other" as part of one divine unity. The Hindu value of compassion for all living things and the concept of suffering as an essential part of the human condition are influential in Ayurveda's ancient codes of conduct (Francis 1992).[9] As a result, Ayurveda's view of the physician's duty to his patients is more holistic than biomedicine's, incorporating physical and spiritual dimensions of health and sickness. It is also more paternalistic, granting the physician greater authority to make treatment decisions than is the case in biomedicine's rights-based approach.

In the modern context, the philosophical foundations of the great medical traditions continue to shape ethical thinking in healing activities. Renée Fox and Judith Swazey (1984) concluded from their research in a Chinese hospital that Confucianism, Taoism, Chinese Buddhism, *and* Marxism-Leninism-Maoism have all left an imprint on the way health care workers define and resolve ethical problems. They insist that "medical morality" in China is as "Chinese" as bioethics is "American" (p. 349). According to their view, differences outweigh similarities in medical ethics. Context is all-important.

The Development of Bioethics in the United States

Historical Perspective

Ethical concerns and even explicit codes of conduct have been a part of the Western medical tradition at least since the time of Hippocrates in the fourth century B.C. As biomedicine in the United States underwent professionalization in the twentieth century, individual physicians and the American Medical Association issued commentaries and policies on such ethical issues as professional standards, physician authority, and patient disclosure (Rothman 1990).

It was not until the 1960s that ethics in biomedicine came to be considered a topic for nonphysicians to debate.[10] This opening came about first as a result of revelations of unethical conduct in human experimentation (Beecher 1966; Rothman 1990). The discovery that medical researchers had carried out tests and experimental procedures on mental patients, prisoners, servicemen, senile elderly, and other unsuspecting patients created a public demand for the ethical oversight of biomedicine (Fox 1990). The central ethical issues were "informed consent" and "benefit-risk" assessments for persons on whom experimental procedures would be performed (Jonsen 1997:6–8).

Also critical to the physicians' partial loss of autonomy over ethical issues was the public's concern about the implications of new medical technologies (e.g., mechanical life support systems, organ transplantation, and contraception) and the excessive rise in the cost of health care. These developments "exacerbated long standing ethical problems (e.g., distribution of costly or scarce medical resources, balance of responsibilities of physicians to their patients and to other parts of society), as well as creat[ed] new contexts for ethical concern (e.g., prenatal diagnosis of genetic defects and decisions to abort pregnancy)" (Kunstadter 1980:289; see also Marshall 1992).

The field of bioethics emerged from this evolving discussion of rights and obligations in medical research and clinical practice. It was led from the start by philosophers and theologians, who soon institutionalized the new discipline in ethical "think-tanks" like the Institute of Society, Ethics, and the Life Sciences (The Hastings Center, New York), the Center for Bioethics at Georgetown University's Kennedy Institute of Ethics (Washington, DC), and the Society of Health and Human Values (now in McLean, Virginia) (Fox 1990:203). An impressive production of books and articles on bioethical matters soon followed.

Manifestations of Bioethics in Public Life

Medical sociologist Renée Fox (1990) observes that "one of the most remarkable features of the way in which bioethics has developed is the extent to which it has pervaded the public domain" (p. 204). She cites the introduction of bioethical concerns into the courts,[11] the creation of congressional and presidential commissions to study ethical issues,[12] and the proliferation of stories about bioethics in print media and television. One wonders where the script writers for the ubiquitous medical programs on television (e.g., *ER*, *Grey's Anatomy*, and *Saint Elsewhere*) would find material were it not for ethical dilemmas associated with medical interventions.

The biomedical profession has sought to understand and control the unruly ethical dilemmas that research and clinical care create. Statements on ethics are now drafted and periodically revised by general medical organizations (e.g., the American Medical Association) as well as by professional societies for medical specialties (e.g., the American Society of Transplant Surgeons). Medical schools have incorporated bioethics into their curricula, and hospitals have established "Institutional Review Boards" and "Ethics Committees" to review research proposals and to advise medical professionals who are forced to deal with difficult clinical cases. These developments were prompted by medical professionals' recognition of how complex ethical issues had become and how important ethical standards were to the public at large, by a fear of legal and financial accountability,[13] and by federal statutes and administrative rules associated with federal funding.[14] The result is that bioethics has gained an unprecedented place in the U.S. medical system.

Deliberating Bioethics

There is substantial disagreement about how one ought to go about making ethical decisions in medicine. The traditional approach, as I mentioned above, requires that one start with a general ethical theory and then derive a set of basic principles that are logically consistent with that theory. These principles can then be rationally applied in specific cases. For example, the German philosopher Immanuel Kant (1724–1804) included in his influential theory of ethics an imperative to tell the truth in all circumstances and regardless of the consequences. The basic principle of full disclosure to patients necessarily follows from this Kantian imperative. Armed with this principle, there can be no dispute about the ethical duty of a physician to a specific patient with a terminal diagnosis. The physician must reveal the diagnosis, no matter how difficult that may be.

One problem with this almost mechanical application of basic ethical principles is that it doesn't work very well in the real world. Often two or more basic principles seem equally to apply in a given case, and there is no obvious ground on which one might favored over the other. For example, the duty to disclose a fatal disease may conflict with the equally "basic" principle to act in the patient's best interest (beneficence), as when a patient's quality of remaining life will be seriously diminished by the knowledge that the end is near (Taylor 1988; Muller and Desmond 1992; Gordon 1994).

Also problematic is the mismatch between inflexible principles and dynamic medical situations. At one moment in a disease process it may make sense to talk about truth telling and patient autonomy, but at a later point in time, such considerations may be entirely irrelevant. What value is there in full disclosure to a patient who has slipped into a coma? Another example is the principle of nonmaleficence: Is there a point in the trajectory of a disease when inflicting harm (e.g., terminating life support) becomes the ethically justifiable action?

These and other difficulties (Hoffmaster 1992) have encouraged bioethicists to suggest alternative ways to reach decisions in ethically problematic cases.[15] What the alternatives have in common is the recognition that some balance must be reached between the particular circumstances in which ethical dilemmas arise and a set of often competing values. This is accomplished by "begin[ning] ethical analysis with actual observations of the details of a particular case: the persons, circumstances, and relationships involved in the dilemma. . . . Experience and observation, rather than philosophical principles and theories, provide the premises of ethical argument" (Jecker 1997:120).

Several bioethicists have pointed out that this attention to the context of ethical dilemmas in medicine is essentially a call for an ethnographic approach to bioethics (Jennings 1990; Hoffmaster 1992). This leads us to ask in more detail what role the social sciences in general, and anthropology in particular, have played in the development of bioethics in the United States.

The Social Sciences and Bioethics

The pervasiveness of bioethics in the United States has not been matched by an equivalent level of attention to the subject in the social sciences, even those, like medical sociology, which have a long history of studying biomedicine in the United States

(Fox 1990; Lieban 1990; Marshall 1992). This has been attributed to the marginal status of the social sciences relative to the disciplines that have dominated bioethical discussions: philosophy, religious studies, and the medical sciences. Sociology and anthropology are often disqualified from bioethical debates because they are considered insufficiently humanistic by the philosophers and theologians and too unscientific by the physicians and biologists (Fox 1990:213).

On the other hand, blame for the neglect of bioethics by the social sciences must also be placed on what Renée Fox calls the "ethos of the social sciences" (1990:214). Sociologists, she explains, have preferred social structures over social values; medical sociologists have shown less interest in bioethics than in the "sick role," the institutional structures of biomedicine, and the process of medical socialization. Offering a similar explanation for the neglect of bioethics in medical anthropology, Patricia Marshall (1992) singles out the discipline's prejudice in favor of the culturally relative over the human universal, its historic focus on non-Western societies and their healing traditions (i.e., not on biomedicine), and its preference for viewing the individual as a part of a social system (i.e., not as an autonomous ethical actor).

The obstacles that have inhibited social scientists from studying bioethics and entering into bioethical debates are slowly being overcome. At the research end of the relationship, sociologists and anthropologists have contributed important studies of clinical ethics, in the United States and in other countries. For example, the question of physician disclosure has been studied in a Canadian hospital (Taylor 1988), in clinical settings in Italy (Gordon 1994), and in the United States (Marshall et al. 1991; Muller and Desmond 1992).

In each of these studies, the transmission of bad news (e.g., cancer diagnoses) is analyzed at the microlevel of physician–patient interaction, often with close attention given to the actual dialogue and the communication strategies adopted by different types of doctors. Then, the focus widens to the cultural views that shape expectations and influence behavior in such difficult situations: assumptions about the role of family members, ideas about how authority figures ought to act, and conceptions of how suffering should be borne. As in Deborah Gordon's (1994) sensitive exploration of how breast cancer diagnoses are revealed in Tuscany, Italy, the goal is to show how a rights-based ethic of full and complete disclosure is balanced with the real conditions of uncertainty, hope, and continued living in between knowing and not knowing.

The social sciences have been less interested in the actual practice of bioethics, in either the clinical or public policy arenas. Few have followed the lead of medical anthropologist Patricia Marshall and joined a hospital ethics committee, or emulated Renée Fox's (1995) role as an ethical critic of sociomedical policies. Only rarely do social scientists publish articles in the major bioethics journals (e.g., *The Hastings Center Report*) or submit ethical commentaries to medical publications (e.g., *The Journal of the American Medical Association*). From the viewpoint of the social sciences—with the partial exception of economics—bioethics is a research topic but not a forum for direct participation.[16]

We are left, then, with a paradox. There seems to be a growing consensus that social science methods and interpretations are useful in understanding bioethical dilemmas. More sociologists and anthropologists than ever are engaged in research related to bioethics. Yet, unlike their colleagues in philosophy, religious studies, biology, and medicine—who apply their disciplinary skills in clinical and policy deliberations on ethical issues in medicine—social scientists seem content to remain in the background when it comes to actually *doing* bioethics.

Social Science: Out of the Closet

Before I return to the ethical issue with which I began this chapter—the use of commercial incentives to increase organ donation—I want to describe a rare instance in which a social scientist directly participated in a bioethical debate. The case is especially apt because it also involves transplantation and the problem of an organ shortage. It has helped me to think through my own dilemma.

The Case of the Non-Heart-Beating Cadaver

In 1966, a committee of medical experts met at Harvard University to discuss a revision of the criteria by which people are declared dead. The traditional medical definition of death, the absence of a heart beat for a proscribed period of time, had two disadvantages in the context of advancing medical science. First, it had become possible to mechanically maintain heart activity well beyond the point of irreversible brain damage and/or a negligible prospect of survival without life support. Second, waiting for the heart to cease to declare death limits the potential for organ transplantation because of the rapid deterioration of organs once the blood supply is interrupted.

The committee's solution, which was eventually codified in state and federal legislation, was to provide an alternative criterion for the determination of death, the cessation of all brain activity (cerebral and brain stem). Persons who suffer severe head injuries could now be judged "brain dead" while still on life support systems, making it possible to request donation from the next of kin as continuing blood flow keeps internal organs healthy. One obstacle to organ procurement had been removed.

An adequate supply of organs was made available by this revised definition of death until improvements in antirejection medications caused the demand for transplantation to mushroom. By the late 1980s, transplantation centers and related professional organizations were engaged in a frantic search for more organs. Most initiatives focused on increasing the number of persons who agree to donation, but other avenues were also pursued: mechanical devices as bridges to transplantation, cross-species transplantation (**xenotransplantation**), kidney donations by living nonrelated donors,[17] transplants of liver segments by living donors,[18] and so on.

In 1992, the University of Pittsburgh Medical Center (UPMC), a major transplantation site, adopted a controversial plan that added a new category of potential donors, "non-heart beating cadavers." The term refers to persons whose lives will likely end when mechanical support is withdrawn, but who will not meet the criterion of "brain death" as long as life support is maintained. If such a person or his/her next of kin request that life support be withdrawn, and if there is also a request that his/her organs be donated for transplantation, then the UPMC's new procedures permit the following steps:

- Removal of the person to an operating room where life support may be withdrawn.
- Administration of medication only to minimize the pain associated with the termination of life support.
- Declaration of death based on "irreversible cessation of cardiopulmonary function . . . during an appropriate period of observation" (Arnold et al. 1995:240).
- Organ procurement immediately after death is certified.

A real example will help illustrate how the new procedures work (see DeVita and Snyder 1995:58–59). A male suffers cardiac arrest, is resuscitated, but remains comatose and dependent on a ventilator. Eight days later, his family requests that supportive therapy be ended and that his organs be donated after death. Their decision is based on the determination that he will never regain cognitive function—although he is not "brain dead" by the required criteria. He is moved to the operating room, where the ventilator is turned off. When his heart stops and fails to "auto-resuscitate" (start again on its own), he is declared dead and surgeons remove his liver and kidney for transplantation.

The development of this procedure took five years (1987–1992) and involved consultations with six committees that included hospital administrators and trustees, lawyers, physicians, nurses, social workers, ethicists, anesthesiologists, neurologists, local clergy, businessmen, and civic leaders (DeVita and Snyder 1995:57). In 1993, a special issue of the *Kennedy Institute of Ethics Journal* was devoted to a further exploration of the ethical issues involved in taking organs from persons for whom life support is terminated. Two years later, these journal articles were reprinted with several additional essays (Arnold et al. 1995).

Renée Fox was the only social scientist asked to contribute to the journal collection and subsequent book. Her essay's title reflects her position: "An Ignoble Form of Cannibalism: Reflections on the Pittsburgh Protocol for Procuring Organs from Non-Heart-Beating Cadavers" (Fox 1995). Fox writes that the Pittsburgh protocol is "the most elaborately macabre scheme for obtaining organs that I have encountered. . . . I do not consider it either medically acceptable or morally permissible" (p. 156). She is especially troubled by the following:

- The questionable reduction to two minutes of electrocardiographic inactivity for the declaration of death by irreversible heart failure. The standard had been to wait for twenty minutes.
- The inhumane treatment of the dying patient, whose final moments are away from family in an operating room, "amidst masked, gowned, and gloved strangers, who have prepared his (her) body for the eviscerating surgery that will follow" (p. 160).

- A "planned terminal management" plan for the removal of life support, which requires lower levels of pain medication than would ordinarily be given, so as to avoid even the appearance that death is being hastened to gain faster access to the organs. In other words, the patient may suffer more pain while dying just because he/she has been designated an organ donor.

- The anticipated possibility that after death has been declared, the transplantation surgeon may determine that too much time has passed to use the organs. Under this circumstance, the procedures permit the intensive care unit (ICU) physician to send the patient back to ICU, presumably to be returned to life support.

Fox concludes that the Pittsburgh plan "goes so far beyond the pale of the medically decent, morally allowable, and spiritually acceptable that it strains credulity" (p. 161). She says that the medical center's massive commitment to transplantation and the surrounding community's devotion to potential organ recipients "has eroded respect for the willingness of patients and their families to donate organs, and decreased awareness of the sacred trust with which medical professionals who receive and utilize these 'gifts of life' are invested" (p. 162).

Moral Passion and Social Science?

Renée Fox's essay is a rhetorically powerful and impassioned attack on the Pittsburgh protocol, but on the basis of what authority does her critique rest? Are her implicit standards of a humane death, her references to respect for donors, and her invocation of a "sacred trust" that accompanies the "gift of life" grounded in a social scientific analysis of bioethics or comparative medical ethics? How does Fox's ethical vantage point differ from the perspectives of the philosophers, lawyers, doctors, and clergy who also contributed to the review of the protocol?

Fox and her longtime research colleague, Judith Swazey, are themselves troubled by the difficulty of reconciling their social science with their ethical concerns. Explaining why, after nearly thirty years, they are calling an end to their research on organ transplantation, Fox and Swazey write, "Our problem, we finally admitted to ourselves, was that we had lost much of the detached concern that had enabled us to study and write about this field for so many years" (1992:203). They diagnose the problem as "participant-observation burnout," caused by the emotional and intellectual conflict between their intense connection with dying patients awaiting transplants and an equally powerful set of objections to the values that have dominated transplant medicine.

> By our leave-taking we are intentionally separating ourselves from what we believe has become an overly zealous medical and societal commitment to the endless perpetuation of life and to repairing and rebuilding people through organ replacement—and from the human suffering and the social, cultural, and spiritual harm we believe such unexamined excess can, and already has, brought in its wake (ibid., p. 210).

I understand why Fox and Swazey would conclude that continued fieldwork with the medical staff and patients at transplantation centers is incompatible with their increasingly critical view of transplantation medicine. In a 1979 interview (Glazer 1982), Fox spoke eloquently of the field-worker's close personal relationships with research subjects, of the sharing of their "suffering, joy, secret hopes and desires and disappointments, births, deaths and mortalities" (p. 64). How could she maintain that intimate connection while simultaneously attacking aspects of the medical specialty on which her informants' lives depend?

However, I would also argue that it is precisely the dynamic tension between the intimacy of fieldwork and the dispassionate analysis of social and cultural patterns that authorizes Fox to speak out in a bioethical debate. Unlike any other participant in such debates, Fox—as a social scientist—offers a moral intuition informed by an empathy for the plight of the potential organ recipient, a recognition of the symbolic power of the donated organ, an understanding based on cross-cultural comparisons of the "American-ness" of biomedical values, and a comprehension of the social equity issues entailed by organ transplantation. She writes passionately in the essay I have reviewed here precisely because of the deep understanding of the issue she acquired as a social scientist.[19]

Medical Anthropology in Bioethics

I conclude from the example of Renée Fox's critique of the Pittsburgh protocol that there is a special social science vantage point on bioethical issues that justifies the move from analysis to advocacy. The social scientist understands ethical dilemmas by tacking back and forth between the particulars of individual cases and the broader cultural context in which they occur.[20] Medical anthropologists, and sociologists like Fox, add a cross-cultural dimension which can help to correct the bioethical myopia that sees universals in Western values. Social scientists should be free to apply the insights of their discipline to an ethical position, just as scholars from other disciplines do routinely.

Where did this leave me as I contemplated a response to the cash for organs proposal I heard at the Washington conference? First, I had to think about my interviews with organ recipients and ask how their experience would have differed had the organ they received been purchased. Then I had to look more broadly at the variety of circumstances in which body parts are presently commodified and ask where the cultural hesitation lies in extending this principle to internal organs. This exploration took me back in time—for example, to the period when medical schools in England paid grave robbers for corpses—as well as into possible futures. It also took me to other countries, where the same reluctance to put a price tag on body parts is more or less intense.

My anthropology also required me to consider the treatment of the dead, in the United States and cross-culturally, and how this relates to ideas about the connection between body and soul. An analysis of mortuary rituals indicated what meanings are attached to the corpse by survivors and how the connections to the dead are attenuated over time.

When the research was complete, I was ready to enter the fray and stake out a position on the marketing of organs . . . and do so as a medical anthropologist. The resulting essays (Joralemon 2001; Joralemon and Cox 2003) appear in bioethics journals.

Organ transplantation is an example of a wider arena in which medical anthropologists have confronted ethical issues: biotechnology in medicine. In the next chapter, I explore ethical disputes at the beginning and end of life that have either been complicated by biotechnologies or significantly shaped by the screening and treatment capacities they introduce. This research represents an exciting new direction for medical anthropology.

SUGGESTED READINGS

I have cited in the text many of the important books, articles, and journals related to the social sciences and medical ethics. I would call special attention to the reviews by Marshall (1992), Muller (1994), and Weisz's (1990) collection of essays.

Paul Unschuld's *Medical Ethics in Imperial China: A Study in Historical Anthropology* (1979) is an excellent source for medical ethics in one of the "Great Traditions" of medicine.

A selection of anthropological accounts that include medical ethics includes Margaret Lock and Deborah Gordon's (eds.) *Biomedicine Examined* (1988), Myra Bluebond-Langer's *The Private World of Dying Patients* (1978), Beatrix Pfleiderer and Giles Bibeau's (eds.) *Anthropologies of Medicine* (1991), Rayna Rapp's "Accounting for Amniocentesis" (1993), Robert Hahn's "Perinatal Ethics in Anthropological Perspective" (1987).

Arnold et al. (1995) and Fox and Swazey (1992) provide the background on the organ transplantation debates discussed in this chapter.

NOTES

1. Some would prefer that "bioethics" be reserved for the general issues related to medical research and experimentation, while "clinical ethics" would encompass physician/patient issues.

2. Lieban is making the same argument here as others have made for using the term "ethnomedicine" as a blanket term that includes biomedicine.

3. These terminological clarifications parallel those made by Patricia Marshall (1992:50).

4. There are, of course, exceptions. Barry Hoffmaster (1990), for example, does not retreat from a contextual view of ethics in favor of a universal set of principles.

5. For example, Patricia Mazzarella's introduction to *Transcultural Dimensions in Medical Ethics* (Pellegrino et al. 1992) concludes that the international experts whose essays are included in the collection each acknowledges—"in his own way"—the values of beneficence, autonomy, nonmaleficence, and justice (p. 11).

6. Fox (1990:212–215) reviews the various factors that have inhibited the involvement of sociologists in bioethics. Lieban (1990:221–222) does the same for anthropology.

7. The idea that the same powers that permit a healer to cure sickness can also be used to harm should not seem so foreign. For example, one of the most common reasons people cite for not signing organ donation cards is their fear that a doctor might hasten a patient's death if the possibility of harvesting valuable organs entered into the calculation.

8. Anthropologists have written a great deal about the connection between culturally formulated views of personhood and self/other responsibilities (e.g., Shweder and Bourne 1984; Marsella et al.

1985; Morris 1994). This material offers an important anthropological angle for the study of medical ethics and will be introduced more fully in the following chapter.

9. There are more ambiguities in the Ayurvedic codes than this brief statement indicates (see Zimmerman 1987).

10. There were earlier efforts to take ethical issues to nonmedical forums, especially by Catholic theologians on issues related to the termination of pregnancy, but these did not generate the widespread attention that subsequent developments brought to medical ethics (Rothman 1990). An exception to the general monopolization of ethical debate by physicians is the antivivisection campaigns of the 1920s and 1930s (Beecher 1970).

11. The list of relevant examples would be nearly endless. It would range from the famous Karen Ann Quinlan case, in which the New Jersey Supreme Court permitted the termination of life support (Ramsey 1976), to more recent litigation over the ownership of biological material (e.g., Rabinow 1992).

12. Fox (1990) mentions the National Commission for the Protection of Human Subjects of Biomedical and Behavioral Research (1974) and the President's Commission for the Study of Ethical Problems in Medicine and Biomedical and Behavioral Research (1978). Many federal agencies have also sponsored national forums for the debate of ethical issues in medicine—the Division of Transplantation is one example.

13. This is especially clear in the "Risk-Management Committees" in hospitals, which are called into action when a case threatens legal action.

14. An example of a federal statute is the "Patient Self-Determination Act" (1990), which requires that hospitals provide patients at admission with information about and forms for advanced directives. The mandate for institutional review boards came from a Federal Drug Administration rule rather than from congressional action.

15. I do not have space to explain each of the alternatives (e.g., casuistry, narrative ethics, and virtue ethics). A general description of each can be found in Marshall (1992); many of the related articles are included in an anthology edited by Jecker et al. (1997).

16. Patricia Marshall (1992) observes that "a decided absence of moral judgment" has characterized anthropological contributions to bioethics. In some cases, anthropologists seem to feel that they even need to apologize when their research on an ethical issue dovetails with their advocacy of a specific ethical position (Kaufert 1990:123).

17. Since a person can survive with a single kidney, transplantation from a living donor is possible. At first, only close relatives were selected because of a concern about diminishing the risk of rejection through genetic matching. However, immunosuppressant drugs have reduced this concern. The remaining reason to prefer donation from close relatives is the fear that a non-related donor, who is not motivated by the emotional bonds of kinship, might be coerced into an operation that entails significant discomfort and risk. On the other hand, expanding the pool of potential donors to include nonrelatives can significantly increase the chance of finding a kidney to transplant.

18. Liver tissue can regenerate, so the donor survives and the recipient has the chance of "growing" a new liver.

19. Nancy Scheper-Hughes (1992) writes about the mortal neglect of children in a Brazilian squatter settlement with equal passion and on the basis of a similarly profound ethnographic foundation.

20. I do not mean to suggest that only social scientists have the capacity to bring this kind of perspective to ethical debates. Ordinary citizens can bring similar insights about the social context of ethical dilemmas.

CHAPTER

9 Body, Self, and Biotechnologies

Biotechnologies disrupt some experiences that we used to take for granted. Getting pregnant, for example, was a pretty straightforward enterprise—even if it wasn't always predictable—before assisted conception technologies, sex realignment surgeries, prenatal diagnostic procedures, stem cell research, and cloning techniques were developed. Building a physically powerful body was just a matter of exertion and discipline, that is, before performance-enhancing drugs confused matters. We all knew what getting older meant for our appearance and stamina, until hormonal replacement therapies, Botox, and Viagra arrived. Selecting "natural foods" once meant making sure pesticides hadn't touched them, but then genetically modified plants and animals joined the family farm. Unlike our ancestors, we rarely puzzled over whether or not a person was really dead until resuscitation and life support technologies became standard, and debates began about how to define "death." For that matter, we were once certain that a corpse was to be mourned and buried or cremated until organ transplantation made the body useful in new ways, the digital revolution created cyber corpses,[1] and cryonics promised future resurrections.

Medical anthropologists have recently pushed their research beyond the conventional topics of disease and healing to explore this brave new world of technological innovations. Common to the medical anthropology of biotechnologies is a concern for the social relations and economic interests that shape the development of new instruments and procedures in medicine. These investigations allow us to see that biotechnologies do not emerge from neutral scientific research, but are powerfully influenced by the sources of funds that support them and by the professional priorities and cultural assumptions of the experts engaged in research and development. Medical anthropologists often also demonstrate how a technology that appears novel is, in fact, built on a long history of cultural formulations related to life stages, identities, and illnesses.

Biotechnologies related to reproduction have stimulated an impressive amount of attention from medical anthropologists, many of whom are women whose own experiences led to research projects related to conception, pregnancy, and childbirth. Taken as a whole, this body of work reveals how reproductive technologies can simultaneously sustain and challenge physician authority over women's lives. It also shows how the push and pull of gender politics and conflicting ethical positions about the status of the fetus can result in competing views of the "product" of the technologies—from test-tube babies to fetal sonograms—and even transform the way the technologies are used.

In this chapter, I survey some compelling examples of medical anthropology applied to biotechnologies and show what this research tells us about divisive debates in the United States, specifically about the beginnings and ends of meaningful life. Before presenting the cases, let me set the theoretical context with some reflections on the anthropology of the self.

Cross-Cultural Views of the Self

In nineteenth-century India, it was accepted practice for a widow to burn on the funeral pyre of her husband, a tradition known as *suttee*. In one remarkable case, the wife was convinced not to self-immolate when her high-caste Brahman spouse died, but another woman, of a lower caste and from a different village, begged to die in the flames. She explained that in three prior lives she had been married to the deceased and, each time, had joined him on the pyre. She had been separated from him in this life as a result of a karmic mistake in her previous existence. Her only chance of being reunited with him in the next life was to die once again alongside his burning corpse.

The American anthropologist Irving Hallowell tells this story in a classic essay on how the "self" is understood across cultures (Hallowell 1955). His argument, now accepted as a basic tenet in **ethnopsychology**, is that while self-awareness is a universal characteristic of humankind, the defining features of selfhood/personhood are differently constructed in every human society. Hallowell pointed to five "basic orientations" to the self that may vary from culture to culture: (1) how the self is or is not distinguished from other selves; (2) how the self is linked to objects in the world; (3) how the self is located in space and time; (4) what motivates the self; and (5) what normative rules apply to the self.

The Indian case illustrates several of these orientations. Most strikingly, it reveals how a culture that subscribes to the idea of reincarnation pushes the boundaries of the self both backward and forward in time. The low-caste woman sees her "self" as continuous through many rebirths, which contrasts with the Western view of a self defined within the limits of one lifespan. Also, she sees her identity as linked to that of the deceased Brahman in a way that challenges Western notions of an autonomous person by blurring the line between self and other; her self is so intertwined with the Brahman that they are connected to one another without even having met in their current existence. Her motivation to burn on the funeral pyre only makes sense, short of psychiatric interpretations, because she embraces a self theory that compels actions based on consequences for future lives.

In the discussion to follow, I suggest that biotechnologies related to the beginnings and ends of life are best understood in the context of competing views of the self even within one culture. The technologies themselves are rooted in specific understandings of the self, but they are also marshaled to promote alternative constructions of personhood. The ethical debates that swirl around the use of these technologies are apparently irresolvable precisely because they trace back to self theories that differ profoundly in several of Hallowell's orientations, especially self/other and time/space.

The Stem Cell Debate

> A free and virtuous society, which America aspires to be, must reject practices that devalue and violate human life at any stage from conception until natural death. In defending the right to life, in law and through a vibrant culture of life, America can show the world the path to a truly humane future in which man remains the master, not the product, of his technology. (Pope John Paul II)[2]

> The bottom line is that there are 400,000 frozen embryos in the United States, and a large percentage of those are going to be thrown out. Regardless of what you think the moral status of those embryos is, it makes sense to me that it's a better moral decision to use them to help people than just to throw them out. It's a very complex issue, but to me it boils down to that one thing. (James Thomson, first scientist to isolate and culture embryonic stem cells)[3]

Proponents and opponents of stem cell research[4] stake out positions that often seem resistant to mediation, cast as they are in the ideologically loaded language of "fundamental human values" versus "scientific progress." Notice that the Pope's argument appeals to absolute moral principles, while Thomson offers a **utilitarian** argument that asks us to weigh the destruction of surplus embryos against the potential for lifesaving treatments. Where the Pope sees bright lines and moral certainty, Thomson asserts a gray area where a balance of benefits and harms should be struck.

At the center of the controversy about stem cell research is an organic entity that serves almost as a Rorschach test for all parties in the debate, an organic inkblot that each viewer interprets according to the perspective he/she brings to the task (Photo 9.1). The web site for the International Society for Stem Cell Research says an embryonic stem cell is "like a blank microchip that can ultimately be programmed to perform particular tasks," and the entity from which embryonic stem cells are taken is "is a hollow ball of about 150 cells called the blastocyst" (http://www.isscr.org/science/faq.htm). What could possibly be troublesome about programming a microchip taken out of a hollow ball?

Bishop Joseph A. Fiorenza, as president of the U.S. Conference of Catholic Bishops, looked at the same entity and saw something entirely different: "a defenseless human being" (http://www.americancatholic.org/Newsletters/CU/ac0102.asp). The Bishop echoed Pope John Paul's warning to President George W. Bush in 2001 that the scientific use of embryonic stem cells constitutes an "assault on innocent human life in the womb." This language takes us a long way from "hollow balls" and "blank microchips."

Proponents of research that utilizes stem cells taken from the early stage of human gestation have trouble understanding how the entity in Photo 9.1 can be seen as human life. They accept that a developmental line potentially connects this entity to an embryo that eventually has the characteristics of a human being, but insist that it is nonsensical to assign human status to the organism at the earliest stage of cell division after fertilization. To invest the entity termed a "blastocyst" with protections due human life is, according to this perspective, religiously inspired but scientifically un- or misinformed. If opponents just understood the biology involved, they would see that

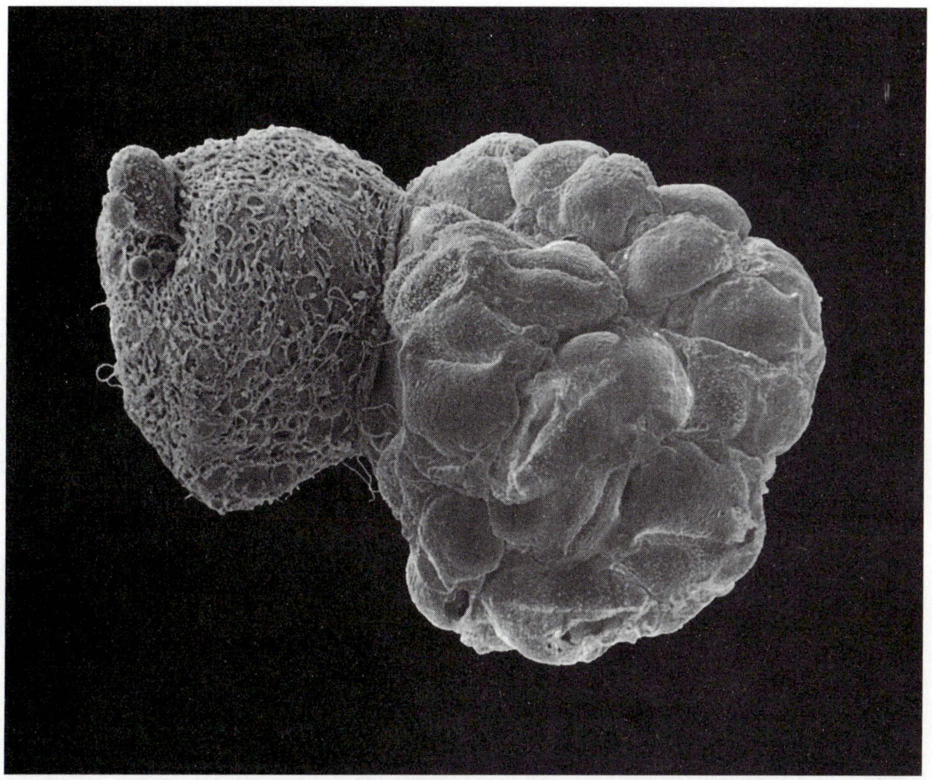

Photo 9.1 Colored scanning electron micrograph (SEM) of a human embryo at the blastocyst stage, five days after fertilization. It is seen at right hatching from a hole in the zona pellucida (at left), a protein shell that originally surrounded the unfertilized egg. (Dr. Yorgos Nikas/Photo Researchers, Inc.)

none of the defining features of personhood are present in the earliest stage of embryonic development, and therefore no moral violation is involved when that entity is destroyed in the process of removing stem cells.

The scientists who organized a conference on the stem cell controversy at Smith College (2005) showed that they believe better education is the key to resolving ethical disagreements. My colleagues from biology and chemistry talked about setting the "foundation" for the two-day gathering with a presentation on the science of cell biology and human reproduction. This would, they argued, allow participants, including the general public, to approach the subsequent ethical and policy issues in a more informed fashion. Although never directly expressed, their guiding assumption was that opponents are insufficiently versed in the biology of human gestation and that, once better educated, they would have to see the illogic of attributing human status to a "pre-embryo" (Franklin and Roberts 2006:56).

Unfortunately, knowing more about biotechnologies doesn't necessarily translate into opposing less. For example, a study on "Public Perceptions of Cloning" undertaken by the Welcomme Trust's Medicine and Society Programme found that public confidence in the research actually dropped as scientific literacy increased (Franklin 2003:110). In short, the more people knew, the less they trusted. Similar evidence comes from research on organ donation, which shows that knowledge about transplantation does not seem to reduce the nearly 50 percent refusal rate when families in the United States are asked to donate. Likewise, a sensitive ethnography of how women respond to bad news from prenatal testing indicates that detailed counseling about the medical facts of genetic abnormalities does not determine whether or not an individual will continue a pregnancy (Rapp 1999).

The contested views of early-stage embryos arise from different conceptions of the person/self and not deficient educational backgrounds. It is not just that the temporal boundaries of the self are differently understood by opponents and proponents, but that the former defines meaningful life as the outcome of a discrete event—conception—while the latter see life as an emerging set of characteristics. Those who see a "defenseless human being" in a blastocyst look to the moment of conception as the clear dividing line between cells and selves—a precise event that offers an unambiguous entitlement to the rights of personhood. Those who see a "hollow ball" in the image of a blastocyst adopt a gradual definition of personhood, which waits for the progressive development of distinctly human traits and capacities before assigning human status.

The important point to keep in mind is that neither view is illogical or uninformed; both are equally embedded in culturally derived notions of the self. Furthermore, the moral reasoning that flows from these interpretations of self is not refutable by rational argument because they start from different premises and apply different standards for ethical decisions (i.e., absolute principals versus utilitarian calculations). The scientist who favors the use of embryonic stem cells in research has no better chance of persuading the opponent who sees conception as the start of personhood than did the family of the deceased Brahman in discouraging the stranger from a fiery death.

"Baby" Pictures

Today's baby book typically starts not with the newborn, swaddled in blankets and held in its mother's arms, but with an image from the womb, taken months before birth with an **ultrasound** machine. The black and white picture may be rather hard to decipher, but it typically reveals major anatomical features—including the all-important genitalia—of a being floating in the amniotic sac. Once used primarily to screen for physiological abnormalities, the "sonogram," as the image is labeled, has become a must-have memento of pregnancy. If the still image is not enough, a video version is now available.

The development of ultrasound technology, along with other scanning instruments that have made our insides visible, is a fascinating story. So too is the evolution of a new medical identity, "ultrasound technician" or "**sonographer**," a profession heavily dominated by women. But I want to focus on the cultural manipulation of the ultrasound image, or sonogram, as the technology moved from the doctor's office to freestanding clinics and from limited diagnostic use to a routine ritual of pregnancy.

Janelle Taylor's *The Public Life of the Fetal Sonogram* (2008) documents the many uses to which sonograms have been put, including in an advertisement for Volvo cars that underscores the vehicles' reputation for safety: "Is something inside telling you to buy a Volvo?" (Taylor 2008:2). She traces the "biography" of a sonogram that achieved notoriety when it became central to an antiabortion media campaign, gaining a name and gender along the way: George. Most interesting to me, however, is Taylor's critical look at the justification for nonmedically necessary ultrasounds based on the claim that they facilitate mother-infant bonding by increasing awareness of the fetus and by reassuring the woman that all is well with her pregnancy.

It is, on the face of it, an odd idea that a blurry moving image on a screen promotes a mother's awareness of her developing fetus, as though the physical changes associated with pregnancy and the direct experience of fetal movements aren't enough to stimulate maternal feelings. The fact that this idea has become conventional wisdom is all the more peculiar since, as Taylor shows, there is virtually no scientific evidence to support the purported effect on a woman's feelings of attachment. Taylor takes a close look at the one research report that is frequently cited as proving the positive psychological benefits of ultrasounds and shows that this is a complete misreading of the study's aims and conclusions.

The question for us to ask is this: Whose interests are served by promoting the idea that sonograms contribute to maternal attachment and, thereby, fetal well-being? There is the obvious correspondence between this view and the priorities of abortion opponents; a woman who is encouraged to believe that she should bond with the fetus imaged in the sonogram is, presumably, a woman less likely to terminate her pregnancy. There is also a clear reason for those who manufacture and market ultrasound equipment to provide an additional rationale for routine imaging, that is, in addition to the diagnostic purposes for which the technology was originally designed. If women are convinced that an ultrasound is critical for the development of ideal maternal emotions, they will secure screenings with or without physician approval. More screenings mean more demand for the latest and best technology, which results in more income for the suppliers.

Less obvious, but equally compelling, is the link Taylor establishes between the idea that sonograms foster emotional attachment, and therefore healthier maternal behavior during pregnancy, and a wider ideology of maternal bonding that emerged in the United States in the 1970s. Originally directed at postnatal practices, the theory applied biological models derived from animal experiments to argue that immediate and direct physical contact between mother and infant is critical for the formation of strong bonds. Dire consequences, including "diseases of nonattachment" (Selma Fraiburg, cited in Taylor 2008:98), were said to result from even a brief delay in mother-infant contact. Although this biologically-based bonding theory had the salutary effect of helping to humanize hospital delivery room practices, it also extended the control physicians could exercise over women's reproductive lives by creating yet more medically justified regulations over maternal behavior. Worse, it effectively blamed women for failing to "bond," even when normative postdelivery conduct was impossible due to circumstances beyond a woman's control (e.g., premature delivery requiring intensive care and postsurgical complications associated with caesarian sections).

Taylor reviews the withering criticism leveled at the postnatal bonding theory—that it radically oversimplified complex human relationships on the basis of seriously flawed and inadequate research—and then points out that despite this criticism essentially the same erroneous theory of maternal attachment was applied to prenatal conditions via the theory of ultrasound bonding. With even less research to support it and with the same consequences for medical surveillance and control of pregnant women, sonograms were promoted as being just as important as prenatal vitamins and behavioral restrictions to the production of a healthy infant. Indeed, "production" is precisely the point, according to Taylor: "When doctors act as managers, and fetuses appear as products, then women come to be regarded as unskilled workers, alienated from their own reproductive labor" (p. 120).

The construction of self/personhood at work here is a complicated mix of the very old and very modern. It did not require the development of screening technologies to convey the idea that the fetus is an "other" for which the woman is directly responsible. Taylor and others have shown that historically and across cultures pregnant women were restricted from eating certain foods and engaging in specific behaviors because of the perceived impact on fetal development. Abnormalities seen at birth have long been interpreted as the result of a woman's violation of prenatal taboos.

What distinguishes "ultrasound bonding" from previous prenatal notions of maternal feelings is that it associates the mother's responsibility for the developing fetus with an emotional attachment stimulated by a sonogram. It uncritically accepts the idea that women "naturally" bond with their infants and asserts that this emotional connection can be pushed back in time to early fetal stages with the help of a visual image. A scanning technology gives a nudge to a biologically driven maternal drive. Seeing is, in this argument, feeling.

Taylor points out that the absence of scientific evidence to support the claim that sonograms make a pregnant woman feel more attached to her developing fetus matters little if popular culture accepts it as fact. If women feel a rush of maternal emotions during their ultrasounds, it is not because of the technology itself but because of "all the social and cultural work that goes on around it" (Taylor 2008:114). At least some of that work traces back to a view of the infant-as-person that a veritable baby-industrial-complex has promoted to sell all the goods and services a mother "needs." If personhood can be extended back into the womb, if we come to believe that the fetus is an autonomous consuming self, imagine the marketing opportunities: self-help books, prenatal supplements with or without proven benefit, soothing or educational recordings to play through the abdomen, and, yes, repeated ultrasounds with memento images for the baby book.

Rights, Death, and the Autonomous Self

Vivian Bearing, the central character in Margaret Edson's play *Wit* (1999), is dying of ovarian cancer. A radical and tortuous experimental treatment has failed. Her nurse, one of the few caring individuals in what remains of her life, helps her to add a "Do Not Resuscitate" (DNR) order to her medical chart so that she may die without further medical interventions. Her heart stops, and the monitoring equipment sends the alarm before the nurse is able to silence it. In rushes the "crash team," ready to inject and shock her back to life. The nurse battles to stop them, insisting that they honor the DNR order. They finally desist, but only after subjecting Vivian to one more round of medical violence.

In the months prior to March 2005, a video of Florida resident Theresa Marie Schiavo was featured on national television news programs and on an Internet site developed by supporters of her parents. Her eyes are open; she displays facial gestures and makes unintelligible noises. It seems that she tracks the movement of a balloon passed in front of her. The images were presented as a part of a campaign waged to stop her husband, Michael Schiavo, from proceeding with his plan to withdraw the feeding tube that was keeping his wife alive. Michael agreed with the preponderance of medical opinion: Terri's cardiac arrest fifteen years earlier, on February 25, 1990, had stopped blood flow to her brain for so long that she would never recover any conscious life. She was diagnosed as being in a "permanent vegetative state"; only the survival of her brain stem, which regulates basic organic functions like respiration, kept her from being declared brain dead.

The fictional Vivian and the very real Terri represent different kinds of medical disputes that arise at the end of life—thanks to the medical technologies that delay death. The first speaks to the conflict between a medical system determined to do more and an individual wishing for less. The second is a textbook example of a medical declaration of futility confronting a family's insistence on hope. Disputes like these have worked their way through our court system ever since the widely publicized case of Karen Ann Quinlin, a twenty-one-year-old New Jersey woman whose irreversible brain damage in 1975 led to a battle between her parents, who wanted to "pull the plug" on the life-maintaining respirator, and a hospital that insisted on continued treatment.

In the United States, when and whether medical interventions at life's end should be undertaken or withdrawn is typically discussed in the language of individual rights. Did the emergency response team have the right to override Vivian's declared preference for no resuscitation? Did Terri ever declare herself to her husband or others on the question of whether she would want to be kept alive in circumstances like those she now faced? The presumption, in popular consensus and legal statutes, is that each person has the right to make his/her own treatment choices. This rights-based framework resonates with a prominent view of the self in America, as an autonomous self-determining actor. It stands in contrast to cultures that embed the self in the nexus of social relations and substitutes individual choice with decisions made either by a collective (e.g., an entire extended family) or by discrete group leaders (e.g., a clan leader).

A self-construction that enfranchises the individual to make all important decisions can result in trouble in a medical setting when the person's ability to make decisions is compromised or questioned. Vivian's previous willingness to turn over medical decisions to her physician, who then treated her purely as an experimental subject without volition, runs up against her reassertion of control in a DNR order. Terri, by never having made a record of her preference in a living will, opened the door to competing claims over decision-making power. It is the technology and its capacity to rescue and sustain life that requires adjudication, oftentimes in the courts, of these conflicting assertions of decisional authority.

Biotechnologies applied at the end of life are interesting for more than what they reveal about views of the self. For example, why does the removal of a feeding tube engender so much more controversy than turning off a respirator, when the patient is known to have no capacity to experience pain in either case? Why do the most publicized cases of disagreements over withdrawing life support almost uniformly involve women patients? If we are culturally committed to an ethic of individual autonomy in medical decision making, why do we accept a stated preference not to be resuscitated but, in all but two states, refuse to allow a person in an advanced stage of a terminal illness to choose to end his/her life with the assistance of a willing physician? How can family members insist that their opposition to the withdrawal of life support constitutes a choice in favor of a "natural" death—what is natural when intensive medical attention is all that preserves life?

Conclusion

Medical decisions at the end of life are often troublesome for some of the same reasons as are those made at the start of life. Just as a microscopic slide of a blastocyst or an ultrasound image of a fetus can't answer the question of when personhood begins, a respirator and feeding tube can't tell us when meaningful life has ended. These are cultural judgments, tied to different constructions of the self and influenced by political and economic interests. Biotechnologies add dimensions to the dilemmas, by revealing life stages that were once invisible and by extending a degree of control over the timing of death, but the underlying questions of what constitute the boundaries and meanings of life did not arise as a result of these medical innovations.

The medical anthropology of biotechnologies literally puts science in its place, by situating it in the working world where it develops, by stripping back its veil of objectivity to reveal the play of vested interests that determine its direction, and by placing its discoveries in the cultural contexts in which they find application. Its most important contribution is to debunk the view that somehow we are at the mercy of biotechnologies that are out of control. If we understand the very human dynamics behind the research that creates medical technologies and get a better grasp of the interplay between scientists, technicians, physicians, patients, and the commercial interests that promote new machines and procedures, we will see just how domesticated our biotechnologies really are.

SUGGESTED READINGS

Relevant studies have been cited in previous sections, especially by Sarah Franklin, Marcia Inhorn, Linda Hogel, Margaret Lock, Rayna Rapp, and Lesley Sharp. Important edited collections on the topic include *Remaking Life and Death* (2003, Sarah Franklin and Margaret Lock, eds.), *Living and Working with the New Medical Technologies* (2000, Margaret Lock, Allan Young, and Alberto Cambrosio, eds.), and *Biotechnology and Culture* (2000, Paul E. Brodwin, ed.).

Two excellent review articles are also worth noting: Sharon R. Kaufman and Lynn M. Morgan's "The Anthropology of the Beginnings and Ends of Life" (2005, *Annual Review of Anthropology*) and Linda F. Hogle's "Enhancement Technologies and the Body" (2006, *Annual Review of Anthropology*).

NOTES

1. The National Library of Medicine's Human Body Project created digital images of two donated cadavers by photographing thousands of anatomical slices of each one and then posting them to the Internet for students and scholars to reassemble at any number of structural levels. The bodies are nicknamed "Adam" and "Eve" (see: http://www.nlm.nih.gov/research/visible/visible_human.html).

2. Excerpt from the Pope John Paul II's address to President Bush at Castel Gandolfo, Italy, July 23, 2001, http://www.americancatholic.org/News/StemCell/pope_to_bush.asp, accessed on August 19, 2008.

3. James Thomson, first scientist to isolate and culture embryonic stem cells, June 2005, http://pewforum.org/docs/?DocID=320, accessed on August 19, 2008.

4. A good source for information about stem cell research is the National Institute of Health's web site: http://stemcells.nih.gov/index.asp

CHAPTER 10 A Look Back and a Glance Ahead

Think of the unrelenting cascade of medical stories that each new year brings to our collective attention. There are the seemingly endless reports on technological innovations—such as computed axial tomography (CAT) scans and ultrasound and magnetic resonance imaging (MRI)—and improved surgical procedures (e.g., heart bypass, multiple organ transplantation, neural and microscopic surgeries, and fetal surgeries). New and newly named diseases appear regularly: all the re/emerging infections cited in Chapter 5, fetal alcohol syndrome (FAS), attention deficit disorder (ADD), premenstrual syndrome (PMS), a seemingly endless number of cancers, posttraumatic stress disorder (PTSD), and toxic shock syndrome—so many new ways to be ill!

In addition to the accounts of scientific discoveries and medical innovations, personal medical stories are routinely covered in the media. Sometimes these individual accounts are transformed into medical morality tales of questionable judgments and physician irresponsibility. In a previous edition of this book, I mentioned the 1997 report of a Midwestern woman who gave birth to septuplets after using fertility drugs to produce the pregnancy and declining the opportunity to "selectively reduce" the number of embryos that resulted. In a déjà vu moment, headlines on January 26, 2009, announced another multiple birth, this time involving eight infants born nine weeks prematurely to Nadya Suleman of Bellflower, California. Ms. Suleman had used sperm donation and in vitro fertilization; as in the earlier case, she declined the opportunity to reduce the number of embryos that resulted. The initial story, reported as a feel-good segment on the evening news, quickly became a highly critical account when it was revealed that Ms. Suleman already had six children at home, that she was single, that implanting that many fertilized eggs violates accepted in vitro fertilization (IVF) standards, and that the costs of short- and long-term care for the octuplets would likely become a public expense.

A list of all the health-related reports that have drawn media notice in the United States over the past forty years would be very long indeed. Health, disease, and medicine permeate our shared experience of life in this country. The triumphs and failures of medicine, the personal stories of suffering, and the health effects of social and economic inequities are part of our common history. The challenge is to make sense of what this collective experience means—to understand the significance of each medical story in a broader context.

What does medical anthropology offer by way of wider contexts for our medical stories? How does "thinking anthropologically" help us to understand the significance of developments in medicine, of personal health crises that are turned into public dramas, of policy decisions related to medical care, or of medical encounters across cultural lines? In this final chapter, I review the insights and priorities of medical anthropology (see the Preface) and then illustrate how they can clarify an important health issue in contemporary American society: the prevention of HIV/AIDS. I conclude with brief comments about future direction in medical anthropology and suggestions for advanced training in the field.

Advantages of Medical Anthropology

Sensitivity for Culture and Biology

Medical anthropology encourages us to consider biological and cultural perspectives on disease, and even to ask how much culture influences what we consider "biological" (see Chapter 1). I referred to several cases that reveal links between cultural practices and the biological processes of disease (e.g., malaria, agricultural irrigation, and sickle-cell anemia and cholera and poor sanitation). I showed how the ecological approach in medical anthropology employs an evolutionary framework to analyze the interaction between disease-causing organisms/processes, sociocultural factors, and environmental conditions (Chapters 3 and 4).

Recognition That the Political Economy Has Health Implications

The two chapters on cholera illustrated how different a disease can look when the perspective shifts from biological to political-economic frameworks. Cholera, an evolving bacteria adapting to opportunities in human societies (Chapter 3), becomes an outcome and emblem of underdevelopment, as well as an excuse for oppressing the poor (Chapter 4). The example demonstrates the health effects of social and economic structures, both within individual countries and on a global scale (Chapter 5).

The discussion of biomedicine and of applied medical anthropology (Chapters 6 and 7) similarly drew upon political-economic analyses. The rise of the profession of biomedicine, its global expansion, and challenges to its authority were interpreted in the context of the economic system that supports it (and vice versa), namely, world capitalism. The debate about whether and how medical anthropology should be applied was also related to questions of political and economic interests in health care.

Insistence on the Value of Ethnography

In this book, I have used ethnographic comparisons to explore the cultural content of biomedical concepts and practices (Chapters 1 and 7), to deepen an understanding of the healing role (Chapter 6), and to explore the values applied in healing traditions around the world (Chapter 8). Careful ethnography was shown to be useful even when applied to the unorthodox settings in which biotechnologies are created and applied (Chapter 9).

Commitment to Applying Medical Anthropology

Anthropology has a contribution to make to the alleviation of human suffering, whether it be through its incorporation into the training and practice of medical professionals or by the critique it offers of ill-conceived programs at home and abroad. I have surveyed the ways medical anthropology is applied (Chapter 7)—from the work of "culture experts" on health teams to "social activists" in community organizations—and suggested that a greater role in the domain of medical ethics represents an important future direction (Chapter 8).

Thinking Anthropologically about HIV/AIDS

One of the most important medical stories of our times, the AIDS pandemic, became a major news story in the United States after 1983, when it was clear that the disease would not be confined to discrete segments of the population. Between the last three months of 1982 and the period of April through June of 1983, there was a 60 percent increase in media reports on AIDS (Shilts 1987:267). At about the same time, the number of medical anthropologists carrying out research on AIDS and working on prevention programs began to increase dramatically. The AIDS and Anthropology Research Group, a subunit of the Society for Medical Anthropology, soon had well over two hundred members (Bolton and Orozco 1994).

AIDS and the Culture/Biology Interface

Just as in the case of cholera, the relationship between cultural patterns and the processes of biological evolution explains variations in the HIV virus, which causes AIDS. Since the virus is transmitted by the exchange of blood, semen, or vaginal secretions, its evolutionary trajectory is directly tied to human behaviors that facilitate contact with an infected person's bodily fluids. For example, culturally defined social norms regarding sexual relations, especially concerning the acceptability of multiple partners, create opportunities for different variants of the virus, some more and some less severe (Ewald 1994).

Medical anthropologists have focused on norms governing sexual behavior in different cultures and related these to the spread of the HIV virus, for example, in Uganda (McGrath et al. 1992), Brazil (Parker 1987), Belgium (Bolton 1992), and southern California (Hoffman and Bolton 1996). The research in Zaire summarized in Chapter 7 (Schoepf et al. 1991) illustrates how this line of research can be integrated into a prevention program. This work permits evolutionary biologists to assess the course of the HIV virus's adaptation in different human populations.

Political-Economic Factors in the Pandemic

Medical anthropologists have underscored the relationship between the behaviors that put people at risk of HIV infection (e.g., sex without condoms and intravenous drug use) and the conditions of economic and social disadvantage. The link is especially clear in the case of men and women who are forced by economic necessity to engage in sex work; the Zaire case shows how difficult it is for persons in this position to insist that their clients use condoms (see also Farmer 1992; Biehl 2007). The connection between poverty and intravenous drug use is equally well documented (Wallace 1990).

Baer et al. (1997) refer to an inner-city AIDS **syndemic**, in which the HIV virus acts in a synergistic fashion with many other health and social problems characteristic of urban settings.[1] For example, substance abuse is associated with elevated rates of sexually transmitted diseases, which, in turn, increases the risk of HIV infection. The compromised immune system of a person with HIV leaves him/her more vulnerable to tuberculosis (ibid., p. 178). And so on. The point is that the AIDS pandemic cannot be isolated from a broader analysis of the health consequences of economic and social inequality.[2]

AIDS Ethnography and Its Contribution to Prevention Planning

AIDS prevention measures must be geared directly to the behaviors that favor the transmission of the virus. This requires a detailed understanding of the sexual practices and drug-using behaviors of persons who are most likely to be exposed to infection. Questionnaires and surveys have proven to be inadequate research methods for these social activities; they tend to report "ideal" rather than "real" behavior. Ethnographic inquiry, on the other hand, has yielded important insights that have helped to fine-tune and critique prevention campaigns (see Baer et al. 1997:178–187; Biehl 2007).

For example, Ralph Bolton (1992) carried out participant observation studies in gay bars, saunas, restaurants, and other places in Brussels. He discovered that, contrary to what survey research had indicated, "unprotected anal intercourse was still widely practiced, as were unprotected oral sex and rimming" (p. 135). His report to the Institute of Epidemiology of Belgium's Ministry of Health urged that prevention efforts be redoubled—they were likely to have been reduced on the basis of the previous surveys which were far more optimistic about changes in gay men's sexual behavior.

Bolton insists that AIDS-related sex research must understand sexual behaviors from the actor's point of view—which includes the dangers *and* pleasures of sex—and that it should not impose "a sexophobic ideology on people who are at risk but [instead] help to restructure and re-create a sexuality that is life-sustaining and beneficial" (ibid., p. 154). This is the challenge to which medical anthropology has made a significant contribution.

Future Directions in Medical Anthropology

Brigit Obrist, from the University of Basel, Switzerland, contributed a note to the Society for Medical Anthropology's column in *Anthropology News* (2009, Vol. 50, no. 1, p. 52) regarding the "vibrant" status of medical anthropology in Europe. She noted that there are graduate programs, journals, and regional networks in France, the United Kingdom, Germany, Italy, Spain, the Nordic countries, and Switzerland. More can be learned at the web site for the European Association of Social Anthropology (http://www.easaonline.org/).

A recent collection of essays, *Medical Anthropology: Regional Perspectives and Shared Concerns* (Saillant and Genest 2007), includes reviews of the discipline in Canada, Brazil, and Mexico, in addition to the European countries cited by Obrist. The concluding chapter, by Margaret Lock, offers this optimistic prognosis:

> It is my belief that the discipline is entering a new era, an era that will continue to adopt a critical/interpretive approach, to make use of the techniques of ethnographic research and related empirical evidence, and to question the concepts and truth claims of the world of bioscience as well as those made by politicians and policy-makers . . . For too long the remarkable insights resulting from so much good research in medical anthropology have been mainly unnoticed by society at large. This must change, and will only come about through our own concerted efforts (Lock 2007).

The future is bright for medical anthropology, both because it is gaining a foothold in an increasing number of countries around the world and because its insights are slowly penetrating into the academic, political, and public discourse about health. I agree with Lock's prediction about the continuing importance of the critical/interpretive perspective, especially as we get better at tying macrolevel social and economic analysis with compelling accounts of the lived reality of sufferers. I would add that the synthesis envisioned by those who speak of a biocultural approach (Goodman and Leatherman 1998) also holds great promise, particularly for the study of health and nutrition, genetic and evolutionary factors in disease, infectious disease agents, and human-mediated environmental changes.

Looking forward, Lock is also right to point to medical anthropology's role as a constructive critic of the biosciences. I fully expect that future research will greatly expand on the pioneering studies of biotechnologies reviewed in Chapter 9, and that the ethical context of medical innovations will continue to profit from deep ethnographic and comparative investigations. The study of pharmaceuticals is a particularly rich arena for future work, in regard to access as well as efficacy.

Finally, Lock's call to action is well taken. Too often the work of medical anthropologists, despite being profoundly relevant to how human health and sickness is understood, goes unnoticed by those who provide care, plan interventions, and develop policy. It is frequently our own fault, as we write in jargon unintelligible to any but other anthropologists and publish in sources few others read. It is indeed up to us to make sure our voices are heard and our viewpoints recognized.

Academic and Professional Career Paths Related to Medical Anthropology

The Society for Medical Anthropology published a directory of "Graduate Programs in Medical Anthropology" (1994)[3], which illustrates the variety of options available for post-baccalaureate training. Many graduate anthropology programs have concentrations in medical anthropology, with varying degrees of elaboration, and some offer dual-degree programs with schools of medicine, nursing, public health, and epidemiology (Case Western University, Harvard University, the University of California, Los Angeles, and San Francisco). The dual-degree opportunities are especially attractive for those who wish to use medical anthropology in international health or in public health in the United States.

The graduate anthropology departments that include medical anthropology as a core program sometimes identify a special focus on a particular theoretical perspective. For example, the University of California, Berkeley, identifies itself with the critical/interpretive perspective (see Chapter 4); the University of Alabama, Tuscaloosa, commits itself to a biocultural approach. There are also programs that specialize in medical anthropology in specific regions of the world, such as the University of Hawaii, Honolulu, which encourages research in Asia and the Pacific. Applied medical anthropology is cited by many programs as a priority (e.g., Case Western University, University of South Florida, and University of Maryland).

The research interests of faculty can add another dimension to the defining focus of graduate programs. For example, the University of California, San Francisco, which has a joint program in medical anthropology with the U. C. Berkeley campus, has special strengths in the anthropology of aging, international health, and studies of the experience of illness, disability, and stigmatized conditions. These are the research interests of the program's principle faculty and therefore represent areas the program is particularly interested in supporting.[4]

Conclusion

In this introduction to medical anthropology, I have sought to convey the impressive accomplishments that have marked the field's short history: the breadth of ethnographic work in medical anthropology—from studies of African traditional healers (Turner 1964) to research on laboratories engaged in cloning research (Franklin 2007)—the discipline's blending of biological and cultural perspectives on health, and the partnerships medical anthropologists have forged with health workers abroad and at home. In this chapter, I also illustrated the relevance of medical anthropology to a fuller understanding of health problems that confront contemporary society and suggested avenues for continued explorations in the field.

The next step in an exploration of medical anthropology is to delve directly into the case studies that constitute the heart and soul of the discipline. Many important ethnographies have already been cited in the text; I conclude with an additional selection of recent works.

SUGGESTED READINGS

At several points I have made brief reference to medical anthropologists whose research focuses on women's health issues and/or on reproduction. Recently, Lesley Doyal (*What Makes Women Sick: Gender and the Political Economy of Health*, 1995), Robbie E. Davis-Floyd and Carolyn F. Sargent (*Childbirth and Authoritative Knowledge*, 1997), Marcia C. Inhorn (*Local Babies, Global* Science, 2003), Rayna Rapp (*Testing Women, Testing the* Fetus, 1999), and Sarah Franklin (*Embodied Progress: A Cultural Account of Assisted Conception*, 1997) have made significant contributions to this literature.

Anthropological studies of science and technology in medicine are reviewed in David Hess' *Science Studies: An Advanced Introduction* (1997b); his analysis of alternative cancer treatments is also noteworthy (*Can Bacteria Cause Cancer? Alternative Medicine Confronts Big Science*, 1997a).

Valuable medical anthropology accounts have appeared on Haiti (Paul Brodwin's *Medicine and Morality in Haiti: The Contest of Healing Power*, 1996) and on Native North Americans (Theresa O'Nell's *Disciplined Hearts: History, Identity, and Depression in an American-Indian Community*, 1996).

Two collections which include contributions from medical anthropologists should also be mentioned: *Social Suffering* (edited by Arthur Kleinman et al. 1997) and *The Social Medicine Reader* (edited by Gail E. Henderson et. al. 1997).

For additional sources, turn to the book reviews that appear in the major journals in medical anthropology: *Medical Anthropology Quarterly*, *Social Science and Medicine*, *Culture, Medicine and Psychiatry*, and *Medical Anthropology*.

NOTES

1. These conditions include "high rates of unemployment, poverty, homelessness and residential overcrowding, substandard nutrition, environmental toxins and related environmental health risks, infrastructural deterioration and loss of quality housing stock, forced geographic mobility, family break-up and disruption of social support networks, youth gangs and drug-related violence, and health-care inequality" (Baer et al. 1997:174).

2. Pursuing the same logic, researchers associated with the Hispanic Health Council (Romero-Daza et al. 2003) have proposed another "syndemic" related to HIV-AIDS: SAVA (Substance Abuse, Violence, and AIDS). They demonstrate the links between prostitution, sexual/physical abuse, injection drug use, and HIV infection.

3. The directory is available from the American Anthropological Association's web site: http://www.aaanet.org/

4. It should be remembered that as faculty come and go, the research topics supported by a program can shift.

GLOSSARY

adaptation "biological change effected by evolution to accommodate populations to different environmental conditions" (Boaz and Almquist 1997:550).

anthropometry measurement of the size and proportions of the human body, used by biological anthropologists to assess growth and nutrition.

applied medical anthropology application of anthropological theories and methods to health interventions, for example, in international and domestic health projects.

archaeology study of the material remains of human societies.

autonomy ethical principle that an individual has the right to choose his/her own treatment course.

beneficence ethical principle that health care workers must always act in accordance with the best interests of the patient.

biocultural a theoretical perspective in medical anthropology which considers both the biological and cultural components of health and sickness.

bioethics academic discipline and field of applied studies which considers rights and wrongs in the practice of biomedicine.

biomedicine healing system which developed on the basis of medical scientific research in Europe and the United States.

bioterrorism "use of harmful chemicals, pathogenic microbes, or plant or microbial toxins as weapons of terrorism" (Perrota 2001:328).

case fatality ratio (CFR) proportion of people contracting a disease who die of that disease.

critical medical anthropology theoretical perspective in medical anthropology which stresses the importance of political and economic structures, especially global capitalism, on the health of human populations (also known as the political economy of health).

critical-interpretive theoretical perspective in medical anthropology which blends the "critical" attention to political/economic structures that affect human health with a "cultural" interpretation of the meanings humans assign to conditions of health and sickness.

culture shared ideas characteristic of a given social group and the patterns of behavior that result from them.

cultural authority ability of a person or social group (e.g., a medical profession) to influence the actions and/or decisions of others on the basis of cultural legitimacy.

cultural competency ability to consider cultural factors in the prevention and treatment of disease; includes the cultural influences on caregivers and patients.

cultural-constructivist theoretical perspective in the social sciences in general which analyzes the cultural grounding of ideas and practices, even those which may be considered "objective" (i.e., free from cultural influence).

cultural ecology "study of human adaptation to social and physical environments. Human adaptation refers to both biological and cultural processes that enable a population to survive and reproduce within a given or changing environment" (Elliot Fratkin, personal communication).

cultural materialism study of the material basis (i.e., biologically driven requirements for food, shelter, and so on) of culturally patterned behavior.

curandero (curanderismo) "curer;" in Peru, traditional healers who employ the San Pedro cactus in night rituals centered around curing altars or **mesas**.

daño sorcery-induced "harm" or sickness.

diffusion study of cultural transmission from society to society.

ecological (ecological/evolutionary) theoretical perspective in medical anthropology which analyzes the adaptive relationship between human groups and the biotic and nonbiotic environments they inhabit.

emerging infections "those whose incidence has increased within the past two decades or threatens to increase in the near future" (Lederberg et al. 1992).

epidemic incidence of a disease beyond what is normal and expected for a given region (i.e., in excess of normal expectancy).

epidemiology study of the distribution and determinants of diseases in human populations.

ethnography intensive study of particular societies and/or social groups with a focus on the interrelationships among institutions and the ideas which support them.

ethnopsychology "the way in which people conceptualize, monitor and discuss their own and others' mental processes, behavior and relationships" (Catherine A. Lutz)

extrasomatic beyond the physical characteristics of a life-form.

fitness (reproductive) "the extent to which the genes of an individual survive in its descendants" (Boaz and Almquist 1997:554).

folk sector that part of a society's medical system in which healing is undertaken by "non-professional, non-bureaucratic, specialists" (Kleinman 1980:59).

function (functionalism) theoretical perspective in anthropology which analyzes the contribution that each social institution makes to the continuation of the social system.

genotype an organism's genetic constitution.

global germ governance international monitoring of and response to epidemics by both state and nonstate entities.

healing profession institutionalized body of healers, with formal training requirements, licensing procedures, and collective organizations which enforce standards of practice, share knowledge, and protect the group from competition.

heterozygygous bearing two different alleles at a genetic locus.

holism (holistic) anthropological notion that sociocultural patterns are interrelated.

homeopathy healing tradition premised on the theory that a substance known to cause a disease can, in minute doses, also cure it.

homozygous "bearing two identical alleles at a genetic locus" (Boaz and Almquist 1997:556).

host organism in which a disease-causing agent survives.

iatrogenic an injury or disease process that results directly or indirectly from medical treatment (e.g., surgical errors, hospital-related infections).

incidence rate or frequency of a disease in a population over a specified period of time.

interpretive theoretical perspective in anthropology in general, and in medical anthropology in particular, which focuses on the meanings that human groups attribute to experiences (e.g., sickness episodes).

justice ethical principle which requires that access to treatment be fairly distributed.

maladaptive physical characteristic or behavior that threatens the survival of an organism, and therefore its capacity to reproduce.

medical ecology application of evolutionary and ecological theory to the analysis of human health and sickness.

medical ethics general term for the ethical principles which govern healing activities in a given society.

medical ethnoethics ethical principles which guide healing activities in a culturally distinct society; the term is treated here as synonymous with "medical ethics."

mesa literally "table" in Spanish, but for Peruvian shamans a collection of symbolic healing objects arrayed on a table or on the ground during curing rituals.

morbidity number of individuals suffering from a specific disease in a given area and/or period of time (contrasted to mortality)—absolute numbers or ratios, general for a whole population or distinguished by a segment of that population.

mortality number of deaths from a specific disease in a given area and/or over a period of time (contrasted to morbidity).

mutation "any novel genetic change that may affect both genes and chromosomes. Such changes are spontaneous and random in occurrence" (Boaz and Almquist 1997:558).

natural selection "the process of differential reproduction whereby individuals well-adapted to their environment will be "favored," that is, they will pass on more of their heritable attributes to the next generation than other, less well-adapted individuals" (Boaz and Almquist 1997:558).

nonmaleficence ethical principle which requires that healing professionals "do no harm" to their patients.

paleontological pertaining to life forms from former geologic periods, studied by their fossil remains.

participant observation anthropological fieldwork method by which the investigator lives among the people he/she studies and seeks to take part in daily life while simultaneously observing it.

pandemic outbreak of a disease which has spread beyond a region, nation, or continent.

pathogen disease-causing organism.

phenotype observable features of a living organism (e.g., color of skin, hair, or eyes; height; weight; and circumference of arms or chest).

plural medical systems presence in a society of two or more healing systems; particularly characteristic of modern, industrialized societies.

political ecology application of evolutionary theory and the concept of adaptation in the context of the social and political relations between groups of people.

popular health care sector that part of a society's medical system in which healing is undertaken by nonspecialists and on the basis of generally shared knowledge.

prevalence "total number of people diagnosed with a disease at or over a designated time, divided by the total population at risk of having the disease at that same time or midway through the period" (James Trostle, personal communication).

primary health care (PHC) approach to the provision of medical care which gives priority to prevention over curative services, encourages community participation, guarantees equal access, respects local traditions, and incorporates health planning into general social and economic development.

professional health care sector that part of a society's medical system in which healing is undertaken by persons with specialized knowledge and professional status.

qualitative methods research techniques which explore the meanings that humans attribute to their behavior through interviews and other narrative approaches.

quantitative methods research techniques which measure, count, and/or statistically assess data.

reemerging infections diseases once brought under control, at least in wealthy countries, appearing again due to resistant strains, changes in human settlements, and reductions in public health prevention measures.

rehydration solution (Oral Rehydration Solution) solution used to restore essential water and salts to a dehydrated person. The World Health Organization's official ingredients are 20 gm glucose, 3.5 gm sodium chloride, 2.9 gm trisodium citrate, and 1.5 gm potassium chloride in 1 liter of water.

rites of passage rituals that mark the transition of an individual or group of individuals from one social status to another (e.g., baptism, puberty rituals, marriage, and funerals).

serotype "a serologically distinguishable strain of a micro-organism" (Oxford English Dictionary 1993).

shaman a religious specialist whose personalistic relationship with a spirit being(s) is established and maintained through controlled trance in a community context. Trance is induced by any one or combination of three mechanisms: sensory deprivation, mental concentration, and/or mind-altering substances.

social authority ability of a person or social group to influence the actions and/or decision making of others on the basis of social status and power.

somatic physical or corporeal part of an organism.

Structuralism a theoretical model in anthropology derived from structural linguistics and associated with Claude Lévi-Strauss. It claims that beneath cultural expressions like mythology there is a basic structure reflective of the functioning of the human brain.

syndemic interacting health problems characteristic of a segment of a human society (e.g., inner-city poor).

sonographer a medical technician trained to use an ultrasound scanning device.

ultrasound (sonography) a medical scanning device that uses high-frequency sound waves to produce images of the inside of the body, with special application to pregnancy and fetal development.

utilitarian a philosophical position in ethics, associated with Jeremy Bentham, that uses the "greatest good for the greatest number" calculation to determine what is right and wrong. It is also known as consequentialism.

xenotransplantation cross-species transplantation.

REFERENCES

ABRAHAM, LAURIE

1993 *Mama Might Be Better off Dead*. Chicago: University of Chicago.

ACKERKNECHT, ERWIN H.

1963 "Medical Practices: The Non-Andean Tribes." In *Handbook of South American Indians*, Vol. 5. J. H. Steward, ed., pp. 621–633. New York: Cooper Square.

1971 *Medicine and Ethnology: Selected Essays*. Baltimore: Johns Hopkins University Press.

ADAMS, RICHARD N.

1955 "A Nutritional Research Program in Guatemala." In *Health, Culture and Community: Case Studies of Public Reactions to Health Programs*. B. D. Paul, ed., pp. 435–458. New York: Russell Sage Foundation.

AGAR, MICHAEL

1996 "Recasting the 'Ethno' in 'Epidemiology.'" *Medical Anthropology* 16:391–403.

ALLAND, ALEXANDER, JR.

1970 *Adaptation in Cultural Evolution: An Approach to Medical Anthropology*. New York: Columbia University.

1977 "Medical Anthropology and the Study of Biological and Cultural Adaptation." In *Culture, Disease and Healing*. D. Landy, ed., pp. 41–47. New York: Macmillan.

1987 "Looking Backward: An Autocritique." *Medical Anthropology Quarterly* 1:424–431.

ANDERSON, ROBERT

1991 "The Efficacy of Ethnomedicine: Research Methods in Trouble." *Medical Anthropology* 12:1–17.

1996 *Magic, Science, and Health: The Aims and Achievements of Medical Anthropology*. NY: Harcout Brace.

ARMELAGOS, GEORGE, THOMAS LEATHERMAN, MARY RYAN, AND LYNN SIBLEY

1992 "Biocultural Synthesis in Medical Anthropology." *Medical Anthropology* 14:35–52.

ARMELAGOS, GEORGE, MARY RYAN, AND THOMAS LEATHERMAN

1990 "Evolution of Infectious Disease: A Biocultural Analysis of AIDS." *American Journal of Human Biology* 2:353–363.

ARMS, S.

1975 *Immaculate Deception*. Boston: Houghton Mifflin.

ARNOLD, R. M., S. J. YOUNGNER, R. SCHAPIRO, AND C. SPICER (EDS.)

1995 *Procuring Organs for Transplant: The Debate over Non-Heart-Beating Cadaver Protocols*. Baltimore: Johns Hopkins.

ASSOCIATION OF AMERICAN MEDICAL COLLEGES

2007 *Minority Students in Medical Association: Facts and Figures*. Washington: Association of American Medical Colleges.

ATKINSON, JANE

1992 "Shamanisms Today." *Annual Review of Anthropology* 21:307–333.

BAER, HANS A.

1993 "How Critical Can Clinical Anthropology Be?" *Medical Anthropology* 15:299–317.

1996 "Critical Biocultural Approaches to Medical Anthropology: A Dialogue." Special Issue. *Medical Anthropology Quarterly* 10(4).

BAER, HANS A., MERRILL SINGER, AND JOHN H. JOHNSEN

1986 "Introduction: Toward a Critical Medical Anthropology." *Social Science and Medicine* 23:95–98.

BAER, HANS A., MERRILL SINGER, AND IDA SUSSER

1997 *Medical Anthropology and the World System: A Critical Perspective*. Westport, CT: Bergin and Garvey.

BAKER, P. T., AND J. S. WEINER (EDS.)
1966 *The Biology of Human Adaptability*. Oxford: Clarenden.

BARKER-BENFIELD, G. J.
1976 *The Horrors of the Half-Known Life: Male Attitudes Toward Women and Sexuality in Nineteenth Century America*. New York: Harper and Row.

BARRETT, R., C. W. KUZAWA, T. MCDADE, AND G. J. ARMELAGOS
1998 "Emerging and Re-emerging Infectious Diseases: The Third Epidemiological Transition." *Annual Reviews in Anthropology* 27:247–271.

BASTIEN, JOSEPH
1992 *Drum and Stethoscope: Integrating Ethnomedicine and Biomedicine in Bolivia*. Salt Lake City: University of Utah.

BATTISTELLA, R. M., AND R. M. F. SOUTHBY
1968 "Crisis in American Medicine." *Lancet* 1:581–586.

BEALS, ALAN R.
1976 "Strategies of Resort to Curers in South India." In *Asian Medical Systems*. C. Lesley, ed., pp. 184–200. Berkeley: University of California.

BEAUCHAMP, TOM, AND JAMES CHILDRESS
1994 *Principles of Biomedical Ethics*, 4th Ed. New York: Oxford.

BECKER, H. S., B. GEER, E. C. HUGHES, AND A. L. STRAUSS
1961 *Boys in White: Student Culture in a Medical School*. Chicago: University of Chicago.

BEECHER, HENRY K.
1966 "Ethics and Clinical Research." *New England Journal of Medicine* 274:1354–1360.
1970 *Research and the Individual*. Boston: Little Brown.

BENEDICT, RUTH
1946 *The Chrysanthemum and the Sword*. Boston: Houghton Mifflin.

BERNARD, H. RUSSELL
1994 *Research Methods in Anthropology: Qualitative and Quantitative Approaches*, 2nd Ed. Thousand Oaks, CA: Sage.

BIEHL, JOÃO
2007 *Will to Live: AIDS Therapies and the Politics of Survival*. New York: Oxford University.

BLUEBOND-LANGER, MYRA
1978 *The Private World of Dying Patients*. Princeton: Princeton University.

BOAZ, NOEL T., AND ALAN J. ALMQUIST
1997 *Biological Anthropology: A Synthetic Approach to Human Evolution*. Upper Saddle River, NJ: Simon and Schuster.

BOGIN, BARRY
1988 *Patterns of Human Growth*. Cambridge: Cambridge University.

BOLTON, RALPH
1992 "Mapping Terra Incognita: Sex Research for AIDS Prevention: An Urgent Agenda for the 1990s." In *The Time of AIDS: Social Analysis, Theory and Method*. G. Herdt, and S. Lindenbaum, eds., pp. 124–158. Newbury Park, CA: Sage Publications.

BOLTON, RALPH, AND GAIL OROZCO
1994 *The AIDS Bibliography: Studies in Anthropology and Related Fields*. Arlington, VA: American Anthropological Association.

BONFIL-BATALLA, GUILLERMO
1966 "Conservative Thought in Applied Anthropology: A Critique." *Human Organization* 25:89–92.

BOSTON WOMEN'S HEALTH BOOK COLLECTIVE
1971 *Our Bodies Ourselves*. New York: Simon and Schuster.

BRODWIN, PAUL
1996 *Medicine and Morality in Haiti: The Contest of Healing Power*. New York: Cambridge University Press.
2000 *Biotechnology and Culture: Bodies, Anxieties, Ethics*. Bloomington: Indiana University Press.

BRODY, JANE
2004 "Age-Fighting Hormones Put Men at Risk, Too." *New York Times*, Health and Fitness, Section F, p. 7, Col. 1, Tuesday, February 24.

BROWN, E. RICHARD
1976 "Public Health in Imperialism: Early Rockefeller Programs at Home and Abroad." *American Journal of Public Health* 66:897.
1979 *Rockefeller Medicine Men: Medicine and Capitalism in America*. Berkeley: University of California.

BROWN, MICHAEL F.
1988 "Shamanism and Its Discontents." *Medical Anthropology Quarterly* 2:102–120.
1997 *The Channeling Zone: American Spirituality in an Anxious Age*. Cambridge: Harvard University.

BROWN, PETER
1987 "Microparasites and Macroparasites." *Cultural Anthropology* 2:155–171.

CALLAHAN, DANIEL
1984 "Autonomy: A Moral Good, Not a Moral Obsession." *Hastings Center Report* 14(5):40–42.

CALLENDER, CLIVE O.
1991 "Organ Donation and Blacks: A Critical Frontier." *The New England Journal of Medicine* 325:442–444.

CALLENDER, CLIVE O., A. S. BEY, P. V. MILES, AND C. L. YEAGER
1995 "A National Minority Organ/Tissue Transplant Education Program: The First Step in the Evolution of a National Minority Strategy and Minority Transplant Equity in the USA." *Transplant Proceedings* 27:1441–1443.

CAPLAN, ARTHUR L., H. TRISTRAM ENGELHARDT, JR., AND JAMES J. MCCARTNEY (EDS.)
1981 *Concepts of Health and Disease: Interdisciplinary Perspectives*. London: Addison-Wesley.

CARSON, RACHEL
1962 *Silent Spring*. Boston: Houghton Miflin.

CARTWRIGHT, S. A.
1981 "Report on the Diseases and Physical Peculiarities of the Negro Race (1851)." In *Concepts of Health and Disease: Interdisciplinary Perspectives*. A. L. Caplan, H. T. Engelhardt, Jr., and J. J. McCartney, eds., pp. 305–326. London: Addison-Wesley.

CASSELL, JOAN
1991 *Expected Miracles: Surgeons at Work*. Philadelphia: Temple University.

CAUDILL, WILLIAM
1953 "Applied Anthropology in Medicine." In *Anthropology Today*. A. L. Kroeber, ed., pp. 771–806. Chicago: University of Chicago Press.

CHAGNON, NAPOLEON A.
1997 *Yanomamo*. 5th Ed. New York: Harcourt Brace.

CHRISMAN, NOEL J., AND THOMAS M. JOHNSON
1990 "Clinically Applied Anthropology." In *Medical Anthropology*. T. M. Johnson, and C. F. Sargent, eds., pp. 93–113. New York: Praeger.

CHRISMAN, NOEL J., AND THOMAS W. MARETZKI (EDS.)
1982 *Clinically Applied Anthropology: Anthropologists in Health Settings*. Dordrecht: D. Reidel.

CHRISTOPHER, G. W., T. J. CIESLAK, J. A. PAVLIN, AND E. M. EITZEN

1999 "Biological Warfare: A Historical Perspective." In *Biological Weapons: Limiting the Threat*. J. Lederberg, ed., pp. 18–19. Cambridge, MA: MIT Press.

CLIFFORD, JAMES, AND GEORGE MARCUS (EDS.)

1986 *Writing Culture: The Poetics and Politics of Ethnography*. Berkeley: University of California.

CLOUSER, K. DANNER

1978 "Bioethics." In *Encyclopedia of Bioethics*, Vol. 1. W. Reich, ed., pp. 115–127. New York: Free Press.

COHEN, LLOYD R.

1995 *Increasing the Supply of Transplant Organs: The Virtues of an Options Market*. New York: Springer.

COHEN, MARK N.

1989 *Health and the Rise of Civilization*. New Haven: Yale University.

COREIL, JEANNINE, AND J. DENNIS MULL (EDS.)

1990 *Anthropology and Primary Health Care*. Boulder, CO: Westview.

CRIGGER, B., C. CAMPBELL, AND P. HOMER (EDS.)

1988 "International Perspectives on Biomedical Ethics." *Hastings Center Report* (Special Supplement) 18(4):1–39.

CROSBY, A. W.

1972 *The Columbian Exchange: Biological and Cultural Consequences of 1492*. Westport, CT: Greenwood.

CROSS, T., B. BAZRON, K. DENNIS, AND M. ISAACS

1989 *Toward a Culturally Competent System of Care*, Vol. 1. Washington, DC: Georgetown University.

CROWCROFT, N. S.

1994 "Cholera: Current Epidemiology." *Communicable Disease Report—CDR Review* 4(13): 157–164.

CROWLEY-MATOKA, M.

2001 *Organ Donation and Receiving in Mexico*. PhD thesis, University of California, Los Angeles.

CSORDAS, THOMAS J.

1988 "The Conceptual Status of Hegemony and Critique in Medical Anthropology." *Medical Anthropology Quarterly* 2:416–421.

1994 *The Sacred Self: A Cultural Phenomenology of Charismatic Healing*. Berkeley: University of California.

DAVIS-FLOYD, ROBBIE E.

1992 *Birth as an American Rite of Passage*. Berkeley: University of California.

DAVIS-FLOYD, ROBBIE E., AND CAROLYN F. SARENT

1997 *Childbirth and Authoritative Knowledge*. Berkeley: University of California.

DESOWITZ, ROBERT S.

2002 *Federal Bodysnatchers and the New Guinea Virus: People, Parasites, Politics*. New York: W. W. Norton and Company.

DEVITA, MICHAEL A., AND JAMES V. SNYDER

1995 "Development of the University of Pittsburgh Medical Center Policy for the Care of Terminally Ill Patients Who May Become Organ Donors after Death Following the Removal of Life Support." In *Procuring Organs for Transplant*. R. A. Arnold, S. J. Younger, R. Schapiro, and C. M. Spicer, eds., pp. 55–68. Baltimore: Johns Hopkins.

DIAMOND, JARED

1992 "The Return of Cholera." *Discover* 13:60–66.

DOUGHERTY, MOLLY C.

1991 "Anthropologists in Nursing-Education Programs." In *Training Manual in Applied Medical Anthropology*. C. E. Hill, ed., pp. 161–179. Washington: American Anthropological Assocation.

DOYAL, LESLEY

1995 *What Makes Women Sick: Gender and the Political Economy of Health*. New Brunswick, NJ: Rutgers University.

DRESSLER, WILLIAM W.

1984 "Social and Cultural Influences in Cardiovascular Disease: A Review." *Transcultural Psychiatric Research Review* 21:5–42.

1989 "Cross-Cultural Differences and Social Influences in Social Support and Cardiovascular Disease." In *Social Support and Cardiovascular Disease*. S. A. Shumaker, and S. M. Czajowski, eds. New York: Plenum Publishing.

DURHAM, WILLIAM H.

1991 *Coevolution: Genes, Culture and Human Diversity*. Stanford: Stanford University.

EDSON, MARGARET

1999 *Wit: A Play*. New York: Faber and Faber.

EHRENREICH, BARBARA, AND DEIDRE ENGLISH

1978 *For Her Own Good: 150 Years of the Experts' Advice to Women*. New York: Doubleday.

1981 The Sexual Politics of Sickness *In The Sociology of Health and Illness: Critical Perspectives*. P. Conrad and R. Kern, eds., pp. 281–295. New York: St. Martins.

EHRENREICH, JOHN (ED.)

1978 *The Cultural Crisis of American Medicine*. New York: Monthly Review.

ENGELHARDT, H. TRISTRAM, JR.

1981 "The Disease of Masturbation: Values and the Concept of Disease." In *Concepts of Health and Disease: Interdisciplinary Perspectives*. A. L. Caplan, H. T. Engelhardt, Jr., and J. J. McCartney, eds., pp. 267–280. London: Addison-Wesley.

ENGELS, F.

1969 *The Condition of the Working Class in England*. London: Granada.

EPSTEIN, PAUL R.

1992 "Link with Cholera." *New York Times*, Tuesday March 10 (Letters).

ESCOBAR, ARTURO

1993 *Encountering Development: The Making and Unmaking of the Third World*. Princeton: Princeton University.

ESTROFF, SUE

1988 "Whose Hegemony? A Critical Commentary on Critical Medical Anthropology." *Medical Anthropology Quarterly* 2:421–426.

EWALD, PAUL W.

1994 *Evolution of Infectious Disease*. New York: Oxford.

FÁBREGA, HORACIO, JR.

1977 "The Scope of Ethnomedical Science." *Culture, Medicine and Psychiatry* 1:201–228.

1990 "An Ethnomedical Perspective of Medical Ethics." *Journal of Medicine and Philosophy* 15:593–625.

1997 *Evolution of Sickness and Healing*. Berkeley: University of California.

FADIMAN, ANNE

1997 *The Spirit Catches You and You Fall Down*. New York: Farrar, Straus, & Giroux.

FARMER, PAUL

1992 *AIDS and Accusation: Haiti and the Geography of Blame*. Berkeley: University of California.

2003 *Pathologies of Power: Health, Human Rights and the New War on the Poor*. Berkeley: University of California.

FEE, ELIZABETH, AND NANCY KRIEGER

1994 *Women's Health, Politics, and Power: Essays on Sex/Gender, Medicine, and Public Health*. Amityville, NY: Baywood.

FIDLER, DAVID P.

2003 "Germs, Governance, and Global Public Health in the Wake of SARS." *Journal for Clinical Investigation* 113(6):799–804.

FINERMAN, RUTHBETH, K. RIVERS, AND J. TURVEY

2003 *Role Negotiation Among Medical Interpreters: Culture Broker or Culture Breakdown*? Paper presented at the Annual Meeting of the American Anthropological Association, Chicago, IL.

FINKLER, KAJA

1985 *Spiritualist Healers in Mexico: Successes and Failures in Alternative Therapeutics*. South Hadley, MA: Bergin and Garvey.

FIRTH, RAYMOND

1981 "Engagement and Detachment: Reflections on Applying Social Anthropology to Social Affairs." *Human Organization* 40:193–201.

FOREIGN ASSISTANCE ACT

1979 *Legislation on Foreign Relations through 1978: Current Legislation and Related Executive Orders*, Vol. 1. Washington, D.C.: US Senate-House of Representatives, Joint Committee.

FOSTER, GEORGE M.

1982 "Applied Anthropology and International Health: Retrospect and Prospect." *Human Organization* 41:189–197.

1987 "Bureaucratic Aspects of International Health Agencies." *Social Science and Medicine* 25:1039–1048.

FOSTER, GEORGE. M., AND BARBARA G. ANDERSON

1978 *Medical Anthropology*. New York: John Wiley and Sons.

FOX, RENÉE

1990 "The Evolution of American Bioethics: A Sociological Perpsective." In *Social Science Perspectives in Medical Ethics*. B. Weisz, ed., pp. 201–217. The Netherlands: Kluwer Academic.

1995 "'An Ignoble Form of Cannibalism:' Reflections on the Pittsburgh Protocol for Procuring Organs from Non-Heart- Beating Cadavers." In *Procuring Organs for Transplant*. R. M. Arnold, S. J. Youngner, R. Schapiro, and C. Mason Spicer, eds., pp. 155–163. Baltimore: Johns Hopkins.

FOX, RENÉE, AND JUDITH SWAZEY

1974 *The Courage to Fail: A Social View of Organ Transplants and Dialysis*. Chicago: University of Chicago.

1984 "Medical Morality is Not Bioethics: Medical Ethics in China and the United States." *Perspectives in Biology and Medicine* 27:336–360.

1992 *Spare Parts: Organ Replacement in American Society*. New York: Oxford.

1997 "Medical Morality is Not Bioethics." In *Bioethics*. N. S. Jecker, A. R. Jonsen, and R. A. Pearlman, eds., pp. 237–251. Sudbury, MA: Jones and Bartlett.

FRANCIS, C. M.

1992 "Ancient and Modern Medical Ethics in India." In *Transcultural Dimensions in Medical Ethics*. E. Pellegrino, P. Mazzarella, and P. Corsi, eds., pp. 175–196. Frederick, MD: University Publishing.

FRANKENBERG, RONALD

1988 "Gramsci, Culture and Medical Anthropology: Kundry and Parsifal? or Rat's Tail to Sea Serpent." *Medical Anthropology Quarterly* 2:324–337.

FRANKLIN, SARAH

1997 *Embodied Progress: A Cultural Account of Assisted Conception*. London: Routledge.

2003 "Ethical Biocapital: New Strategies of Stem cell Cultures." In *Remaking Life and Death: Towards an Anthropology of Biomedicine*. S. Franklin and M. Lock eds, pp. 97–129. Santa Fe, NM: School of American Research Press.

2007 *Dolly Mixtures: The Remaking of Genealogy*. Durham: Duke University Press.

FRANKLIN, SARAH, AND MARGARET LOCK (EDS.)

2003 *Remaking Life and Death: Toward an Anthropology of the Biosciences*. Santa Fe: School of American Research.

FRANKLIN, SARAH AND CELIA ROBERTS

2006 *Born and Made: An Ethnography of Preimplantation Genetic Diagnosis*. Princeton: Princeton University Press.

FREIDSON, ELLIOT

1970 *Profession of Medicine: A Study of the Sociology of Applied Knowledge*. New York: Harper and Row.

FRENK, JULIO, T. FREJKA, J. L. BOBADILLA, C. STERN, R. LOZANO, J. SEPÚLVEDA, AND M. JOSÉ

1991 "La transición epidemiológica en america latina." *Boletín de la Oficina Sanitaria Panamericana* 111:485–496.

FREUND, P. E. S., AND M. B. MCGUIRE

1995 *Health, Illness, and the Social Body: A Critical Sociology*. Englewood Cliffs, NJ: Prentice Hall.

FRIEDMAN, GARY D.

1987 *Primer of Epidemiology*, 3rd Ed. New York: McGraw Hill.

FRISANCHO, A. ROBERTO

1981 *Human Adaptation: A Functional Interpretation*. Ann Arbor: University of Michigan.

GALANTI, GERI-ANN

1991 *Caring for Patients from Different Cultures: Case Studies from American Hospitals*. Philadelphia: University of Pennsylvania.

GALL, NORMAN

1993 *The Death Threat*. Manuscript, Fernand Braudel Institute of World Economics, Sao Paulo, Brazil.

GARRETT, LAURIE

2000 *Betrayal of Trust: The Collapse of Global Public Health*. New York: Hyperion.

GEE, ELIZABETH, AND NANCY KRIEGER (EDS.)

1994 *Women's Health, Politics and Power: Essays on Sex/Gender, Medicine, and Public Health*. Amityville, NY: Baywood.

GENNEP, ARNOLD VAN

1960 *The Rites of Passage*. London: Routledge and Paul.

GLASSER, RONALD J.

2004 "We are not Immune: Influenza, SARS, and the Collapse of Public Health." *Harpers's Magazine* 309(1850):35–42.

GLAZER, MYRON

1982 "The Threat of the Stranger: Vulnerability, Reciprocity, and Fieldwork." In *The Ethics of Social Research*. J. E. Sieber, ed., pp. 49–70. New York: Springer-Verlag.

GOOD, BYRON J.

1977 "The Heart of What's the Matter: The Semantics of Illness in Iran." *Culture, Medicine and Psychiatry* 1:25–58.

1994 *Medicine, Rationality, and Experience: An Anthropological Perspective*. New York: Cambridge University.

GOOD, BYRON J., AND MARY-JO DELVECCHIO GOOD

1980 "The Meaning of Symptoms: A Cultural Hermeneutic Model for Clinical Practice." In *The Relevance of Social Science for Medicine*. L. Eisenberg, and A. Kleinman, eds., pp. 165–196. Dordrecht: D. Reidel.

1981 "The Semantics of Medical Discourse." In *Sciences and Cultures, Sociology of the Sciences*, Vol. 5. E. Mendelsohn, and Y. Elkana, eds., pp. 177–212. Dordrecht: D. Reidel.

1982 "Toward a Meaning-Centered Analysis of Popular Illness Categories: 'Fright Illness' and 'Heart Distress' in Iran." In *Cultural Conceptions of Mental Health and Therapy*. A. J. Marsella, and G. M. White, eds., pp. 141–166. Dordrecht: D. Reidel.

1993 "'Learning Medicine:' The Constructing of Medical Knowledge at Harvard Medical School." In *Knowledge, Power and Practice*. S. Lindenbaum, and M. Lock, eds., pp. 81–107. Berkeley: University of California.

1995 *Medicine, Rationality and Experience: An Anthropological Perspective*. New York: Cambridge.

GOOD, MARY-JO DELVECCHIO

1995 *American Medicine: The Quest for Competence*. Berkeley: University of California.

GOOD, M. D., PAUL BRODWIN, BYRON GOOD, AND ARTHUR KLEINMAN (EDS.)

1992 *Pain as a Human Experience: An Anthropological Perspective*. Berkeley: University of California.

GOODMAN, ALAN, R. BROOKE THOMAS, ALAN SWEDLUND, AND GEORGE J. ARMELAGOS

1988 "Biocultural Perspectives on Stress in Prehistoric, Historical and Contemporary Population Research." *Yearbook of Physical Anthropology* 31:169–202.

GOODMAN, ALAN, AND THOMAS LEATHERMANN

1998 *Building a New Biocultural Synthesis: Political-Economic Perspectives in Biological Anthropology*. Ann Arbor: University of Michigan.

GORDON, DEBORAH R.

1988 "Tenacious Assumptions in Western Medicine." In *Biomedicine Examined*. M. Lock, and D. R. Gordon, eds., pp. 19–56. Dordrecht: Kluwer.

1994 "The Ethics of Ambiguity and Concealment Around Cancer: Interpretations Through a Local Italian World." In *Interpretive Phenomenology*. P. Benner, ed., pp. 279–322. Thousand Oaks, CA: Sage.

GORER, GEOFFREY, AND JOHN RICKMAN

1949 *The People of Great Russia*. New York: Norton.

GOULD, DUNCAN C., AND RICHARD PETTY

2000 "The Male Menopause—Does it Exist?" *British Medical Journal* 320:858–861.

GREENWOOD, D., S. LINDENBAUM, M. LOCK, AND A. YOUNG

1988 "Introduction. Theme Issue: Medical Anthropology." *American Ethnologist* 15(1):1–3.

GRIFFITHS, MARCIA

1990 "Using Anthropological Techniques in Program Design: Successful Nutrition in Indonesia." In *Anthropology and International Health*. J. Coreil, and J. D. Mull, eds., pp. 154–170. Boulder, CO: Westview.

GUERRANT, R. L.

1994 "Twelve Messages from Enteric Infections for Science and Society." *American Journal of Tropical Medicine and Hygiene* 51:26–35.

GUSSOW, ZACHARY

1989 *Leprosy, Racism, and Public Health: Social Policy in Chronic Disease Control*. Boulder: Westview.

GUTHMANN, J. P.

1995 "Epidemic Cholera in Latin America: Spread and Routes of Transmission." *Journal of Tropical Medicine and Hygiene* 98:419–427.

HAHN, ROBERT A.

1987 "Perinatal Ethics in Anthropological Perspective." In *Ethical Issues at the Outset of Life*. W. Weil and M. Benjamin, eds., pp. 213–238. Boston: Blackwell Scientific.

1995 *Sickness and Healing: An Anthropological Perspective*. New Haven: Yale University.

HAHN, ROBERT, AND ATWOOD D. GAINES (EDS.)

1985 *Physicians of Western Medicine: Anthropological Approaches to Theory and Practice*. Dordecht: D. Reidel.

HAHN, ROBERT, AND ARTHUR KLEINMAN

1983 "Belief as Pathogen, Belief as Medicine." *Medical Anthropology Quarterly* 12:305–333.

HALLOWELL, A. IRVING

1955 "The Self and its Behavioral Environment." In *Culture and Experience*, pp. 75–110. Phildadelphia: University of Philadelphia.

HARWOOD, ALAN
1977 *RX: Spiritist as Needed. A Study of a Puerto Rican Community Mental Health Resource*. New York: Wiley.

HENDERSON, GAIL E., NANCY M. P. KING, RONALD P. STRAUSS, SUE E. ESTROFF, AND LARRY R. CHURCHILL
1997 *The Social Medicine Reader*. Durham, NC: Duke University.

HESS, DAVID J.
1997a *Can Bacteria Cause Cancer? Alternative Medicine Confronts Big Science*. New York: New York University.
1997b *Science Studies: An Advanced Introduction*. New York: New York University.

HEURTIN-ROBERTS, SUZANNE
1995 "Exiting the Ivory Tower for the Real World: A Comment on Critical Praxis." *Medical Anthropology Quarterly* 9:110–112.

HILL, CAROLE E. (ED.)
1991 *Training Manual in Applied Medical Anthropology*. Washington: American Anthropological Association.

HOBEN, ALLAN
1982 "Anthropologists and Development." *Annual Review of Anthropology* 11:349–375.

HOFFMAN, VALERIE, AND RALPH BOLTON
1996 "Patterns of Sexual Risk-taking Among Heterosexual Men." *Medical Anthropology* 16:341–362.

HOFFMASTER, BARRY
1990 "Morality and the Social Sciences." In *Social Science Perspectives on Medical Ethics*. G. Weisz, ed., pp. 241–260. Dordrecht: Kluwer.
1992 "Can Ethnography Save the Life of Medical Ethics?" *Social Science and Medicine* 35(12): 1421–1431.

HOGLE, LINDA
1996 "Transforming 'Body Parts' into Therapeutic Tools: A Report from Germany." *Medical Anthropology Quarterly* 10:675–682.
1999 *Recovering the Nation's Body: Cultural Memory, Medicine and the Politics of Redemption*. New Brunswick, NJ: Rutgers University.
2006 "Enhancement Technologies and the Body." *Annual Reviews of Anthropology and Neuroscience* 34:695–716.

HSU, FRANCIS L. K.
1955 "A Cholera Epidemic in a Chinese Town." In *Health, Culture and Community*. B. D. Paul, ed., pp. 135–154. New York: Russell Sage Foundation.

HUBBARD, R., M. S. HENIFIN, AND B. FRIED (EDS.)
1979 *Women Look at Biology Looking at Women: A Collection of Feminist Critiques*. Boston: G. K. Hall.

ILLICH, IVAN
1975 *Medical Nemesis: The Expropriation of Health*. London: Calder and Boyars.

INGMAN, S., AND A. THOMAS (EDS.)
1975 *Topias and Utopias in Health*. The Hague: Mouton.

INHORN, MARCIA C.
2003 *Local Babies, Global Science: Gender, Religion, and In Vitro Fertilization in Egypt*. New York: Routledge.

JARET, P.
1986 "Our Immune System: The Wars Within." *National Geographic* 169(6):702–734.

JECKER, NANCY S.
1997 "Introduction to the Methods of Bioethics." In *Bioethics*. N. S. Jecker, A. R. Jonsen, and R. A. Pearlman, eds., pp. 113–125. Sudbury, MA: Jones and Bartlett.

JECKER, N. S., A. R. JONSEN, AND R. A. PEARLMAN (EDS.)
1997 *Bioethics: An Introduction to the History, Methods, and Practice*. Sudbury, MA: Jones and Bartlett.

JENNINGS, BRUCE
1990 "Ethics and Ethnography in Neonatal Intensive Care." In *Social Science Perspectives on Medical Ethics*. G. Weisz, ed., pp. 261–272. Boston: Kluwer Academic.

JOHNSON, THOMAS M.
1991 "Anthropologists in Medical Education: Ethnographic Prescriptions." In *Training Manual in Applied Medical Anthropology*. C. E. Hill, ed., pp. 125–160. Washington: American Anthropological Association.
1995 "Critical Praxis Beyond the Ivory Tower: A Critical Commentary." *Medical Anthropology Quarterly* 9:107–110.

JOHNSON, THOMAS M., AND CAROLYN F. SARGENT (EDS.)
1990 *Medical Anthropology: Contemporary Theory and Method*. New York: Praeger.

JONES, JAMES H.
1993 *Bad Blood: The Tuskegee Syphilis Experiment*. New and Expanded Ed. New York: Free Press.

JONSEN, ALBERT R.
1997 "Introduction to the History of Bioethics." In *Bioethics*. N. Jecker, A. R. Jonsen, and R. A. Pearlman, eds., pp. 3–11. Sudbury, MA: Jones and Bartlett.

JORALEMON, DONALD
1982 "New World Depopulation and the Case of Disease." *Journal of Anthropological Research* 38:108–127.
1990 "The Selling of the Shaman and the Problem of Informant Legitimacy." *Journal of Anthropological Research* 46:105–118.
1995 "Organ Wars: The Battle for Body Parts." *Medical Anthropology Quarterly* 9:335–356.
2001 "Shifting Ethics: Debating the Incentive Question in Organ Transplantation." *Journal of Medical Ethics* 27:30–35.

JORALEMON, D., AND P. COX
2003 "Body Values: The Case Against Compensating for Transplant Organs." *Hastings Center Report* 33(1):27–33.

JORALEMON, DONALD, AND KIM M. FUJINAGA
1996 "Studying the Quality of Life After Organ Transplantation: Research Problems and Solutions." *Social Science and Medicine* 44:1259–1269.

JORALEMON, DONALD, AND DOUGLAS SHARON
1993 *Sorcery and Shamanism: Curanderos and Clients in Northern Peru*. Salt Lake City: University of Utah Press.

JUSTICE, JUDITH
1986 *Policies, Plans and People: Foreign Aid and Health Development*. Berkeley: University of California.

KASISKE, B. L., J. F. NEYLAN, R. R. RIGGIO, G. M. DANOVITCH, L. KAHANA, S. R. ALEXANDER, AND M. G. WHITE
1991 "The Effect of Race on Access and Outcome in Transplantation." *New England Journal of Medicine* 324:302–306.

KAUFERT, PATRICIA A.
1990 "Ethics, Politics and Contraception: Canada and the Licensing of Depo-Provera." In *Social Science Perspectives on Medical Ethics*. G. Weisz, ed., pp. 121–141. Dordrecht: Kulwer.

KAUFMAN, SHARON R.
1993 *The Healer's Tale: Transforming Medicine and Culture*. Madison, WI: University of Wisconsin.

KAUFMAN, SHARON R., AND LYNN M. MORGAN
2005 "The Anthropology of the Beginnings and Ends of Life." *Annual Review of Anthropology* 34:317–341.

KIDDER, TRACY

2003 *Mountains Beyond Mountains: Healing the World, The Quest of Dr. Paul Farmer*. New York: Random House.

KIPLE, KENNETH F. (ED.)

1993 *The Cambridge World History of Human Disease*. Cambridge: Cambridge University Press.

KLEINMAN, ARTHUR

1980 *Patients and Healers in the Context of Culture*. Berkeley: University of California.

REIDEL

1988 *Rethinking Psychiatry: From Cultural Category to Personal Experience*. New York: Free Press.

KLEINMAN, ARTHUR, VEENA DAS, AND MARGARET LOCK (EDS.)

1997 *Social Suffering*. Berkeley: University of California.

KLEINMAN, ARTHUR, AND J. GALE

1982 "Patents Treated by Physicians and Folk Healers: A Comparative Outcome Study in Taiwan." *Culture, Medicine and Psychiatry* 6:405–423.

KONNER, MELVIN

1987 *Becoming a Doctor: A Journey of Initiation in Medical School*. New York: Viking.

KRIEGER, NANCY

1994 "Epidemiology and the Web of Causation: Has Anyone Seen the Spider?" *Social Science and Medicine* 39:887–903.

KRIEGER, NANCY, AND STEPHEN SIDNEY

1996 "Racial Discrimination and Blood Pressure: The CARDIA Study of Young Black and White Adults." *American Journal of Public Health* 86:1370–1378.

KUNSTADTER, PETER

1980 "Medical Ethics in Cross-Cultural and Multi-Cultural Perspectives." *Social Science and Medicine* 14B:289–296.

LANDY, DAVID (ED.)

1977 *Culture, Disease and Healing: Studies in Medical Anthropology*. New York: MacMilan.

LASHLEY, FELISSA R., AND JERRY D. DURHAM (EDS.)

2003 *Emerging Infectious Diseases: Trends and Issues*. New York: Springer.

LAURENCE, LESLIE, AND BETH WEINHOUSE

1994 *Outrageous Practices: The Alarming Truth About How Medicine Mistreats Women*. New York: Fawcett Columbine.

LEATHERMAN, THOMAS

1996 "A Biocultural Perspective on Health and Household Economy in Southern Peru." *Medical Anthropology Quarterly* 10:476–495.

LEATHERMAN, THOMAS, J. S. LUERSSEN, L. MARKOWITZ, AND R. B. THOMAS

1986 "Illness and Political Economy: The Andean Dialectic." *Cultural Survival Quarterly* 10(3):19–22.

LEDERBERG, J., R. E. SHOPE, AND S. C. OAKS, JR. (EDS.)

1992 *Emerging Infections: Microbial Threats to Health in the United States*. Washington, DC: Institute of Medicine, National Academic Press.

LEE, RICHARD

1993 *The Dobe Ju/'hoansi*. Fort Worth, TX: Harcourt Brace.

LESLIE, CHARLES

1968 "The Professionalization of Ayurvedic and Unani Medicine." *Transactions of the New York Academy of Sciences*, series II, 30:559–572.

1977 "Pluralism and Integration in the Indian and Chinese Medical System." In *Culture, Disease and Healing*. D. Landy, ed., pp. 511–518. New York: Macmillan.

Leslie, Charles (ed.)
1976 *Asian Medical Systems: A Comparative Study*. Berkeley: University of California.

Lieban, Richard W.
1990 "Medical Anthropology and the Comparative Study of Medical Ethics." In *Social Science Perspectives on Medical Ethics*. G. Weisz, ed., pp. 221–240. Dordrecht: Kluwer.

Lindenbaum, Shirley
1979 *Kuru Sorcery: Disease and Danger in the New Guinea Highland*. Palo Alto: Mayfield.

Lindenbaum, Shirely, and Margaret Lock (eds.)
1993 *Knowledge, Power, and Practice: The Anthropology of Medicine and Everyday Life*. Berkeley: University of California.

Livingstone, F. B.
1958 "Anthropological Implications of Sickle Cell Distribution in West Africa." *American Anthropologist* 60:53–62.

Lock, Margaret
1988 "Introduction." In *Biomedicine Examined*. M. Lock, and D. R. Gordon, eds., pp. 3–10. Berkeley: University of California.
1993 *Encounters with Aging: Mythologies of Menopause in Japan and North America*. Berkeley: University of California.
2002 *Twice Dead: Organ Transplants and the Reinvention of Death*. Berkeley: University of California.
2007 "Medical Anthropology: Intimations for the Future." In *Medcial Anthropology*. F. Saillant, and S. Genest, eds., pp. 267–288. Malden, MA: Blackwell.

Lock, Margaret, and Deborah R. Gordon (eds.)
1988 *Biomedicine Examined*. Dordrecht: Kluwer.

Lock, Margaret, and Christina Honde
1990 "Reaching Consensus about Death: Heart Transplants and Cultural Identity in Japan." In *Social Science Perspectives on Medical Ethics*. G. Weisz, ed., pp. 99–120. Dordrecht: Kluwer.

Lock, Margaret, and Nancy Scheper-Hughes
1990 "A Critical-Interpretive Approach in Medical Anthropology: Rituals and Routines of Discipline and Dissent." In *Medical Anthropology: Contemporary Theory and Method*. T. M. Johnson, and C. F. Sargent, eds., pp. 47–72. Westport, CT: Praeger.

Macdonald, John J.
1993 *Primary Health Care: Medicine in its Place*. West Hartford, CT: Kumarian Press.

MacPherson, Kathleen I.
1981 "Menopause as Disease: The Social Construction of a Metaphor." *Advances in Nursing Science* 3(2):95–113.

Marcus, George, and Michael Fischer
1986 *Anthropology as Cultural Critique: An Experimental Moment in the Human Sciences*. Chicago: University of Chicago.

Marks, Jonathan
1995 *Human Biodiversity: Genes, Race and History*. New York: Aldine.

Marmot, M.
1994 "Social Differentials in Health Within and Between Populations." *Daedalus* 123:197–216.

Marsella, Anthony J., George DeVos, and Francis L. K. Hsu
1985 *Culture and Self: Asian and Western Perspectives*. New York: Tavistock.

Marshall, Patricia A.
1991 "Research Ethics in Applied Medical Anthropology." In *Training Manual in Applied Medical Anthropology*. C. E. Hill, ed., pp. 213–235. Washington: American Anthropological Association.
1992 "Anthropology and Bioethics." *Medical Anthropology Quarterly* 6:49–73.

1995 "Representations of Morality in Narratives of Organ Transplantation in India: How Much Do You Want for Your Kidney?" Paper presented at the 94th Annual Meeting of the American Anthropological Association, November 16. Washington, D.C.

MARSHALL, PATRICIA A., DAVID THOMASMA, AND PAUL O'KEEFE
1991 "Disclosing HIV Status: Ethical Issues Explored." *Journal of the American Dental Association* 122:11–15.

MARTIN, EMILY
1987 *The Woman in the Body: A Cultural Analysis of Reproduction*. Boston: Beacon Press.
1990 "Toward an Anthropology of Immunology: The Body as Nation State." *Medical Anthropology Quarterly* 4(4):410–426.
1994 *Flexible Bodies: Tracking Immunity in American Culture From the Days of Polio to the Age of AIDS*. Boston: Beacon Press.

MATSUMOTO, ALVIN M.
2003 "Fundamental Aspects of Hypogonadism in the Aging Male." *Reviews in Urology* 5(suppl 1):S3–S10.

MAUSS, MARCEL
1954 *The Gift: Forms and Functions of Exchange in Archaic Societies*. Glencoe, IL: Free Press.

MCELROY, ANN
1996 "Should Medical Ecology be Political?" *Medical Anthropology Quarterly* 10:519–522.

MCELROY, ANN, AND PATRICIA K. TOWNSEND
1985 *Medical Anthropology in Ecological Perspective*. Boulder, CO: Westview.
2004 *Medical Anthropology in Ecological Perspective*, 4th Ed. Boulder, CO: Westview.

MCGRATH, JANET, D. SCHUMANN, J. PEARSON-MARKS, C. RWABUKWALI, R. MUKASA, B. NAMANDE, S. NAKAYIWA, AND L. KAKYOBE
1992 "Cultural Determinants of Sexual Risk Behavior for AIDS among Baganda Women." *Medical Anthropology Quarterly* 6:153–161.

MCKEOWN, T.
1976 *The Role of Medicine: Dream, Mirage, or Nemesis*? Princeton: Princeton University.

MCKINLAY, JOHN B., AND SONJA M. MCKINLAY
1977 "The Questionable Contribution of Medical Measures on the Decline of Mortality in the United States in the Twentieth Century." *Milbank Memorial Fund Quarterly. Health and Society* 55:405–428.

MCNEILL, W. H.
1976 *Plagues and Peoples*. New York: Anchor.

MORAN, E. F. (ED.)
1990 *The Ecosystem Approach in Anthropology: From Concept to Practice*. Ann Arbor: University of Michigan.

MORGAN, LYNN M.
1987 "Dependency Theory in the Political Economy of Health: An Anthropological Critique." *Medical Anthropology Quarterly* 1:131–155.
1990 "The Medicalization of Anthropology: A Critical Perspective on the Critical-Clinical Debate." *Social Science and Medicine* 30:945–959.

MORRIS, BRIAN
1994 *Anthropology of the Self: The Individual in Cultural Perspective*. Boulder, CO: Pluto.

MORSY, SOHEIR
1979 "The Missing Link in Medical Anthropology: The Political Economy of Health." *Reviews in Anthropology* 6:349–363.
1981 "Towards a Political Economy of Health: A Critical Note on the Medical Anthropology of the Middle East." *Social Science and Medicine* 15(B):159–163.

MULL, J. DENNIS

1990 "The Primary Health Care Dialectic: History, Rhetoric and Reality." In *Anthropology and Primary Health Care*. J. Coreil, and J. D. Mull, eds., pp. 28–47. Boulder, CO: Westview.

MULLER, JESSICA H.

1994 "Anthropology, Bioethics, and Medicine: A Provacative Triology." *Medical Anthropology Quarterly* 8:448–467.

MULLER, JESSICA, AND B. DESMOND

1992 "Ethical Dilemmas in a Cross-Cultural Context: A Chinese Example." *Western Journal of Medicine* 157:323–327.

NATIONS, MARILYN K., AND CRISTINA M. G. MONTE

1996 "'I'm Not Dog, No!:' Cries of Resistance Against Cholera Control Campaigns." *Social Science and Medicine* 43(6):1007–1024.

NAVARRO, VICENTE

1976 *Medicine and Capitalism*. New York: Prodist.

1993 *Dangerous to Your Health: Capitalism in Health Care*. New York: Monthly Review Press.

NICHTER, MARK

1991 "Ethnomedicine: Diverse Trends, Common Linkages. Commentary." *Medical Anthropology* 13:137–171.

NICHTER, MARK, AND MIMI NICHTER

1996 *Anthropology and International Health: Asian Case Studies*. Buffalo: Gordon and Breach.

O'CONNOR, BONNIE BLAIR

1995 *Healing Traditions: Alternative Medicine and the Health Professions*. Philadelphia: University of Pennsylvania.

OLSHANSKY, S. J., AND B. A. AULT

1986 "The Fourth Stage of the Epidemiological Transition: The Age of Delayed Degenerative Diseases." *Milbank Memorial Fund Quarterly* 64:355–391.

OMRAN, ABDEL R.

1971 "The Epidemiological Transition." *Milbank Memorial Fund Quarterly* 49:509–538.

O'NELL, THERESA D.

1996 *Disciplined Hearts: History, Identity, and Depression in an American-Indian Community*. Berkeley: University of California.

O'REILLY, KEVIN R.

1991 "Applied Anthropology and Public Health." In *Training Manual in Applied Medical Anthropology*. C. E. Hill, ed., pp. 88–100. Washington: American Anthropological Association.

OSHERSON, SAMUEL, AND LORNA AMARASINGHAM

1981 "The Machine Metaphor in Medicine." In *Social Contexts of Health, Illness and Patient Care*. E. G. Mishler, ed., pp. 218–249. Cambridge: Cambridge University Press.

PARKER, R.

1987 "Acquired Immunodeficiency Syndrome in Urban Brazil." *Medical Anthropology Quarterly* 1:155–175.

PAUL, BENJAMIN D. (ED.)

1955 *Health, Culture and Community: Case Studies of Public Reactions to Health Programs*. New York: Russell Sage Foundation.

PEAR, ROBERT

2004 "Health Spending Rises to Record 15% of Economy." *New York Times*, Jan 9, Section A, Pg. 16, Col. 3.

PEDERSEN, DUNCAN

1996 "Disease Ecology at a Crossroads: Man-Made Envronments, Human Rights and Perpetual Development Utopias." *Social Science and Medicine* 43:745–758.

PELLEGRINO, EDMUND D.

1992 "Prologue: Intersections of Western Biomedical Ethics and World Culture." In *Transcultural Dimensions in Medical Ethics*. E. Pellegrino, P. Mazzarella, and P. Corsi, eds., pp. 13–20. Frederick, MD: University Publishing Group.

PELLEGRINO, E., P. MAZZARELLA, AND P. CORSI (EDS.)

1992 *Transcultural Dimensions in Medical Ethics*. Frederick, MD: University Publishing Group.

PELTO, PERTTI J., AND GRETEL H. PELTO

1978 *Anthropological Research: The Structure of Inquiry*, 2nd Ed. Cambridge: Cambridge University.

PERROTA, DENNIS M.

2001 "Bioterrorism." In *Emerging Infectious Diseases*. R. R. Lashley, and J. D. Durham, eds., pp. 325–348. New York: Springer.

PERSON, B., F. SY, K. HOLTON, B. GOVERT, A. LIANG, AND NCID/SARS EMERGENCY OUTREACH TEAM

2004 "Fear and Stigma: The Epidemic Within the SARS Outbreak." *Emerging Infectious Diseases* [serial online] Feb [cited 6/16/04]. URL: http://www.cdc.gov/ncidod/EID/vol10no2/03-0750.htm.

PETERS, LARRY, AND DOUGLAS PRICE-WILLIAMS

1980 "Towards an Experiential Analysis of Shamanism." *American Ethnologist* 7:398–418.

PFLEIDERER, BEATRIX, AND GILES BIBEAU (EDS.)

1991 *Anthropologies of Medicine: A Colloquium of West European and North American Perspectives*. Heidelberg: Vieweg, Bertelsmann.

PILLSBURY, BARBARA L. K.

1982 "Policy and Evaluation Perspectives on Traditional Health Practitioners in National Health Care Systems." *Social Science and Medicine* 16:1825–1834.

1991 "International Health: Overview and Opportunities." In *Training Manual in Applied Medical Anthropology*. C. E. Hill, ed., pp. 54–87. Washington: American Anthropological Association.

POPOVIC, TANJA, O. OLSVIK, AND P. A. BLAKE

1993 "Cholera in the Americas: Foodborne Aspects." *Journal of Food Protection* 56:811–821.

PRESS, IRWIN

1971 "The Urban Curandero." *American Anthropologist* 73:742–756.

1990 "Levels of Explanation and Cautions for a Critical Clinical Anthropology." *Social Science and Medicine* 30:189–197.

PRESTON, RICHARD

1994 *The Hot Zone*. New York: Random House.

PURNELL, LARRY D., AND BETTY J. PAULANKA

1998 *Transcultural Health Care: A Culturally Competent Approach*. Philadelphia: F. A. Davis Company.

QUI, REN-ZONG

1992 "Medical Ethics and Chinese Culture." In *Transcultural Dimensions in Medical Ethics*. E. Pellegrino, P. Mazzarella, and P. Corsi, eds., pp. 155–174. Frederick, MD: University Publishing.

RABBANI, G. H.

1986 "Cholera." *Clinical Gastroenterology* 15(3):507–528.

RABINOW, PAUL

1992 "Severing the Ties: Fragmentation and Dignity in Late Modernity." *Knowledge and Society: The Anthropology of Science and Technology* 9:169–187.

RAMSEY, PAUL

1976 "Prolonged Dying: Not Medically Indicated." *Hastings Center Report* 6:14–16.

RAPP, RAYNA

1993 "Accounting for Amniocentesis." In *Knowledge, Practice and Power*. S. Lindenbaum, and M. Lock, eds., pp. 55–78. Berkeley: University of California.

1999 *Testing Women, Testing the Fetus: The Social Impact of Amniocentesis in America*. New York: Routledge.

RATZAN, SCOTT C. (ED.)
1998 *The Mad Cow Crisis: Health and Public Good*. New York: New York University Press.

REICHEL-DOLMATOFF, GERADO
1950 *Los Kogi: una tribu de la Sierra Nevada de Santa Marta, Colombia*. 2 vols. Bogota: Instituto Etnológico Nacional.

REUBEN, DAVID
1966 *Everything You Always Wanted to Know About Sex*. New York: Bantam.

RHODES, LORNA A.
1990 "Studying Biomedicine as a Cultural System." In *Medical Anthropology*. T. M. Johnson, and C. F. Sargent, eds., pp. 159–173. New York: Praeger.

RICHARDSON, RUTH
1989 *Death, Dissection and the Destitute*. New York: Penguin.

RIVERS, WILLIAM H. R.
1924 *Medicine, Magic and Religion*. London: Kegan Paul, Trench, Trubner and Co., Ltd.

ROCKETT, I. R. H.
1994 *Population and Health: An Introduction to Epidemiology*. Washington, D.C.: Population Reference Bureau.

ROMERO-DAZA, N., M. WEEKS, AND M. SINGER
2003 "'Nobody Gives a Damn if I Live or Die:' Violence, Drugs, and Street-Level Prostitution in Inner-City Hartford, Connecticut." *Medical Anthropology* 22:233–259.

ROSENBERG, TINA
2004 "What the World Needs Now is DDT." *New York Times*, Magazine, Sunday, April 11, pp. 38–43.

ROSSER, SUE V.
1994 *Women's Health: Missing From U. S. Medicine*. Bloomington, IN: Indiana University.

ROTHMAN, DAVID J.
1990 "Human Experimentation and the Origins of Bioethics in the United States." In *Social Science Perspectives on Medical Ethics*. G. Weisz, ed., pp. 185–200. Dordrecht: Kluwer.

RUBEL, ARTHUR J., AND MICHAEL R. HASS
1990 "Ethnomedicine." In *Medical Anthropology*. T. Johnson, and C. Sargent, eds., pp. 115–131. New York: Praeger.

RUXIN, JOSH N.
1994 "Magic Bullet: The History of Oral Rehydration Therapy." *Medical History* 38:363–397.

SAILLANT, FRANCINE, AND SERGE GENEST
2007 *Medical Anthropology: Regional Perspectives and Shared Concerns*. Malden, MA: Blackwell.

SARGENT, CAROLYN F., AND THOMAS M. JOHNSON (EDS.)
1996 *Handbook of Medical Anthropology: Contemporary Theory and Method*, Revised Ed. Westport, CT: Greenwood.

SAVITT, TODD
1978 *Medicine and Slavery: The Diseases and Health Care of Blacks in Antebellum Virginia*. Urbana: University of Illinois.

SCHEPER-HUGHES, NANCY
1990 "Three Propositions for a Critically Applied Medical Anthropology." *Social Science and Medicine* 30:309–319.
1992 *Death Without Weeping: The Violence of Everday Life in Brazil*. Berkeley: University of California.

SCHEPER-HUGHES, NANCY, AND MARGARET LOCK
1986 "Speaking 'Truth' to Illness: Metaphors, Reification, and a Pedogogy for Patients." *Medical Anthropology Quarterly* 17:137–140.

SCHOEPF, B. G., W. ENGUNDU, R. W. NKERA, P. NTSOMO, AND C. SCHOEPF

1991 "Gender, Power, and Risk of AIDS in Zaire." In *Women and Health in Africa*. M. Turshen, ed., pp. 187–203. Trenton: World Press.

SCOTCH, NORMAN A.

1963 "Medical Anthropology." In *Biennial Review of Anthropology*. S. J. Siegel, ed., pp. 30–68. Stanford: Stanford University Press.

SCULLY, D. H.

1980 *Men Who Control Women's Health: The Miseducation of Obstetrician-Gynecologists*. Boston: Houghton Miflin.

SEDGWICK, PETER

1981 "Illness—Mental and Otherwise." In *Concepts of Health and Disease: Interdisciplinary Perspectives*. A. L. Caplan, H. T. Engelhardt, Jr., and J. J. McCartney, eds., pp. 119–130. London: Addison-Wesley.

SELYE, HANS

1956 *The Stress of Life*. New York: McGraw-Hill.

SHARON, DOUGLAS

1978 *Wizard of the Four Winds: A Shaman's Story*. New York: Free Press.

SHARP, LESLEY A.

1995 "Organ Transplantation as a Transformative Experience: Anthropological Insights into the Restructuring of the Self." *Medical Anthropology Quarterly* 9:357–389.

2006 *Strange Harvest: Organ Transplants, Denatured Bodies, and the Transformed Self*. Berkeley: University of California.

SHATTUCK, G. C.

1933 *The Pennisula of Yucatan: Medical, Biological, Meteorological and Sociological Studies*. Washington: Carnegie Institution, Publication No. 431.

SHILTS, RANDY

1987 *And the Band Played On*. New York: St. Martin's Press.

SHWEDER, RICHARD, AND EDMUND J. BOURNE

1984 "Does the Concept of the Person Vary Cross-Culturally?" In *Culture Theory*. R. A. Shweder, and R. A. LeVine, eds., pp. 158–199. New York: Cambridge University.

SINGER, MERRILL

1987 "Cure, Care, and Control: An Ectopic Encounter with Biomedical Obstetrics," In *Case Studies in Medical Anthropology*, H. Baer, ed., pp. 249–265. New York: Gordon and Breach.

1989a "The Coming of Age of Critical Medical Anthropology." *Social Science and Medicine* 28: 1193–1203.

1989b "The Limitations of Medical Ecology: The Concept of Adaptation in the Context of Social Stratification and Social Transformation." *Medical Anthropology* 10:223–234.

1990 "Reinventing Medical Anthropology: Toward a Critical Reallignment." *Social Science and Medicine* 30:179–187.

1995 "Beyond the Ivory Tower: Critical Praxis in Medical Anthropology." *Medical Anthropology Quarterly* 9:80–106.

1996 "Farewell to Adaptationism: Unnatural Selection and the Politics of Biology." *Medical Anthropology Quarterly* 10:496–575.

SINGER, MERRILL, AND HANS BAER

1995 *Critical Medical Anthropology*. Amityville, NY: Baywood.

SNODGRASS, MARY ELLEN

2004 *World Epidemics: A Cultural Chronology of Diseases from Prehistory to the Era of SARS*. Jefferson, NC: McFarland and Company.

SNOW, LOUDELL F.

1993 *Walking' Over Medicine*. Boulder, CO: Westview.

Sobo, E. J., and M. Seid

2003 "Cultural Issues in Health Services Delivery: What Kind of 'Competence' is Needed?" *Annals of Behavioral Science and Medical Education* 9(2):97–100.

Sontag, Susan

1977 *Illness as Metaphor*. New York: Doubleday.

Starr, Paul

1982 *The Social Transformation of American Medicine*. New York: Basic Books.

Stein, Howard F.

1990 *American Medicine as Culture*. Boulder: Westview.

1995 "Cultural Demystification and Medical Anthropology: Some Answers in Search of Questions." *Medical Anthropology Quarterly* 9:113–117.

Steward, J. H.

1955 *Theory of Culture Change: The Methodology of Multilinear Evolution*. Urbana: University of Illinois.

Swerdlow, David L., E. D. Mintz, and M. Rodriguez

1992 "Waterborne Transmission of Epidemic Cholera in Trujillo, Peru: Lessons for a Continent at Risk." *Lancet* 340:28–32.

Taylor, Carl E.

1976 "The Place of Indigenous Medical Practitioners in the Modernization of Health Services." In *Asian Medical Systems*. C. Lesley, ed., pp. 285–299. Berkeley: University of California.

Taylor, Janelle S.

2003 "The Story Catches You and You Fall Down: Tragedy, Ethnography, and 'Cultural Competence.'" *Medical Anthropology* 17(2):159–181.

2008 *The Public Life of the Fetal Sonogram*. New Brunswick, NJ: Rutgers University.

Taylor, Katheryn M.

1988 "Physicians and the Disclosure of Undesirable Information." In *Biomedicine Examined*. M. Lock and D. R. Gordon, eds., pp. 441–463. Boston: Kluwer Academic.

Thomas, R. Brooke

1997 "Wandering Toward the Edge of Adaptability: Adjustments of Andean People to Change." In *Human Adaptability*. S. J. Ulijaszke, and R. Huss-Ashmore, eds., pp. 183–232. Oxford: Oxford University.

Timmreck, T. C.

1993 *An Introduction to Epidemiology*. San Bernadino, CA: Health Care Management Development Association.

Trevathan, Wenda R., E. O. Smith, and J. J. McKenna (eds.)

2008 *Evolutionary Medicine and Health: New Perspectives*. New York: Oxford University Press.

Trostle, James A.

1995 *Political, Economic and Behavioral Aspects of the Re-emergence of Cholera in Latin America*. Paper presented at the Annual Meetings of the American Anthropological Association, Washington, D.C.

2005 *Epidemiology and Culture*. New York: Cambridge University Press.

Trostle, James A., and Johannes Sommerfeld

1996 "Medical Anthropology and Epidemiology." *Annual Reviews in Anthropology* 25: 253–274.

Trotter, Robert T.

1991 "Ethnographic Research Methods for Applied Medical Anthropology." In *Training Manual in Applied Medical Anthropology*. C. E. Hill, ed., pp. 180–212. Washington: American Anthropological Association.

Trotter, Robert, and Juan Antonio Chavira

1981 *Curanderismo: Mexican American Folk Healing*. Athens: University of Georgia.

TRUMPER, RICARDO, AND LYNNE PHILLIPS

1995 "Cholera in the Time of Neoliberalism: The Cases of Chile and Ecuador." *Alternatives* 20:165–194.

TURNER, VICTOR

1964 "An Ndembu Doctor in Practice." In *Magic, Faith and Healing*. Ari Kiev, ed. New York: Free Press.

1969 *The Ritual Process: Structure and Anti-Structure*. Chicago: Aldine.

ULIJASZEK, STANLEY J., AND REBECCA HUSS-ASHMORE (EDS.)

1997 *Human Adaptability: Past, Present and Future*. Oxford: Oxford University.

UNITED NATIONS CHILDREN FUND (UNICEF)

1996 *The Progress of Nations 1996, Health*. Geneva: UNICEF.

UNITED STATES, DEPARTMENT OF HUMAN RESOURCES SERVICE ADMINISTRATION, BUREAU OF PRIMARY HEALTH CARE

2000 *Cultural Competency: A Journey*. Bethesda, MD: US Department of Human Resources Service Administration, Bureau of Primary Health Care.

UNSCHULD, PAUL U.

1979 *Medical Ethics in Imperial China: A Study in Historical Anthropology*. Berkeley: University of California.

1985 *Medicine in China: A History of Ideas*. Berkeley: University of California.

VEATCH, ROBERT M.

1989 *Cross Cultural Perspectives on Medical Ethics: Readings*. Boston: Jones and Bartlett.

WAITZKIN, HOWARD

1991 *The Politics of Medical Encounters: How Patients and Doctors Deal With Social Problems*. New Haven: Yale University.

WALLACE, RODERICK

1990 "Urban Desertification, Public Health and Public Order: 'Planned Shrinkage,' Violent Death, Substance Abuse and AIDS in the Bronx." *Social Science and Medicine* 31:801–813.

WALLERSTEIN, E.

1974 *The Modern World-System*, Vol. 1. New York: Academic Press.

WARDWELL, WALTER I.

1988 "Chiropractors: Evolution to Acceptance." In *Other Healers: Unorthodox Medicine in America*. N. Gevitz, ed., pp. 157–191. Baltimore: Johns Hopkins University.

WEISZ, GEORGE (ED.)

1990 *Social Science Perspectives on Medical Ethics*. Boston: Kluwer Academic.

WELLIN, EDWARD

1955 "Water Boiling in a Peruvian Town." In *Healing, Culture and Community*. B. Paul, ed., pp. 71–103. New York: Russell Sage.

1977 "Theoretical Orientations in Medical Anthropology: Continuity and Change Over the Past Half-Century." In *Culture, Disease and Healing*. D. Landy, ed., pp. 47–58. New York: Macmillan.

WHITEFORD, LINDA

1991 "Need Assessment and Program Evaluation in Community Health." In *Training Manual in Applied Medical Anthropology*. C. E. Hill, ed., pp. 101–124. Washington, D.C.: American Anthropological Association.

WILBERT, JOHANNES

1993 *Mystic Endowment: Religious Ethnography of the Warao Indians*. Cambridge: Harvard Unviersity.

WILLS, CHRISTOPHER

1996 *Yellow Fever, Black Goddess: The Coevolution of People and Plagues*. Reading, MA: Addison-Wesley.

WILSON, ROBERT

1966 *Feminine Forever*. New York: M. Evans and Co.

WINN, PETER
1992 *Americas: The Changing Face of Latin America and the Caribbean*. Berkeley: University of California.

WOLF, ERIC
1982 *Europe and the People Without History*. Berkeley: University of California.

WOMEN'S HEALTH INITIATIVE, WRITING GROUP
2002 "Risks and Benefits of Combined Estrogen and Progestin in Healthy Menopausal Women: Principal Results from the Women's Health Initiative Radonized Controlled Trial." *Journal of the American Medical Association* 288:321–333.

WORLD HEALTH ORGANIZATION (WHO)
1978 *Primary Health Care: Report of the International Conference on Primary Health Care, Alma Ata*, USSR, 6–12 September 1978.
1981 *Traditional Birth Attendants: A Field Guide to Their Training, Utilization and Evaluation*. Geneva: WHO.
1991 "Cholera in Peru." *Weekly Epidemiological Record* 66(20):141–148.

WRIGHT, A. L., AND T. M. JOHNSON (EDS.)
1990 "Symposium on Critical Perspectives in Clinically Applied Anthropology." Special Issue. *Social Science and Medicine* 30(9).

WRIGHT, PETER W. G., AND ANDREW TREACHER (EDS.)
1982 *The Problem of Medical Knowledge: Examining the Social Construction of Medicine*. Edinburgh: University of Edinburgh.

YODER, P. STANLEY (ED.)
1997 "Knowledge and Practice in International Health." Special Issue. *Medical Anthropology Quarterly* 11(2).

ZBOROWSKI, MARK
1969 *People in Pain*. San Francisco: Jossey-Bass Inc.

ZIMMERMAN, F.
1987 *The Jungle and the Aroma of Meats: An Ecological Theme in Hindu Medicine*. Berkeley: University of California.

INDEX

Note: Page reference with *n* notation refer to a note on that page